The Field of
Life and Death
and
Tales of
Hulan River

CHINESE LITERATURE
IN TRANSLATION

Editors

Irving Yucheng Lo
Joseph S. M. Lau
Leo Ou-fan Lee

TWO NOVELS BY *Hsiao Hung*

The Field of Life and Death

Translated by Howard Goldblatt and Ellen Yeung

and

Tales of Hulan River

Translated by Howard Goldblatt

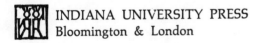

INDIANA UNIVERSITY PRESS
Bloomington & London

Manufactured in the United States of America

Library of Congress Cataloging in Publication Data
Chang, Nai-ying, 1911-1942.
The field of life and death.
(Chinese literature in translation)
Translation of Sheng ssu ch'ang and Hu-lan ho chuan.
Includes biliographical references.
I. Chang, Nai-ying, 1911-1942.   Hu-lan ho chuan.
English. 1979.   II. Title. III. Series.
PZ3.C36415Fi 1979 [PL2740.N3] 895.1'3'5 78-19549
ISBN 0-253-15821-4   1 2 3 4 5 83 82 81 80 79

For Jessica and Erica

Contents

TRANSLATORS' PREFACE

Each of the novels included here presents its own problems to the translator. For *Tales of Hulan River*, the translation of which was begun in mid-1975, the foremost consideration has been a faithful rendering of the unique writing style—simple yet precise, intimate without being gushy. Another problem has been the occasional unclear passage or local expression. The resolution of these problems owes a great deal to many people and, where unavoidable, some educated guesswork. Owing to the noninflected nature of the Chinese language, a writer can move undetected from the general to the specific, from tense to tense, without affecting the readability of the work. In *Tales of Hulan River* the translator has rendered the narration of the first two chapters in the present tense, moving occasionally to the past when specific, isolated incidents demanded it. The remainder of the work and the whole of *The Field of Life and Death* have, for the most part, been translated in the past tense. Chapter titles for *Tales of Hulan River* have been added by the translator. Although the formal name of the city in the title is simply Hulan, the inhabitants referred to it as Hulan River; it is the town, of course, and not the river that is the author's concern. Nicknames in both novels have been translated, while formal names generally have not been translated.

A 1966 photocopy of the 1954 Shanghai edition of *Tales of Hulan River* (which was, in turn, based on a 1947 edition) was used for the present translation. This edition is presently available in a 1975 Hong Kong reprint. The present translation does not include the final two chapters of the original work, for once the decision was made to include two novels under one cover, problems of length and other considerations made necessary some cuts. The two chapters are certainly detachable from the novel as a whole, and both are covered in translation elsewhere (see Introduction, note 6). The translators feel that the gain of *The Field of Life and Death* easily compensates for the loss of these two chapters of *Tales of Hulan River*.

The translation of *The Field of Life and Death*, a cooperative venture that took much less time to complete, proved as challenging as that of *Tales of Hulan River*. The major problems were in re-creating the earthy language and staccato rhythm of the original (the punctuation made this task more difficult). There were other problems created by textual variances between the original 1935 edition and the 1957 Hong Kong republication. While the earlier version has been used as the standard, the bowdlerizing editor of the later edition has made some corrections and clarifications that have been incorporated into this translation.

In both works the modified Wade-Giles system of Romanization has been used, and the months given in the original have been set back by one month to correspond more closely with their lunar counterparts.

The cause of readability for the Western reader has motivated a large-scale rearrangement of paragraphing in both novels; the same principle has held true for the omission of many lead-ins to dialogue. With these exceptions, the translators have taken pains to keep as close to the original as possible.

A great many people have made the translators' task considerably easier and their product more accurate. Our thanks to Professor Michael Berkvam of Indiana University and Professor K. Y. Hsu and Mr. George Cheng of San Francisco State University for reading the manuscript of *Tales of Hulan River* and for their suggested improvements. Thanks, too, to Professor Roger Williams of San Francisco State University, whose critical reading of *The Field of Life and Death* and his comments on it improved not only the translation but our understanding of the novel itself. We are also in debt to Professors Joseph Lau of The University of Wisconsin and Leo Ou-fan Lee of Indiana University for their expert editing and unflinching support of the project from its inception. Through the efforts of Dr. Leo Young, Dean of the School of Humanities, San Francisco State University, a grant-in-aid was made available for the typing of the entire manuscript. The translator of *Tales of Hulan River* was aided in his work by Syosuke Tatsuma's Japanese translation of the entire *Tales of Hulan River*, published in Tokyo in 1972. Thanks also to Ms. Gloria Shen of the East Asian Languages and Cultures Department at Indiana University, who checked the translation against the original.

To those who have willingly lent their advice and ideas—colleagues, students, and friends—our heartfelt thanks. For the remaining infelicities and errors, the translators alone are responsible.

H. G.
E. Y.

San Francisco

INTRODUCTION   *Howard Goldblatt*

Hsiao Hung wrote *The Field of Life and Death* in Tsingtao, Shantung, in 1934; she was 23 years old. Six years later she completed *Tales of Hulan River* in Hong Kong. Within a year, at the age of 30, she was dead of a chronic respiratory infection. In strictest terms these two novels cannot be considered the alpha and omega of her creative life, yet they were the high points of her writing career and, we can suppose, of her tragically short life.

In 1936 Hsiao Hung was asked by the renowned journalist and China-watcher Edgar Snow to write a brief autobiographical sketch for his short-story anthology *Living China*. Though noticeably short on factual data, this piece goes a long way toward describing the author's emotional state at the time of its writing and her feelings toward her family and herself.

> In 1911, in a small county seat I was born into a petty landlord family. That county seat is in what is probably the easternmost and northernmost part of China—Heilungkiang province—and so for four months of any given year there are snow flurries.
>
> My father often gave up his humanity over his own covetousness. His relationships with servants, or with his own children, as well as with Granddad were all characterized by his stinginess, aloofness, and even hard-heartedness.
>
> Once, over rent payment due on a house, my father took possession of a tenant's entire team of horses and his wagon. The tenant's family wept, pleaded, and prostrated themselves at the feet of Granddad, who

then unharnessed two tawny horses from the wagon and gave them back to them.

My father quarrelled with Granddad all night long over those two horses. "Two horses to us mean nothing, but to a poor man those two horses mean his very existence," Granddad said, but my father continued to quarrel with him.

When I was nine my mother died. My father changed even more; when someone would on occasion break a glass, he would shout and carry on until the person was shaking in his boots. Later on, even my father's eyes underwent a change, and each time I passed by him I felt as though there were thorns stuck all over my body; he would cast an oblique glance at you, and that arrogant glance of his would shift from the bridge of his nose, down past the corner of his mouth, and continue moving down.

So at dusk during snowstorms I stayed near the radiator and by Granddad where I would listen to him reading poetry and watch his slightly reddened lips as he read the poems.

Whenever my father beat me, I would go to Granddad's room and stare out the window from dusk to late into the night—the white snow beyond the window floated there like white fleece, while the lid of the water jug on the radiator vibrated, sounding like the accompaniment of a musical instrument.

Granddad would often place his two wrinkled hands on my shoulders, then place them on my head, and my ears would ring with sounds of:

"Hurry and grow up! It will be fine once you have grown up."

The year I reached the age of twenty, I fled from the home of my father, and ever since I have lived the life of a drifter.

I've "grown up," all right, but things are not "fine."

But I learned from Granddad that besides coldness and hatred, life also includes warmth and love.

And so, in my bosom there is a perpetual longing and pursuit to find this warmth and love.[1]

According to Hsiao Hung's second husband, Tuan-mu Hung-liang, she was born on the day of the Tuan-yang or Dragon-Boat Festival, which falls on the fifth day of the fifth lunar month. Local superstition had it that it was unlucky to be born on that day, so her birthday was moved forward to the eighth day of the fifth month.[2]

Hsiao Hung (her true name was Chang Nai-ying) was born into what, by all accounts, was a wealthy landlord family. It is the family that is portrayed in chapters three through five of *Tales of Hulan River*. There seems little doubt that she led a cloistered and troubled childhood in Hulan county, where she was raised, and it is not difficult to reason, from her writings and the comments of her friends, that the source of the emotional and psychological problems she later experienced can be traced to these early years. Her first extended contact with the world outside of Hulan county came when she attended middle school in Harbin, some twenty miles away, in 1928. The initially pleasant and exciting nature of her stay in Harbin came to an end a few years later, when she began cohabiting with a local teacher, was expelled from school, and was subsequently abandoned by the man. Pregnant, destitute, and unwilling or unable to return home, she found herself with no one to turn to.

It was during this time, too, that the opening shots of the Sino-Japanese conflict were fired. On September 18, 1931, a rather minor anti-Japanese incident occurred near the southern Manchurian city of Mukden. Retaliation was swift and decisive and led to the formalization of Japanese control over all of Manchuria with the establishment of the puppet regime of Manchukuo in early 1932.

A few months after this incident Hsiao Hung met and began living with a contributor of stories and poems to a Harbin newspaper who wrote under the penname of San Lang. Over the ensuing year and a half, Hsiao Hung (who had adopted the pseudonym Ch'iao Yin—"Gentle Moanings") also contributed works to the newspaper. In August 1933 she and San Lang privately published a joint anthology of stories and essays entitled *Trudging* (Pa-she); it was quickly proscribed by the Japanese and never reprinted.

By the spring of 1934 the Japanese occupation of Manchuria had become intolerable to patriotic Chinese youths. Following a brush with the Japanese authorities, Hsiao Hung and San Lang fled to Shantung, where they stayed for six months before traveling on to Shanghai. During their brief stay in the city of Tsingtao, the two writers worked on their first full-length novels. San Lang's *Village in August* (Pa-yüeh ti hsiang-ts'un), which he wrote under the pseudonym T'ien Chün, was not completed until after his arrival in Shanghai, in August 1935. It is the story of a band of guerrilla patriots and their anti-Japanese activities. Hsiao Hung, on the other hand, completed her manuscript prior to her departure from Tsing-tao for Shanghai. It was sent ahead to Lu Hsün, the most popular and influential literary figure of the time, with the hope that he would help to get the work published. This novel, untitled at the time, was *The Field of Life and Death*. It was, in fact, published un-der Lu Hsün's auspices, but not until late 1935, when Hsiao Hung had been in Shanghai for over a year and had already had several short pieces published in Shanghai magazines. By then her relation-ship with her domineering husband, who had now adopted the pseudonym by which he is best known—Hsiao Chün—was becoming strained. Fortunately for her, the unhappiness she was experiencing in her life with him was balanced by the intimate friendship she had formed with Lu Hsün and his family.

Following the appearance of *The Field of Life and Death*, which made its author an overnight literary sensation, Hsiao Hung pub-lished a long reminiscence of her life with Hsiao Chün in Harbin from 1932 to 1933, entitled *Market Street* (Shang-shih chieh), and a collection of short stories and essays entitled *The Bridge* (Ch'iao). But in early 1936, when her treatment at the hands of Hsiao Chün was growing unbearable, and Lu Hsün was beset not only by physi-cal ailments but was also embroiled in a heated battle over National Defense Literature, Hsiao Hung left Shanghai for Japan. There, for the remainder of 1936, she licked her wounds, studied a little, and did some writing.[3] Lu Hsün died on October 19, 1936; this was an unparalleled emotional blow to Hsiao Hung, and precipitated her return to Shanghai from Japan. She had now lost the second person in her life who had treated her with kindness, understanding, and warmth (her grandfather, of course, was the first). The death of Lu Hsün was a prime reason why, over the next two years, Hsiao Hung's literary output nearly ceased. But there were other reasons as well, on both the national and personal levels.

The full-scale opening of war with Japan in July and August 1937 drove large numbers of writers out of besieged Shanghai and into the interior. Hsiao Hung and Hsiao Chün joined the exodus, settling for a few months in Wuhan. There she met another writer from Northeast China, Tuan-mu Hung-liang, who, for good or ill, was to be the most important figure in her life from that point on. In early 1938, following a one-month journey to Northern China (the stay there cut short by the approach of the Japanese army), Hsiao Hung and Hsiao Chün separated, and she eventually returned to Wuhan in the company of Tuan-mu Hung-liang, with whom she lived, off and on, for the next four years. She was pregnant again, and was left alone in Wuhan when Tuan-mu Hung-liang traveled to the new capital of Chungking. The accumulation of physical and emotional ills that beset her pushed her to the brink of despair. In September she, too, went to Chungking, where she was delivered of a dead infant. Following her subsequent reunion with Tuan-mu Hung-liang, her life returned to normal: she began to write again, and slowly regained some of her health.

The war, from which Hsiao Hung had been fleeing for most of her adult life, caught up with her again in Chungking, so she and Tuan-mu Hung-liang fled to Hong Kong in early 1940.[4] A year or so later her second novel, *Ma Po-lo*, was published. It is a humorous satire set in Tsingtao and Shanghai and, though generally condemned by contemporary critics who were demanding wartime literature of a more strident, propagandistic variety, is an entertaining and rather successful novel.[5]

In December 1940 Hsiao Hung completed her manuscript of *Tales of Hulan River*, a work which was begun in Chungking but whose origins go back even further, to one of the stories she had written in Japan in 1936.[6] A sequel to this novel was planned, but she never had the opportunity to put her plan into effect. Her physical condition, which had been poor from as early as her days in

Harbin and was adversely affected by her almost nomadic and bo-hemian life throughout the first stages of the war with Japan, grew even worse during her stay in Hong Kong. Bothered by a recurring stomach ailment, tuberculosis, and complications during child-bearing, in December 1941 she was forced into the hospital be-cause of a respiratory condition. On January 22, 1942, slightly over a month after the Japanese occupation of the city, Hsiao Hung died in a temporary hospital set up by the Red Cross; she had not reached her thirty-first birthday. Her remains were cremated and buried in Repulse Bay, where they stayed until August 1957, when they were transferred to the city of Canton for permanent burial.

The Field of Life and Death

Hsiao Hung's first novel was published in Lu Hsün's Slave Society Series by the Jung-kuang Book Company in Shanghai in December 1935. It has long been heralded by Chinese critics as one of the two earliest and most important examples of anti-Japanese literature (Hsiao Chün's *Village in August* is the other). Yet the anti-Japanese theme is not the dominant one. Rather the novel is a grim and powerful portrait of the lives of peasants in Northeast China. The effect of the work on its contemporary readers was anger, pity, and a sense of outrage, outrage not only against the outside forces that so demeaned and brutalized the villagers, but also against the fatalis-tic, passive, conservative mentality of the peasants themselves. To readers of our generation, the forceful impact is lessened only slightly by the knowledge that the events portrayed belong to his-tory. Humanity being what it is we can never be assured that such suffering, cruelty, and ignorance are very far away.

The Field of Life and Death is not the story of any particular in-dividual. Many of the characters we find in it are little more than types, and although the spotlight shifts from one individual or family to another, it seldom stops long enough to give much definition. It is the aggregate village that has the starring role, and with the author's skill, it comes alive.

It is unfortunate that this broad aspect and many finer points have escaped the attention of most critics in the years since the novel was first published, for by focusing only on the final portion of the work and its patriotic message, Hsiao Hung's artistic skill and the subtle workings of her creative mind have gone largely neglected. There is, for example, the strong Buddhist flavor that runs through much of the novel: the villagers' fatalistic attitudes, repeated mention of the four distresses (birth, old age, sickness, and death), and even the title itself (samsāra in Sanskrit) are unquestionable and, we can assume, conscious references to the Buddhist faith. Beyond this, we might ponder the possibility of Christian influences on the author (who lived in an apartment below a Catholic nun in Tsingtao and was friendly with several Russian emigrès in Harbin); the sacrificial goat is but one possible manifestation of this influence.[7]

The role of animals, generally, is yet another neglected aspect of this novel (see Hu Feng's Epilogue for the major exception). Whether it is Mother Wang's old mare, Two-and-a-Half Li's goat (which both opens and closes the novel), the stray dog that shares Golden Bough's lodging in Harbin, or Chao San's ox, animals are often used to heighten the dramatic effect of an episode or scene. Animal imagery, too, is a significant facet of Hsiao Hung's descriptive art; in the first two chapters alone, the characters' appearance and actions are portrayed with the aid of animal images nearly twenty times. The visual effect of this device on the reader is substantial.

Finally, the related themes of feminism and autobiography deserve detailed investigation. These two themes are most obvious in the chapters dealing with Golden Bough's liaison and subsequent marriage to Ch'eng-yeh, the almost horrifying chapter on births, and the episode concerning Golden Bough's adventures in Harbin. That Golden Bough is, in some respects and to some degree, a fictional representation of the author herself is hard to dispute. Her ambi-

valent and often contradictory view of men seems to parallel what
we know of Hsiao Hung's experiences in this regard. Hsiao Hung's
dependence upon men, her willingness to allow them to use her for
their own ends, and the anger that erupted when she was abandoned
or mistreated are nearly exactly duplicated in Golden Bough. Beyond
this, the agonies of childbirth and the demeaning act of prostitution
by an impoverished woman were also experienced by Hsiao Hung
no more than two years before she wrote The Field of Life and
Death.

All of this brings us to the final portion of the novel and the introduction of the anti-Japanese theme. When it is viewed in political
terms (as it has been by most Chinese critics and literary histor-
ians), this portion of The Field of Life and Death makes it the important novel it is, but when it is viewed from a more detached literary perspective (as a few more recent critics, myself included, have
attempted to do), this portion is the weakest and least well-integrated
part of the work.[8]

Upon further reflection and analysis, however, I believe there may
be yet a third approach, one in which the true significance of this
portion of the novel may be discerned. For with all its literary flaws
and political overtones, it is here that we perceive the author's
understanding of the burning issue of the day—Japanese aggression
and approaching war—and the force of her implicit message is clear.
The uncharacteristically (for her) sketchy, ill-defined descriptions;
the abrupt, loosely connected transition from the first to the second
parts of the novel; and the role of hearsay as regards the actions of
the Japanese all point to a fragmented and clouded comprehension
of events taking place around her. What Hsiao Hung puts before
the reader is not the idealized, patriotic-romantic view of war, but
the isolated and extremely personal effects it has on real people in
everyday situations. Rather than viewing the war in its broad his-
torical sense, she has subtly yet forcefully described the individual
tragedies experienced by people who, like the author herself, are
brutalized by this violence they do not really understand. The epi-
sodic and loosely connected nature of this portion in particular and

of the novel as a whole makes one think of a series of individual photographs, each with its own clarity and significance. That is, after all, how Hsiao Hung observed the lives of her villagers, before and after the advent of war. In this she may well be representative of the vast majority of her feminine contemporaries who, raised in a patriarchial society that relegated women to domestic functions, relied upon their menfolk and gossip for their knowledge and understanding of the world beyond their family circles.

Tales of Hulan River

The careful reader of *The Field of Life and Death* and *Tales of Hulan River*, while acknowledging the almost totally disparate nature of the two novels, will find a great many similarities in style, themes, and specifics. The same issues, for the most part, were the author's concern in both works written six years apart. The plight of the peasants, the role of women, the scenic beauty, all these are at the core of Hsiao Hung's literary creations. In almost every case these themes are most powerfully and vividly drawn where they are inextricably tied up with Hsiao Hung's personal experiences and observations. In other words, she is at her finest when she is most openly autobiographical, and *Tales of Hulan River* is an autobiographical novel. Regarding this type of work, Northrop Frye has written:

> Autobiography merges with the novel by a series of insensible gradations. Most autobiographies are inspired by a creative, and therefore fictional, impulse to select only those events and experiences in the writer's life that go to build up an integrated pattern. This pattern may be something larger than himself with which he has come to identify himself, or simply the coherence of his character and attitudes.[9]

Tales of Hulan River is not merely an exercise in nostalgia, nor is its purpose to feed the author's ego, for while recounting the experiences and images of her youth, it clearly captures her attitudes as an adult, her concerns about the society in which she lives, and her philosophical position. Her descriptions of the incidents, people, and scenery that made up her early life hold deeper meaning than is at first apparent.

Chapter five, the tragic story of the child-bride, is the author's most powerful indictment of the cruel and dehumanizing effects of traditional society. It is a tale of suffering, insensitivity, selfishness, morbid curiosity, superstition, and compassion made impotent in the face of more powerful forces. It is not an isolated theme, for the victims of this complex social order people many of the other chapters as well. The young women whose lives are the counterpoints to the outwardly convivial activities of the various festivals are all sacrificed in the name of traditional morality and wisdom. This is not, as Mao Tun and others have suggested, merely a result of the author's melancholia in her final years, but as we can see with equal clarity while reading *The Field of Life and Death*, it is an idée fixe with Hsiao Hung. The effect is heightened by the way in which she deals with more or less commonplace events and contrasts the ostensibly serene and simple daily life of the town as a whole with the horrors experienced by the individuals whose lives are swallowed up in this grand design (in chapter one she has given the reader a microcosmic view of this paradox in her description of the products of the ornament shops and the lives of the craftsmen themselves). As we have seen in the autobiographical sketch, however, warmth and love are irrepressible, if generally in retreat, in Hsiao Hung's world; this is evident in *Tales of Hulan River*. Beyond the obvious figure of the narrator's grandfather, the people in this novel are eminently worthy of love and compassion, and goodness can be its own reward. The good will triumph, and the evil will suffer cosmic retribution (represented by the breakup of the Hu family in chapter five and the poetic justice meted out to its members).

Among the most striking features of *Tales of Hulan River* are the simple beauty of Hsiao Hung's rhetorical style and the vivid quality of her descriptions. The Western reader may occasionally find her repetitive passages tedious, her frequent summarizations redundant, and her language too prosaic. Taken as a whole, however, the un-adorned and unpretentious style brings to the work highly evocative and intimate qualities. Her genius in capturing detail and nuance (the camera-like quality already apparent in *The Field of Life and Death*) makes this work appeal to the reader's visual as well as verbal senses. It should come as no surprise to the discerning reader that Hsiao Hung was a budding artist in her youth and continued to paint for most of her adult life.

In the final analysis, *Tales of Hulan River* must stand as Hsiao Hung's representative work; it is her most personal and artistic creation and is a lasting testimony to her artistic genius.

Notes

1. Edgar Snow, comp. and ed., *Living China: Modern Chinese Short Stories* (New York, 1937). We do not know which of Hsiao Hung's stories Snow planned to include, for none was used. The Chinese original of this sketch was printed in the inaugural issue of *Pao-kao* (Reportage), January 1937, pp. 73–77. The reader who is interested in examining the life of Hsiao Hung more closely may consult my *Hsiao Hung* (Boston, 1976). New data which have appeared more recently will be cited below.

2. See Tuan-mu Hung-liang, "Chi-nien Hsiao Hung, hsiang tang chih-ching" (Remembering Hsiao Hung while Paying Respects to the Party), *Ta Kung Pao*, August 15, 1957, p. 57. See *Tales of Hulan River*, chapter two, for a description of the consequences of being born during the Festival of the Hungry Ghosts, the fifteenth day of the seventh month.

3. She wrote a total of four stories and one essay which first appeared in-dividually in Shanghai magazines, then were published together in 1937 in the collection *On the Oxcart* (Niu-ch'e shang).

4. See Mao Tun's Introduction (Appendix III) for some details of her life in Hong Kong.

5. According to a recent source, a sequel to *Ma Po-lo* appeared in serialized form just prior to Hsiao Hung's death. This, her last piece of creative writing, was never published in book form. See Liu Yi-ch'ang, "Hsiao Hung ti *Ma Po-lo* hsü-kao" (The Sequel to Hsiao Hung's *Ma Po-lo*), *Ming Pao Monthly*, No. 144 (December 1977), pp. 72–75.

6. "The Family Outsider," which was the basis for chapter six of the novel (not included here), is scheduled for inclusion in C. T. Hsia, Joseph S. M. Lau, and Leo Ou-fan Lee, eds., *Modern Chinese Stories and Novellas, 1918–1949* (forthcoming from Columbia University Press). An English translation of chapter seven, entitled "Harelip Feng," appeared in the magazine *Chinese Literature* (see Bibliography).

7. Christianity portrayed in negative terms plays an important role in *Ma Po-lo*.

8. See *Hsiao Hung,* pp. 44–49, 122–23.

9. Northrop Frye, *Anatomy of Criticism* (Princeton, 1957), p. 307.

. . . for those whose lives are at
Heaven's mercy, who hasn't experienced
Heaven's wrath?
                    —Hsiao Hung

Hsiao Hung

The Field of
Life and Death

*Translated by Howard Goldblatt
and Ellen Yeung*

1 THE WHEAT FIELD

A goat gnawed at the exposed roots of an elm tree by the side of the road.

The long road outside the city had been partitioned into shady patches by the elm trees. Walking down this road was like walking under a huge swaying umbrella that blocked out the sky.

As the goat gnawed at the bark of the elm, threads of saliva trickled down its whiskers. When these threads of saliva were caught up by the wind they looked like soap lather, or like sluggishly floating strands of silk. The goat's legs were covered with them. The huge scars on the elm tree bore witness to the fact that it was badly ulcerated. Yet the goat lay down to sleep in the tree's shade, the white pouch that was its stomach rising and falling.

A little boy made his way slowly through the vegetable plot. With his straw hat on he resembled a big mushroom. Was he hunting for butterflies, or was he stalking grasshoppers, this little boy under the midday sun?

Before long a limping farmer also appeared in the vegetable plot. The color of the patch of cabbages was almost the same as that of the goat.

Adjacent to the southern end of the vegetable plot was a patch of green-tasseled sorghum. The little boy wormed his way in among the sorghum, brushing against the tassels with his head and knocking them to the ground. Some of them struck him on the face. The leaves rubbed against each other, at times pricking his skin. He was in a world of verdant sweetness, a world that was obviously cooler than the one outside. Soon the little boy fought his way to the last stalk. At that instant the sun began to scorch his crown, and he nimbly pulled his hat back on. Under the canopy of blue sky the sun sent its rays to dance atop the vegetable plot. There wasn't a cloud to be seen. The little boy carried a willow switch tucked under his arm. He was so bowlegged and pigeon-toed that, as he walked, it almost looked as though he were holding a bowl between his legs. The limping farmer had long since discerned that it was his son, and from that distance he hailed the boy in a raspy voice: "Hey, Tunnel Legs! Didn't you find it?"

The name fit the boy just perfectly. "No," he answered.

The narrow path at the edge of the vegetable plot was fringed by wild vegetables. At the other end of this short path was Two-and-a-Half Li's* house. In front of his house stood a poplar tree, the leaves of which rustled and shook. Every day, as Two-and-a-Half Li passed beneath the tree, he invariably stopped to listen to the rustling sound of its leaves and watch their movement. So it was with the poplar day after day, and day after day he stopped. On this day, however, he abandoned his routine. His mind was a complete blank. His limp had become more pronounced, and with each stride he seemed to be stepping into a hole.

A fence woven of twigs surrounded the mud house. Half of the yard was covered with the shade of the poplar, and in this shade Old Mother Pockface was doing the laundry. In the fields the midday calm was broken only by butterflies that waltzed among the flowers, unafraid that the sun would singe their wings. Everything had gone into seclusion. Even the dog had found a shady spot for its nap. Insects, too, were hidden and silent.

Perspiration gathered on the face of Old Mother Pockface like pearl drops or peas, seeping into every pockmark and then flowing

---

*Li, a unit of measurement, approximately one-third of a mile.

downwards. Old Mother Pockface was not a butterfly. She could not sprout wings. Only pockmarks.

Two butterflies flitted by Old Mother Pockface, and she swatted at them with her wet hands, bringing them down. One fell into the tub and drowned. As her body continued its fore-and-aft movement, perspiration flowed down to her lips, salty to the taste. When the perspiration ran into her eyes, stinging them, she quickly rubbed them with her wet hands, but she never stopped her washing. Her eyes looked as though they were red from crying, and where she had wiped them with her hands, funny-looking smudges appeared. Seen from afar, she looked to have been made up as a clown for the stage. Her eyes were frighteningly large, larger even than those of a cow. Irregular lines crisscrossed her face.

The windows and the door of her house looked like mere holes. Old Mother Pockface stepped through the doorway. She was looking for another garment to wash, but when she tried unsuccessfully to pick up a shadow from the k'ang,* she knew that her eyes had been momentarily dazzled by the sun. It was like passing from light into complete darkness. After resting for a while, she felt much cooler. Then from beneath the mattress she pulled out a pair of her own pants, with which she dabbed at her brow as she returned to her tub in the shade. Into the muddy water went the pants. The pants were probably not thoroughly clean, but she hung them on the fence anyway. Or maybe they were clean after all. Old Mother Pockface's chores came one right after the other. And if necessary, before finishing one, she would lay it down and start on another.

From the chimney of the nearby house surged clouds of thick smoke. Scattered by the wind, it filled the whole yard and assailed her eyes. Realizing that her family would soon be home for dinner, she grew flustered. With her mud-covered hands, she grabbed a handful of straw from the corner, and with straw still sticking to

---

*K'ang, a heated brick bed used in Northern China.

her hands, she started to cook. She never bothered to rinse her hands with clean water. Soon smoke was curling out of her chimney, too. She came out for more firewood. She gathered up an armful of straw, and half of it trailing on the floor and the other half dangling from her apron, she waddled along. With her hair falling down over her face, she looked like a she-bear. The she-bear carried the straw into her cave.

As the thick smoke obliterated the sun, the yard suddenly turned dark. The smoke hung in the air like clouds. Water dripped from the clothes hanging on the fence and evaporated into muddy-looking steam. The whole village was suffocating in the stifling heat. The midday sun ruled over everything.

"Damn. . . . It must have been stolen."

When Two-and-a-Half *Li* limped badly, his buttocks protruded, and always in the same configuration. He rapped on the fence of the goat pen, but where was the goat?

"Damn. . . . Who'd steal my goat . . . the son-of-a-bitch."

Hearing her husband swear, Old Mother Pockface came out with bulging eyes. "Are you complaining about dinner being late? I thought you weren't coming, so I did some washing." When Old Mother Pockface spoke, she sounded like a pig. Perhaps she had the vocal cords of a pig, for the sounds she made were pig noises.

"Aiya, the goat is gone. Why would I be bawling out a stupid wife like you?"

When Old Mother Pockface heard that the goat was gone, she went right over and began to dig through the stack of firewood. She remembered that once the goat had hidden itself in there. But that had been in the winter when the goat was trying to get warm, and she did not realize that only a goat that was as stupid as she would go into the stack to get warm in the month of July. She kept digging through the stack, without even thinking. Her hair was covered with wisps of straw. Her husband tried to stop her, asking her what she was doing, but she didn't answer him. She was hoping that her actions would produce a miracle, one that would make people look up to her from then on. In order to show that she was not stupid, to show that her intelligence would rise to the occasion when necessary, she tired herself out, the way a dog playing in a stack of firewood would do. She finally sat down and picked at the wisps of straw in her hair. She sensed, to her surprise, that her intelligence had failed her; to her surprise, she also experienced disappointment in herself.

Before long the neighbors fanned out under the sun to look for the goat. The rice in Old Mother Pockface's rice pot was already letting off steam, but she, too, joined the search.

Before he had traveled very far, Two-and-a-Half *Li* ran across Tunnel Legs. "Papa, I'm hungry," the boy said.

"Go home for dinner then," Two-and-a-Half *Li* answered him.

But when he wheeled around he saw his wife, looking like a bundle of straw, trailing after them.

"You, woman, what are you doing here? Take him home to eat." With this, he turned around and limped on ahead.

Only stubble remained on the yellow and yellowing patches of wheat field. Viewed from a distance, the wheat field was a distressing sight. At the edge of the field someone was drawing water from a well. Two-and-a-Half *Li* shaded his eyes with one hand and peered around. He suddenly made up his mind to go over to the well. When he got there he looked down the sides. Nothing. He lowered the bucket to the bottom of the well to check. Again nothing. Finally he raised the bucket and, leaning against the rim of the opening, he drank, the water gurgling in his throat. He sounded like a horse at the trough.

Old Mother Wang was resting on the grassy patch of ground in front of her house.

"How's the wheat threshing coming along? My goat's gone." Two-and-a-Half *Li*'s pale face had grown even paler because of the goat's disappearance.

"*Baa-aa . . . baa-aa . . . .*" The bleating of a goat? No, it was not a goat; only someone looking for the goat.

Under the shade of the trees a line of carts carrying bricks passed, the drivers making loud noises. The goat woke from its nap. Still half asleep, it scratched itself all over with its horns. The green of the leaves made its coat look a pale yellow. Alongside the road, a melon seller was eating his own melons. The line of brick-carrying carts stirred up clouds of dust as it moved from the shade onto the road leading into the city.

The goat grew lonesome. It had already finished its nap and its meal of bark and was ready to go home. But no, it was not going home. It passed under every tree and listened to every whispering leaf. Could the goat be heading into the city, too? Yes, it was trotting toward the road leading into the city.

"*Baa-aa . . . baa-aa . . . .*" The bleating of a goat? No, it was not a goat; only someone looking for the goat. Two-and-a-Half *Li* made the loudest noises of all, but he didn't sound like a goat. He sounded more like a cow.

In the end, Two-and-a-Half *Li* came to blows with a neighbor. His hat, like a kite separated from its string, drifted down from his head and sailed off some distance away.

"How dare you walk on my cabbages . . . you . . . you . . . ."

The tall man with the red face looked exactly like the Prince of Demons. Two-and-a-Half *Li* was beaten till he saw stars. He pulled up a small tree beside him, a defenseless, guiltless little tree. The tall man's wife came running out and handed her husband a rake used to stir bean sauce. The rake was still dripping sauce.

When Two-and-a-Half *Li* saw the rake he fled home carrying the small tree. The straw hat lay by itself beside the well, the straw hat that he had worn for countless years.

Two-and-a-Half *Li* swore at his wife. "Fool, who wants to eat your burnt rice?"

His face was as long as that of a horse. Old Mother Pockface was alarmed, and her movements grew clumsy. She knew that the goat had not been found. Before long she was weeping beside the rice pot. "My . . . my goat. I fed it every single day . . . and it grew. I raised it with my own hands." By nature, Old Mother Pockface was uncomplaining. Whenever she was unhappy, or was being scolded by her husband, or had a quarrel with a neighbor, or when the children gave her trouble, she would act like a pool of melted wax. By nature she did not like to resist, nor did she like to fight. She seemed to be forever storing sorrow in her heart, which forever seemed to be like a piece of worn-out cotton. Racked by sobs, she mechanically went outside to take down the clothes that were already sun-dried; she did not notice the goat at all.

As for the errant goat, it scratched itself from time to time in the pen, nearly knocking down the door, which banged noisily.

It was already afternoon, but Two-and-a-Half *Li* was still sitting on the *k'ang*. "Damn . . . let it be lost then. It's bad luck to have a goat around, anyway."

But his wife did not understand how keeping a goat could bring bad luck, and she said: "Humph, are we going to just let it disappear like that? I'll go right out and look for it. I think it must be out in the sorghum field."

"You're going to go looking for it again? Don't bother. Let it stay lost."

"I'm sure I can find it."

"Aiya, looking for the goat can create other problems." His mind kept returning to the beating he had taken—his hat drifting down like a kite broken from its string, the rake dripping bean sauce. Quick, grab the small tree! Grab it! These unhappy thoughts kept running through his mind.

His wife knew nothing of what had happened. She walked off toward the sorghum field, which was alive with butterflies and other insects, and in which farmers were working. She did not stop to chat with the women in the fields, and as she passed through the stubby wheat field, she looked like a tiny crawling insect. The sun's rays were weaker than they had been at midday. The buzzing of insects grew louder and louder, and more and more of the insects took flight.

Old Mother Wang was forever telling her endless life story during her leisure time. As she recounted her tale, her teeth would grind against each other in an expression of indignation and anger. Under the stars, the wrinkles on her face seemed greener; her eyes were big

circles that shone with a pale light. Sometimes, when she talked
about something exciting, she would emit funny sounds. Children
from the neighborhood called her an owl, which usually infuriated
her. How could she possibly be a hideous creature like that? she
would think. And as if she were chewing on something, she would
begin to spit.

The mothers would then beat their children, who would run to
the side and cry. By this time Mother Wang would be at the end of
her story, so she would crawl through the window into her house
for the night. But once in a while she would ignore the cries of the
children and, acting as though she could not hear them, would continue her tale. She would talk about a year when the harvest was
so good that she had bought an additional cow; about how the cow
had given birth to a calf; and about what had happened to that calf.
Her talks always had climaxes and anticlimaxes. And when it came
to the cow, she never ran short of words. She would describe its
color, the amount of grass it could consume in a day, and even the
position it slept in.

But, on this particular night, not a single one of those obnoxious
children had come to the yard. Mother Wang and two women from
the neighborhood sat on the trough from which the pigs fed, and
their stories overflowed into the evening air like water.

There were some fleeting clouds in the sky, which, whenever they
obscured the moon, looked like smoke, or like a mountain of coal
ready to burst into flame. Before long, the moon was completely
buried in the clouds. Not even the croaking of frogs could be heard.
There were only the twinkling lights of fireflies. From the cavelike
house came the sound of snoring, which gradually spread over the
whole yard. The winking stars at the edge of the sky went on and off.
Mother Wang's story continued on like the passing clouds in the
sky:

"The child was three when I let her fall to her death. If I had kept
the child, I would have become a vegetable. That morning . . . let me
think . . . yes, it was morning. Anyway, I placed her on the haystack
when I went to feed the cow. Our haystack was behind the house.

When I remembered the child, I ran to get her. But she wasn't there. Then I saw the rake under the haystack, and I knew at once that it was an evil sign. She had fallen right on top of the rake. At first I thought she was still alive, but when I picked her up . . . aah!"

A streak of lightning rent the sky, and in that eerie light Mother Wang looked like a frenzied phantom. The entire wheat field, the sorghum field, and the vegetable plot were all visible in the light. The women were startled as if something cold had brushed across their faces. After the lightning had passed, Mother Wang continued:

"Aah . . . I threw her in the haystack, with blood flowing all over the hay. Her little hand was trembling and blood was trickling from her nostrils and her mouth. It was like her throat had been cut. I could still hear a rumbling in her stomach. It was just like a puppy run over by a cart. I've seen that happen with my own eyes. I've seen everything. Whenever a family in this village decided not to keep a child, I would take a hook, or maybe a paring knife, and I would dig the child out from its mother's womb. A child's death is nothing. Do you really think I'd moan and wail because of that? At first I trembled. But when I saw the wheat field before me, I no longer had any regrets. I didn't shed a single tear. After that we had a good harvest of wheat. I was the one who reaped it, who picked up the wheat grains one by one. That entire fall I worked like the devil, never stopping to gossip or even to catch my breath. Then came winter. I compared my grains with the neighbors', and mine were so much larger. That winter I had terrible pains in my back from all that bending over, but in my hands I held those big full grains. But when I noticed that my neighbors' children were growing, I paused to think of my own Hsiao Chung."* Mother Wang nudged the woman next to her as she shook her head.

"My child's name was Hsiao Chung. For several nights I suffered. I couldn't sleep. What was all that wheat worth? From then on,

---

*Hsiao literally means "little," and is commonly used in childhood appellations.

grains of wheat didn't matter much to me. Even now, nothing matters to me. I was only twenty then."

Flashes of lightning, one after another. The phantom who had been speaking sat mutely in the light. The women looked at each other, suddenly feeling chilled. A snarling dog ran over from the wheat field. The night was filled with silent clouds. Suddenly another flash of lightning, and the yellow dog ran with its tail between its legs to Two-and-a-Half *Li*. After the lightning, the dog returned to the haystack.

"Is Third Brother home?" a voice asked softly from the tall grass.

"He's asleep." Mother Wang retreated into silence again. Her response seemed to come from an empty bottle or from some empty, hollow vessel. She sat alone on the trough as if petrified.

"Third Brother, did you quarrel with Third Sister-in-Law again? This constant bickering is destroying the harmony between you." Two-and-a-Half *Li*, who was always tolerant of his own wife, was measuring someone else by his own standards.

Chao San lit his pipe; there was a smile on his ruddy face. "I didn't quarrel with anyone."

Two-and-a-Half *Li* untied his tobacco pouch from around his waist and spoke slowly: "My goat was lost, or didn't you know? But it came back. You've got to find a buyer for me. Keeping this goat will bring me bad luck."

Chao San guffawed, the lightning illuminating his big hands and ruddy face. "Haw-haw. You may be right. I hear that your hat flew all around the edge of the well."

Suddenly Two-and-a Half *Li* could see the small tree beside him. Quick, grab the small tree, grab it! His dream came to an abrupt end. He knew that the news of his beating had spread. Lingering over the job of lighting his pipe, he defended himself: "That couple was downright unreasonable. Whoever said you can't go looking for a lost goat? She accused me of walking all over their cabbages. So you see, I couldn't fight with her." He shook his head, his shame having left him dispirited. He sucked on his pipe, sincerely believing that the goat would bring him bad luck and a loss of face.

Lightning flashed again, and Chao San, tall, husky, and big-handed, got up from the *k'ang* and rubbed his eyes with his palms. Suddenly he said in a loud voice: "I'm afraid it's going to rain. That's bad. The threshing isn't finished yet, and the wheat is piled up in the fields."

Chao San had the feeling that raising livestock and planting crops were not enough, that he must try to do something in the city. Every day he went into the city until he had begun to neglect the wheat. He was dreaming of something with a better future.

"That wife of mine, why isn't she taking care of the wheat? It will all be washed away by the rain." Chao San took for granted that his wife would be sitting in the yard. The flashes of lightning came more frequently. Then the sound of thunder and the sound of wind. In the dark night the whole village was astir.

"I'm over here. Get the straw mats from the shed and cover up the grains!" As lightning flashed over the wheat field, the sounds of shouting seemed to be echoing off a body of water. Mother Wang shouted again: "Hurry, you good-for-nothing old man! All that sleeping has made you so soft in the head you can't even find the door."

Chao San was intimidated by the impending heavy rainfall and did not exchange words with her.

The sorghum field seemed to be collapsing, and the elm tree at the edge of the field began to whistle, producing an almost metallic sound. Because of the lightning flashes, the entire village would suddenly appear, then disappear back into the darkness. The village was like a bubble floating on the ocean. From the neighboring families came the sounds of babies crying and adults shouting: "The sauce urn hasn't been covered yet!" "Round up the poultry!" And from the wheat-growing families came other shouts: "The threshing isn't done yet!" The farming community was like a chicken coop: throw in a lighted splinter and the chickens will run amok.

The yellow dog began making a den for itself in the haystack, pawing at the hay with its legs and tearing at it with its mouth. Mother Wang was trembling as she picked up a rake. "Damn you! The threshing should have been finished by now. But once you get into the city, you just won't come back. The wheat is going to spoil now."

Two-and-a-Half *Li* approached his house under the lightning flashes. Raindrops were falling, causing a rustling sound in the leaves. As the rain fell on his head, he touched his crown. That reminded him of his straw hat, and as he walked, he began to curse his goat again.

It was morning, and the rain had stopped. In the east a long rainbow hung suspended in the air. Wet-smelling clouds passed overhead. Above the sorghum in the east the sun trailed behind the clouds, sparkling like red crystal, like a crimson dream. Off in the distance the sorghum stood somberly, looking like a small forest. The villagers were taking advantage of the cool morning air and were busy in the fields.

In front of Chao San's house the little boy was leading a horse onto the threshing floor. Because it was a young foal, it trotted after its young master, its tail swishing in the air. The young foal loved to nuzzle the millstone that lay on the ground; pawing the smooth ground with its front hooves, then looking for something, it gave a slightly discordant whinny.

The horse's whinny brought out its master. It was waiting for the millstone to be put in place. When that was done, the foal swished its tail, swished it over and over. It was very docile and happy.

Mother Wang, dressed in a short jacket with wide sleeves, came out onto the threshing floor. Her hair was disheveled and snarled. The morning sun was on her, and her hair looked like the tassels of the ripening corn, red and curly.

Mother Wang touched the straw mat—it was a little damp. She pulled it over to one side. The little boy came over to help her. Then, with wheat grains covering the floor, Mother Wang stood off to one side holding a rake. The boy ran happily into the middle of the floor and the foal started to trot in a circle. The boy in the middle also turned round and round. Like the compass used in drawing a circle, no matter how the foal ran, the boy remained in the center of the circle. The foal got a little wild; it galloped, playful as a child, causing the tassels of grain to splatter beyond the floor. Mother Wang hit the foal with the rake. But the foal soon tired of its antics and, like a puppy exhausted after playing and in need of rest, it stopped. As if possessed, Mother Wang swung at it with the rake, and the foal lunged wildly, made a couple of turns around the floor, pulling the millstone away from the grain-covered floor. It then began to nibble at the grains. The boy, who was holding its bridle, was soundly scolded.

"You're always trying to sneak that animal in here! How can a horse like that help with the threshing? Get the hell out of here, and don't give me any more trouble!"

The child led the horse away from the threshing floor and back to the horse trough; he was coming to get the old mare. He tied up the foal between the poles. The older horse had shed almost all of its hair, and the boy did not like it; so he hit it with the reins to move it along. But the old horse was immovable as a piece of rock or a plant rooted to the ground. This was the foal's mother. It stopped and nuzzled at the open, bleeding cuts on the foal's abdomen. When the boy saw that his beloved foal was bleeding, his eyes brimmed with tears. He could not understand the love between a mother and her offspring because he had never seen his mother; he was an illegitimate child. The old, nearly hairless animal was forced to leave its foal, and with its nose smeared with blood, it stepped onto the threshing floor.

A train passed over the bridge across the river in front of the village, but no one could see it; they could only hear the rumbling sound. Mother Wang watched the black smoke spiraling up into the sky. Some people from the village up ahead were taking cabbages into the city in a cart, and as they passed by Mother Wang's threshing floor, they threw down a few tomatoes, saying: "You people don't plant tomatoes. These are cheap, worthless things. Now wheat is the thing that brings in money." The husky youth driving the cart moved on, cracking his whip.

The old horse looked at the horse beyond the wall, but did not whinny or snort. The boy picked up the tomatoes and began to eat. They were not very ripe, yet it was the unripe tomatoes that always were plucked.

The horse stood there quietly, not even swishing its tail. It did not nudge the millstone, it did not look into the distance, nor did it shirk its work. When there was work to be done, it worked with resignation. When ropes and chains were fastened onto its body, it obeyed its master's whip. The master's whip rarely fell on its body. But sometimes, when it was too exhausted and could not go on, its steps would slow down, and the master would beat it with a whip or with something else. Yet it would not rear wildly, because its future had already been determined by all the past generations.

Gradually the grains on the floor were smashed all out of shape.

"Here, lead the horse for a while, P'ing."

"I don't want to be with the old mare. All day long it's like she's asleep."

P'ing pocketed the tomatoes and retreated to one side to enjoy the fruit.

"You're quite the boy!" Mother Wang scolded. "Well, I may not be able to manage you, but there's still your daddy."

P'ing ignored her and left the threshing floor, heading toward the east edge of the field where flowers grew. As he strolled, he looked at the red flowers and ate his tomatoes.

The old gray phantom was furious. "I'll get your daddy to teach you a lesson!" And like a huge gray bird she left the threshing ground.

The early morning leaves, the leaves on the trees, the leaves of the flowers all glistened with dewy pearls. The limitless rays of the sun shone down on the sorghum stalks. The families nearby were already preparing breakfast.

The old horse was grinding the wheat by itself, its reins dangling below its mouth. It did not nibble at the grains, nor did it stray from its orbit. It made one revolution, then another, the rope and the reins chafing its hairless body with a regular rhythm. The old animal moved without sound and all alone.

The haystacks of the wheat-growing families were piling higher and higher. Fu-fa's haystack was higher than the wall. His woman sucked on her pipe. She was robust but small. As smoke drifted from her pipe, she combed the grains on the ground with the rake in her hand. Her nephew, cracking his whip as he passed under the shady patch up ahead, quietly sang his lonely song. She was moved by his song and nearly stopped her raking. The song continued to come from the edge of the woods.

> Yesterday morning there was a light rain;
> The young maiden donned her rain cloak;
> The young maiden . . . gone fishing.

2 THE VEGETABLE PLOT

In the vegetable plot the red tomatoes were quietly ripening. Young girls picked the bright red fruit, filling their baskets with it. Other girls were picking turnips and carrots.

When Golden Bough heard the crack of the whip and the whistles, she stood up abruptly and left the vegetable plot nervously, basket in hand. At the eastern edge of the vegetable plot she paused beside the fence to listen. The whistling had grown fainter, and the cracking sound of the whip was moving away from her. She waited patiently. Presently the seductive whistling came again from a point behind her. She was getting close to him. Some of the women in the plot saw her and hailed her from afar: "Why aren't you over here picking tomatoes? What are you doing standing over there?"

She shook her two braids, waved, and answered loudly: "I have to go home."

The young girl pretended to be going home. She circled round the neighbors' fences, evading the eyes from the vegetable plot, and headed toward the bend in the river. The basket that hung from her wrist swung from side to side. The whistling in the distance urgently beckoned to her, and she was attracted to it like a piece of iron to a magnet.

The quiet bend of the river smelled damp. There the man stood, waiting.

Five minutes later, the young girl was pinned to the ground, like a helpless chicken in the grasp of a wild animal. Mad with passion, the man's large hands clutched savagely at her body, as if he wanted to swallow it, to destroy that warm flesh. His veins gorged with blood, he cavorted on top of what had become for him a white cadaver. The naked, round legs of the girl sought to coil around him, but could not. A chorus of sound erupted from these two greedy monsters.

The flowers trembled and swayed, and the long grasses behind them were crushed. Not far off, an old woodcutter was cutting wild grass. Having been interrupted, the well-developed young man went down to the sorghum field with the girl, like a hound with its prey. As they fled, his hand traveled under her clothes.

Whistling and cracking his whip, he felt that life was good to him. His body and soul had been sated. His aunt watched him from a distance, and when he got closer, she said: "You've been with that girl again, haven't you? She's really a nice girl . . . ai . . . ai!"

Troubled, the aunt pressed close to the fence. "Auntie, why are you sighing?" her nephew asked. "I'm going to marry her."

"Ai . . . ai!"

His aunt was overcome with anguish.

"Wait till you marry her, then her looks will change. She won't look the way she does now. Her face will turn sallow, and you'll put her out of your mind. You'll abuse and beat her. It's only when they are your age that men carry their women in their hearts."

In her distress, she placed her hand on her heart as if she wanted to prevent it from undergoing any changes. She spoke again: "The girl is probably pregnant by now. If you want to marry her, you'd better do it quickly."

"Her mother doesn't know yet. I have to get a matchmaker."

Fu-fa was coming back, leading a cow. As soon as the woman saw her husband, she hurriedly returned to the yard, pretending to be tidying the stack of firewood. Her husband went up to the well to let the cow drink, then he left again, leading the cow behind him. Like a mouse, the aunt's head shot up, and she resumed her talk with her nephew:

"Ch'eng-yeh, let me tell you. When I was a young girl I also fished by the river. One drizzly October morning I sat at the edge of the river in my rain cloak. I never expected . . . I didn't want it to happen. I know it's a bad thing to sleep with a man, but your uncle, he led me from the river over to the stable. There in the stable everything ended for me. But I wasn't afraid at all, because I wanted to marry your uncle. But look at me now; I'm afraid of men. A man's as hard as a rock, and I don't dare even touch one.

"You're always singing about drizzles, and donning a rain cloak to go fishing. Well, I don't want to hear that song again. You young men aren't to be trusted. Your uncle sang the same song, but now he never thinks of the past. The past is a dead tree that can never be revived."

The young man did not want to listen anymore to his aunt's ramblings, so he turned and went into the house for some wine. Later, emboldened by the wine, he told his uncle everything. At first Fu-fa could only shake his head. "The girl is only seventeen," he finally said, "and you are twenty. What could a young girl like that do in our house to help out?"

Instantly on the defensive, Ch'eng-yeh said: "But she's really pretty. She has jet black braids. She can do anything, and she's very strong."

The uncle could tell from Ch'eng-yeh's words that he was drunk.

So he said nothing more and just sat there musing for a while. Then he laughed and looked at his woman. "Ha, we were like that once. Have you forgotten? Those days . . . I guess you've forgotten them by now. Those were the days. It's nice to think back to our youth."

The woman came over and held his arm. She fawned on him, but he didn't move. She sensed that her husband's smiling face was not the smiling face of long ago. Her heart was filled with his many angry faces. Like him, she did not move either. She gave a laugh but immediately wiped the smile from her face. She was afraid that if she laughed too long she might be scolded again. He told her to bring him his wine cup, and she obeyed as if it were a command. Soon her husband was lying on the *k'ang* in a stupor. She went out on tiptoe, stopping by the doorway. The rustling sound of the paper in the window was in her ears. She felt completely drained of strength; a sense of grayness enveloped her. In front of the yard dragonflies buzzed among the sunflowers. But all of this had absolutely nothing to do with her.

The paper window gradually grew visible, and slowly the window frame came into view. The young girl who had gone down to the sorghum field was deep in thought. As she pondered, her tears fell. But she wept so softly that she could not be heard above the rustling sound of the paper window. Her mother turned over and muttered something, occasionally grinding her teeth. Afraid that she might be beaten, Golden Bough dried her tears in the dark. She felt like a mouse sleeping under the tail of a cat. The whole night passed in this way. Each time her mother turned over, it seemed like an eruption, and she would let fly a curse toward where her daughter rested her head.

"Damn you!" After that she would spit. It was like that all night long. She spat, but not on the floor. She would rather the spittle fell on her daughter's face. This time, however, when she turned over she did not spit, nor did she curse.

But in the morning, after her daughter had finished braiding her hair and was on her way out to the fields, she snatched the basket from the girl like a crazed woman. "You still want to go and pick tomatoes? Golden Bough, you're not made for picking tomatoes. You even left your basket behind. I don't think you have any brains at all. It's lucky that the woodcutter turned out to be Chu Ta-yeh. If it had been anyone else, what chance do you think we'd ever have of getting it back? If someone else had found the basket, your reputation would be ruined. The wife of Fu-fa, didn't she come to ruin at the edge of the river? Even the children in the village were talking about it. Ai! . . . What kind of woman is that? Afterwards she couldn't find any man who would have her. She was with child, so she had to marry Fu-fa. Her mother suffered such terrible shame that she couldn't hold her head up among the villagers any more." The mother saw Golden Bough's face grow ashen; she looked so vulnerable that the mother took pity on her daughter. But she did not notice the girl's hand stealing under her coat to feel her belly. Golden Bough was suddenly thrown into a panic as she realized that she might be with child.

"You go on now," her mother continued, "but don't you go to the riverbank again with the other girls. Remember, you're not to go to the riverbank!"

The mother stood outside the door watching the girl. She did not go inside right away but paused before the door for a long time until the girl's figure merged into the crowd of people working in the fields. Then she went inside the house. As she cooked, she sighed, as if she were harboring some sort of disease within her body.

Every day the farming people had to walk home for their breakfast. As Golden Bough walked back on this particular day, her mother saw her put her hand on her belly. "Do you have a stomach-ache?" she asked.

Startled, the girl removed her hand from inside her coat. "My stomach's fine," she quickly denied, shaking her head.

"Are you ill?"

"No."

So they sat down to eat. But Golden Bough had no appetite, and after drinking a little rice porridge she left the table. Her mother cleared the table by herself.

"You didn't even eat a piece of cabbage. You must be ill."

As Golden Bough walked out the door, her mother called to her: "Come back and put on an extra jacket. You must have taken a chill; that's why you have a stomachache." She handed her a jacket. "Maybe you shouldn't go back to the fields. Let me go."

Golden Bough shook her head, turned, and left. Her mother's small jacket, which had been placed around her shoulders, was not buttoned, and, as she walked, it flapped in the wind.

The tomato patch that belonged to Golden Bough's family was as large as a courtyard. When one reached the patch there was a peppery smell in the air, but no one could say just what the odor was. The tallest tomato plant was about two feet high, its branches laden with the golden-red fruit. Every plant carried many fruits, including some green and half-green ones. Of all the vegetable plots in the area, only theirs and one other that adjoined theirs were to-mato patches. In September many of the people were busy raking potatoes, while others were cutting down the cabbages and loading them onto carts to be taken into the city and sold.

Two-and-a-Half *Li* was one of those who had a vegetable plot. Old Mother Pockface went back and forth loading cabbages onto the cart at the edge of the field. Tunnel Legs also ran back and forth, sometimes with two round cabbages in his arms, which made him look as if he were carrying two huge rocks.

Old Mother Pockface saw that the pumpkins in her neighbors' plot had turned red. She glanced around furtively, and when she was sure nobody was looking, she plucked off four large pumpkins growing alongside her vegetable plot. Two of them were as big as small watermelons. She told her son to carry them, but Tunnel Legs strained so much that his face turned as red as the pumpkins. He could not hold them any longer. His arms felt crushed. He had just passed Golden Bough but had not quite reached the edge of the field when he had to yell for help: "Daddy, the waterme . . . watermelons are going to fall. They're going to fall!"

In his anxiety he had called the pumpkins watermelons. There were many people in the vegetable plots, and they all laughed when they saw him. Sister Phoenix glanced at Golden Bough and said: "Would you look at him. Calling pumpkins watermelons!"

Golden Bough glanced at him and gave a perfunctory smile. Two-and-a-Half *Li* came over and gave the boy a kick. Two of the big pumpkins dropped to the ground as a result. The boy did not cry but stood off to one side, dumbfounded. Two-and-a-Half *Li* lashed out at him: "You nitwit, you son-of-a-bitch! I told you to carry the cabbages. Who asked you to pick pumpkins?"

Old Mother Pockface was right behind them. When she saw her son in trouble, she cleverly bent down and rolled the two bigger pumpkins in among the tomato plants. But since everyone could see what she was doing, she was the only one who thought she was being clever. Two-and-a-Half *Li* asked her: "What are you doing, you stupid insect? Don't tell me you . . ."

Old Mother Pockface mumbled, her speech even more incoherent than usual: " . . . I didn't . . ."

From where he stood, off to the side, the boy accused her shrilly: "Didn't you pick them and ask me to carry them to the carts? Don't deny it!"

Desperately signaling with her eyes, she finally blurted out: "I was stealing them, damn you! Not so loud, or we'll get caught!"

There were some people nearby who were usually too preoccupied with their work to watch the fun no matter what was happening, but today even these impassive souls crowded around. Here was a road-show with three members of the same family performing on stage. Two-and-a-Half *Li* berated the boy: "You goddamn nitwit! You can't help us make a living, but you sure know how to botch things up. Who asked you to pick pumpkins?"

Tunnel Legs was not going to stand there and take the blame, so he ran over and rolled the two pumpkins out from among the tomato plants. Everyone rocked with laughter, the sound of their hilarity ringing in the air; but Golden Bough was like a chick stricken with a contagious disease. She blinked her eyes and crouched down among the tomato plants, not paying attention to anything. She had momentarily escaped from the world around her.

Two-and-a-Half *Li* was so furious he could hardly breathe. Not until he finally disclosed that he had grown the pumpkins for the seeds did Old Mother Pockface heave a sigh of relief. She hadn't, after all, done anything wrong. For, as it turned out, they were her own pumpkins. She raised her head and said to no one in particular: "There, you see. I didn't know. I really didn't know that the pumpkins belonged to us."

Not caring whether what she said was comical or not, she pressed her way through the crowd and placed the pumpkins on the cart. The cart that moved toward the road leading to the city with her bowlegged son running lopsidedly alongside it. The horse, the cart, and the people gradually disappeared down the road.

The incident was bandied about in the fields. Rumors, too, were beginning to spread about Golden Bough.

"It's all over for that girl."

"I knew she was up to no good. Imagine, taking half a day to pick one tomato. And yesterday she even left her basket by the river."

"The riverside is not a place where decent folks go."

Two middle-aged women were sitting behind Sister Phoenix digging for carrots. But they were also gossiping and at times using lewd language that she did not quite understand.

Golden Bough's heart was constantly pounding. For her, time seemed to spin out as long as the spider's silken web. She was in a very depressed state, her expression frail and clouded, as if a veil had fallen across her face. The whistle that she was expecting did not come. She could clearly see the wall around Fu-fa's house, but the man of her dreams did not appear. She continued picking tomatoes, even the green ones, for she was oblivious to the color of the fruits; her basket was getting full. But instead of taking them home, she spread the different-colored fruits on the ground.

"She went to the riverside to be with the man," a woman said, her voice purposely raised. "Shameless hussy. I wonder if the man tore her pants off?"

Golden Bough ignored the sights and sounds before her. She pressed hard on her belly, so hard that she could almost feel something moving inside. Suddenly the whitling came. She stood up and crushed a tomato underfoot; it made a squishing sound like a stepped-on toad. She slipped, and the whistling stopped. No matter how hard she listened, she could not hear it again.

Golden Bough was with the man three times. The first time had been two months earlier. At that time her mother had been unaware of anything. It was only yesterday, when the basket had fallen into the hands of the woodcutter, that her mother had had some vague suspicions.

Golden Bough was in torment. Her stomach had become a hideous monstrosity. She felt a hard object inside, which, when she pressed hard on it, became even more apparent. After she was certain that she was pregnant, her heart shuddered as though it were retching. She was seized with terror. When two butterflies wondrously alighted one on top of the other on her knees, she only stared at the two copulating insects and did not brush them off. Golden Bough seemed to have become a scarecrow in a rice field.

Her mother came. Even from that distance the mother's heart reached out to her daughter. But she approached quietly. From afar, her body looked like a perfect square. Gradually her legs could be discerned, working up and down, peeping out from under the hem of her sacklike clothes. Among the old ladies of the village, what seemed to be her particular characteristic? Angry or pleased, there were always a great many laughter lines gathered at the corners of her eyes. Her mouth was also drawn up into the shape of a smile. The only difference was in the upper lip. When she was truly happy the upper lip retreated, but when she was angry it protruded, forming a tiny peak in the middle and making it look like a bird's beak.

The mother stopped. The telltale sign was apparent—her whole face was smiling, except for the beaklike mouth. The sight of all those green tomatoes angered her. Lost in thought, Golden Bough suddenly received a kick from her mother. "Are you crazy? Have you lost your mind? I'm going to tear out your braids. . . ."

Golden Bough offered no resistance. She slumped to the ground. The mother pounced on her own daughter like a tiger, and soon Golden Bough's nose was bleeding. Her mother scolded her in a low voice. In her wrath, her expression became even more jolly as the beak took shape, with more and more lines gathering at the corners of her eyes.

"Well, young missy, you really know how to spoil things. Did you decide to pick green tomatoes? Is it because I scolded you last night, and you didn't like it?"

Her mother had always been like that. She loved her daughter, but when her daughter ruined some vegetables, then she directed her love toward the vegetables. For farming people, even a single vegetable or a single straw was worth more than a human being.

It was time for bed. By the side of the door some incense was burning from a wire that was used for hanging up hand towels. In the house not a single flying mosquito could be heard. On summer nights every family lit incense, which burned slowly and for a long time. Like the joss sticks burning in a temple, the incense would obliterate all sounds and lull the people into slumber, and the fragrance of artemisia would weave itself into the dreams of the tired souls. The mosquitoes were all driven away by the fumes. Golden Bough and her mother were not yet asleep when a man came to the window and coughed softly.

The mother turned at once to light the lamp as they heard the door opening. It was Two-and-a-Half *Li*. But no matter how she tried, the mother could not get the lamp lit. A sizzling sound came from the wick. She held a match in her hand and brought the lamp up to eye level. "There isn't a drop of oil here," she said.

Golden Bough went outside to get oil. During this time, the two elders discussed a matter that she had not expected. The mother, startled by the business, shook her head resolutely, as if ashamed. "That's impossible. My daughter cannot be married into that family."

Two-and-a-Half Li heard the girl replace the cover of the oil can and he stopped talking. Golden Bough, who was standing at the threshold, said to her mother: "There's no more oil. Shall I put in some water?"

After Golden Bough had set up the lamp, she put it down on the edge of the k'ang and lit it. She had no inkling at all that she was the cause of Two-and-a-Half Li's visit. Two-and-a-Half Li kindled his pipe from the burning incense.

The mother, her hands pressing on the pillows, seemed to be deep in thought, knitting her brows till they almost met. Her daughter stood beside her, facing the lamp with bowed head. The tobacco in Two-and-a-Half Li's pipe glowed every time he sucked on it, its smoke mingling with the smell of artemisia, so that the small house seemed as depressing as a dungeon. He coughed a couple of times in embarrassment. Golden Bough replaced the cotton in her bleeding nose with a new piece. Because of the absence of conversation, everyone was unconsciously fidgeting.

Thus they sat. A crackling sound came from the lamp again. The oil floating on top of the water had almost burned out, and the lamp was flickering. Two-and-a-Half Li left with a heavy heart. He had been rejected in his matchmaking mission, and he went home feeling humiliated.

The Mid-Autumn Festival now past, the fields had become a bleak and desolate land. The sun's rays descended moodily from the sky, and a damp smell circulated in the fields. The sorghum in the south had all been reaped, and as one continued the line of vision, one could see the soybean sprouts lying like tousled hair on the ground. There were also plots that had been plucked completely bald.

The mornings and the evenings were the same. The fields continued to wilt while carts drawn by oxen and horses rumbled past, piled high with sorghum tassels and soybean stalks. Saliva drooled from the mouths of the oxen as the rumbling carts passed by.

Fu-fa's nephew was driving a dark-colored ox to cart away the sorghum from their field. He intentionally traveled a circuitous route. There was Golden Bough's door. She was so overwrought she felt her heart would burst. At last she heard the crack of his whip. She put down the red peppers in her hands and said to her mother: "I have to go out to the hut for a moment."

So the old lady was left to string up the peppers by herself, her swift movements those of a weaver.

Golden Bough's braids were coming loose and her face was diffused with blood. But her sickly condition made her look like a paper doll. As if blown by the wind, she appeared at the fence behind her house.

"Are you ill? What's the matter?" But Ch'eng-yeh was a country boy and did not know he should ask such questions. He threw down his whip and, like a bird, soared over the fence. Grabbing the girl, he pulled her down onto the ground, with him on top. It was not because he wanted to kiss her or that he wanted to say sweet things. He was merely driven by a basic desire. Golden Bough struggled. "No," she protested. "My mother will find out. Why hasn't the matchmaker come yet?"

"Didn't Uncle *Li* come around?" he replied. "You mean you didn't even know? He said your mother refused the match. Tomorrow he'll come again with my uncle."

Golden Bough pressed on her belly to show him. She shook her head. "It's not that . . . it's not that. Look what's happening to me."

The young man was unconcerned. Softly he said: "I don't give a damn. Whether she says yes or not, it's going to happen anyway." His eyes glazed over. A man's instinctive craving demanded satiation.

The sound of her mother coughing came faintly through the wall. Beyond the fence the gossamer in the autumn air clung to the horns of the ox.

Mother and daughter were having dinner. Suddenly Golden

Bough vomited. Her mother asked her: "Did you swallow a fly?"
She shook her head.

"Then you must have caught a chill. How come you are always
sick? You can't even eat your rice. You don't have consumption, do
you?" As she spoke she put her hand on her daughter's belly and
felt all around through the jacket. She spread out her fingers on the
belly and mused: "Do you have consumption? There's something
hard in your stomach. Only people with consumption would have
something hard in their stomachs."

Tears welled in the girl's eyes and threatened to brim over. They
finally rolled down her eyelashes. Even at night Golden Bough had to
get up to go outside and vomit. In her sleep the mother could hear
her daughter calling to her. Outside the moon was as bright as day.
She could see Golden Bough, half of her body lying on the floor
and half bent over the pillow. Her face was completely covered by
her hair. When the mother took her hand, the girl sobbed: "Ma . . .
please marry me to Fu-fa's nephew. That thing in my stomach is
not . . . I'm not ill. It's. . . ."

At this juncture she should be beating her daughter, but not this
time. As if she herself were guilty of a wrongdoing, she was paralyzed upon hearing the words. For a long time she seemed not to
exist. After a while she said in a gentle tone that she had never used
before: "You want to marry into his family? The other day Two-and-
a-Half *Li* came to arrange the marriage, but I sent him away. What
should I do now?"

Seemingly calmer now, the mother started to speak again, but
tears stopped up her throat. She felt as if her daughter had strangled
the life out of her. Because of her daughter she would bear this dis-
grace to her grave.

3 THE OLD MARE'S TRIP TO THE SLAUGHTERHOUSE

The old mare stepped onto the road leading into the city. The illegally run slaughterhouse was located just to the east of the city gate. There the knife had been unsheathed in readiness for the frail old animal.

Old Mother Wang was not leading the horse. She was following behind, driving it ahead of her with a switch.

Yellow leaves swirled in the forest, signaling to each other. Seen from a certain direction, the trees in the woods seemed to form a gigantic, half-opened umbrella. Subdued sunlight shone on the naked trees. In the fields one could see the houses far and near. The late-autumn fields stretched out like cold, tanned hides. Houses buried by vegetation in the summer were now exposed, as if they had recently risen out of the ground.

Late autumn brought with it yellow leaves, while chasing away the summer butterflies. A falling leaf landed on Mother Wang's head. It lay there silently. She drove her old mare ahead, wearing a yellow leaf on her head; the old horse, the old woman, the old leaf— they were walking down the road that led into the city.

Up ahead the blurred shape of a person came into view. Gradually she could see that the person was smoking a pipe. It was Two-and-a-Half Li coming toward them and looking like a tame monkey because of his long face and swaying body. "Aiya, it's too early to be up," he said. "Do you have business in the city? Why are you driving the horse into the city instead of having it pull a cartload of grain?"

She shook her sleeves and tucked some stray hairs behind her ears. "It's time," she said, her hands trembling. "Into the soup caldron it goes." Despondently, she watched the horse nibble at the leaves on the roadside and, waving her switch, drove it onward.

Two-and-a-Half *Li* felt very sad, and his body trembled. Before long he turned back and caught up with them. "It's not right to send it to the soup caldron. It's just not right. . . ." But what could he do? He was at a loss for words. He limped forward and patted the horse's mane. The horse snorted in response. Its eyes looked as if they were crying, wet and glassy. Waves of pain stabbed Mother Wang's heart. In a choked-up voice she said: "What is to be must be. If I don't send it to the caldron, the only alternative is starvation."

The bare trees of late autumn, shaken by the harsh winds, wailed like lost souls. The horse walked in front; Mother Wang followed behind. Step by step the slaughterhouse loomed nearer and nearer. Step by step the whistling wind ushered the old mare to its final rest.

Mother Wang was wondering how a person could change so much. How many times had she accompanied old horses and oxen to the slaughterhouse in her youth? She shivered at the horrible vision of the butcher's knife severing her own spine. The switch dropped from her hand. Feeling faint, she stopped by the roadside, her hair so disheveled that she looked like a specter. When she picked up the switch again, the old horse had disappeared. It had gone ahead to the little ditch for a drink. This would probably be its last chance to have a drink. The old mare needed water, and it also needed rest, so it lay down by the ditch. It breathed slowly. Mother Wang called in a low, kindly voice: "Get up. Let's go into town. What else is there?" But the horse just lay there. Mother Wang saw that it was noon already; she had to get back to prepare lunch. But no matter how she tugged at the reins, the horse would not budge. She grew angry. She began to beat the horse with the switch, but even though this forced it to its feet, it would not leave the ditch. Life's afflictions made her irritable, and the switch snapped in two across the horse's back.

They were back on the road, passing deserted houses and dilapidated temples. In front of one of these small temples lay a dead child, bundled up in straw. The child's head and pitiful little feet extended from the straw. Whose child was this, sleeping in front of this temple in the wilderness?

They drew near the slaughterhouse. Now the city gate was directly ahead. Mother Wang's heart turned over.

Five years ago it had been a young horse, but because of farm work it had been reduced to skin and bones. Now it was old. Autumn was almost over and the harvesting done. It had become useless, and for the sake of its hide, the unfeeling master was sending it to the slaughterhouse. And even the price of its hide would eventually be snatched from Mother Wang's hands by the landlord.

When Mother Wang saw the cowhide nailed to the wall, she felt as if her heart, too, were suspended in the air, about to crash to the ground. The street was lined with tumbledown houses. Women and children gathered in groups here and there on both sides. Gray dust kicked up from the street surface covered the shoes and got into the noses of the pedestrians. When the children picked up dirt clods or garbage and threw them at the horse, Mother Wang cursed out at them: "Damn you, you damned bunch of brats!"

It was a short street, at the end of which a double black door stood open. As she drew nearer, she could see bloodstains splattered all over the door. The old lady was frightened by the bloodstains and felt as if she herself were entering an execution ground. She strove for self-control so as not to be put out of sorts by the memories of what she had witnessed on an execution ground in her youth. But the memories unfolded in spite of her efforts: a young man crumpling to the ground; then an old man; the executioner with his axe poised over yet a third man . . . .

As if struck by an arrow, as if seared by flames, Mother Wang did not see the children pelting the horse with their missiles. She had forgotten all about cursing the little ruffians. On and on she walked until she stood in the center of the yard. Nailed to the walls around her were a great many hides. Near the eaves of the building a crossbar was supported by two tall upright stakes, over which several horse and ox hooves tied together with hemp in pairs were draped, neatly suspended there in forked fashion; looped intestines also hung from it in profusion. Having hung there for many days, the now blackened intestines had taken on the appearance of rigidly straight lengths of rope. And then there were the trails of blood running from the site where those leg bones had been dismembered.

Another tall stake rose up on the southern side near the fence, from which hung coils of steaming intestines drying in the sun. This meant that that particular animal had just recently been slaughtered, as its intestines were still warm.

The entire courtyard gave off an overpowering stench, and amidst this world of stench, Mother Wang seemed to have turned to lead. She just stood there as if weighted down, devoid of any emotion.

The old horse, the tawny horse, stood there alone next to the wooden fence, scratching itself by rubbing against a hide nailed to the fence. At the moment it was a horse, but before long it too would be just another hide.

A man with big eyes and a fierce expression ran out, his coat opened at the chest. As he spoke, his heaving chest could be seen. "So you brought it, did you? We'll talk about the price, but let me take a look at it first."

Mother Wang said: "Just give me some money and I'll go. We don't need to fuss over it."

The man flicked the horse's tail and kicked its hoofs. What a torturous moment.

Mother Wang got three bills. That should be adequate to pay the rent for a *mou* of land. She gazed at the money and brightened up a little. With her head down she went out the front gate. She was thinking that she might use the extra money to buy some wine to take home. She had already crossed the threshold when from behind came some loud shouts: "Hey! That's no good! The horse is leaving!"

Mother Wang turned and looked back—the horse was following behind her. Not knowing what was happening, it was heading for home as always. Several men with their hideous faces came running out of the slaughterhouse, prepared to lead the horse back in with them. Finally it lay down at the side of the road; it planted itself there as if it had taken root in the earth. There was nothing Mother Wang could do but walk back into the courtyard, and the horse followed her back in. She scratched the top of the horse's head, and slowly it lay down on the ground, seemingly about to go to sleep. Suddenly Mother Wang stood up and walked briskly toward the gate. At the head of the street she heard the sound of a gate slamming shut.

How could she have the heart to buy wine? She wept all the way home until her two sleeves were completely soaked with tears. It seemed as if she had just returned from a funeral procession.

A servant from the landlord was already waiting by the door. Landlords never let even a single penny go to waste on the peasants. The servant left with her money. For Mother Wang, her day of agony was all for naught. Her whole life of agony was all for naught.

4 THE DESOLATE HILL

Winter. The women gathered together as easily as pine nuts. The entire k'ang at Mother Wang's place was occupied by women. Fifth Sister was making some jute slippers. She had dropped her needle into a crack in the mattress while she was laughing, and she presented a funny sight as she searched for it. Like a nimble pigeon, she stood up and hopped about on the k'ang, shouting: "Who stole my needle? Did a little puppy steal it?"

"No, a little husband did!"

Sister-in-Law Ling-chih, a recent bride, loved to say things like that. Fifth Sister went over and made as if to slap her.

"Don't slap me or you'll get a pockmarked husband."

From the kitchen Mother Wang picked up the threads of conversation. She was usually moody and silent one minute and happy the next; in this she was quite different from the other old ladies of the village. Again her voice floated in from the kitchen: "How many pairs of jute shoes has Fifth Sister made? You must make a few more pairs for your little husband!"

Fifth Sister sat there and made a face as she said: "Whoever heard of an old lady like you who's almost fifty and still says such things?"

"What do you young people know?" Mother Wang said solemnly. "Make a few more pairs. Your little husband will hold you all the more dear."

Everyone cackled with laughter. Fifth Sister didn't dare laugh out loud, but even she was laughing inside. She lowered her head and pretended to be looking for the needle in the mattress. When Sister-in-Law Ling-chih finally returned the needle to her, the room had quieted down. Scraping noises made by Mother Wang, who was scaling a fish in the kitchen, and the sound of the snow falling against the paper window mingled together.

Mother Wang washed the frozen fish with cold water, until her hands were the color of carrots. She walked over to the k'ang and warmed her hands over the brazier. A freckle-faced, recently widowed woman put down the small piece of cloth on which she was working and found an even smaller piece from the rag pile. She quickly mended it. This woman had a face that resembled Mother Wang's—high cheek bones and glassy eyes set deep into the sockets. And like Mother Wang, she had a protruding brow ridge. She did not like to listen to such racy talk, so she asked Mother Wang: "Is your first husband still alive?"

The two hands warming themselves at the fire stank faintly of fish. A scale fell into the fire, crackling slightly and giving off a little smoke. She smothered the smoke with some of the ashes on the side, then slowly shook her head but did not reply. The smoke from the burning scale had such an unpleasant smell that everyone either wrinkled or rubbed her nose. The freckle-faced widow regretted having asked the question. Fifth Sister's elder sister sat in the corner, and as she sewed, the thread rubbed against the shoe sole, producing a monotonous sound. The kitchen door, crusted with ice, creaked in protest.

"Why did you buy this black fish?"

Everybody knew that Second Aunt Li from the fishing village had arrived. From the sound of her voice alone one could visualize her tall, slender figure.

"Is it New Year's yet? Do you really have the money to buy fish like these?"

The sound of her voice rang out crisp and clear in the cold air. As soon as she stepped into the house and saw the *k'ang* full of people, she commented: "All gathered here, eh, you good little wives?"

She was so thin the wind could seemingly snap her in two at the waist. Her breasts were high, like twin hills facing each other. But seen from the side her belly did not seem flat. A middle-aged woman suckling her child near the wall looked her over and made the observation: "Second Aunt, are you pregnant again?"

Second Aunt looked at her own waist. "You think I'm like you, holding one baby in my arms and carrying another in my belly?" She intentionally sidestepped the issue, but then confessed: "This is the third month. You can't tell, can you?" Sister-in-Law Ling-chih leaned over to touch her belly and gave a wicked chuckle. "Shameless hussy, you've probably been doing it all night with your man."

"Who says so? Only new brides like you would do that."

"New brides . . . humph! Not necessarily."

"People like us, we're old. It's nothing to us anymore. But with you young ones, it's really something. It's only your young husbands who get so excited."

Titillated by such talk, each of them began to fantasize about herself. Every heart was pulsating; every face was hot. Even the unmarried Fifth Sister sensed the mystery and began to feel uncomfortable. Bashfully she passed through the kitchen and went home, leaving behind only the married women. Then the conversation grew even bawdier. Mother Wang sat with the group but said nothing, merely joining in the laughter.

In the village, one remained forever unaware. One could never experience the spiritual side of life; only the material aspects gave these people sustenance.

Second Aunt Li asked Sister-in-Law Ling-chih in a low voice (actually they could hear her whispers even more clearly than her normal speaking voice): "How many times a night for you?"

Sister-in-Law Ling-chih was, after all, a new bride. Overcome by shyness, she would not speak. Second Aunt Li, her breasts bouncing, gave her a little push. "Say something. You're young. You must do it every night."

At that moment Two-and-a-Half Li's wife entered the room. Second Aunt nudged Sister-in-Law Ling-chih. "Go on, ask her then."

"How many times do you do it a night?"

She had asked her question of a foolish old woman who was incapable of being anything but blunt: "Ten times or more."

The women in the house roared with laughter till tears ran down their cheeks. The baby in its mother's lap woke up and began to wail.

Second Aunt Li was silent for a while, then she stood up and said: "Oh, I almost forgot: Yüeh-ying wanted to eat some pickles, and I came over to get some."

So Second Aunt Li took her pickles and left, and Mother Wang went to prepare dinner. The rest of the women gradually got up and left for home, leaving Mother Wang by herself in the kitchen frying fish. With the room filled with smoke, it didn't feel quite so lonely.

The fish was laid out on the table, but P'ing had not come back, nor had his father. So in the deepening dusk Mother Wang ate alone, with only the steam to keep her company.

Yüeh-ying was the most beautiful woman in the fishing village. Her family, who lived next door to Second Aunt Li, was also the poorest. She was so gentle that no one had ever heard her raise her voice in laughter or in anger. She had been born with eyes so expressive that in earlier days everyone who met her gaze felt a pleasure and a warmth that could be likened to sinking into a pile of down.

But those days were all in the past. Now Second Aunt Li heard heart-wrenching sobs from next door every night. On a severe winter night in January the moaning grew even more mournful.

The mountain snow blown by the wind seemed to want to bury this little house near the hill. The trees howled; the wind and snow swooped down on the little house. A wind-swept tree on the hillside toppled over. The winter moon, fearful of being shattered by all that pandemonium, retreated to the edge of the sky. At that moment, from next door came a pitiful plea:

"Won't . . . won't you give me a little water? I'm parched." The voice was so weak it trailed off. "My lips are parched. Give me a cup of water."

After a while, since no reply was forthcoming, the quaking entreaties ceased. But the weeping and moaning resumed, and from next door it seemed that the fall of each teardrop could be heard.

During the day the children gathered on the hillside. They climbed up the slope by hanging on to the branches, then tobogganed down the icy path. They adopted different styles for their descent: backward rolls and split swoops, not to mention the daredevils who slid down headfirst, their feet in the air. Often they went home bruised and bleeding. Winter mistreated the village children the way it mistreated the flowers and the crops. Every child's ears swelled up; his hands or feet were frostbitten. The village mothers acted as if the children were their enemies. When they sneaked out with their fathers' woolen caps, their mothers always chased after them, beat and scolded them, and then snatched the caps back. Mothers persecuted their children mercilessly.

Mother Wang went with Fifth Sister to visit Yüeh-ying. Just as they were crossing the slope they saw P'ing; he was wearing his father's big felt boots, which he had stolen from the house. He turned and fled up the slope, but the boots were like the paws of a great bear; he tottered and tumbled back down the slope. This poor child with the big, disproportionate black feet rolled down like a ball, his fall broken by a huge tree trunk at the foot of the slope. Running like the wind, Mother Wang flung herself upon him like a ferocious beast from the wilds seizing its prey. Finally she retrieved the boots, and P'ing had to return home in his bare feet. He dared not tarry, for walking on the ice was like walking on fire. Even after he was some distance away, Mother Wang was still mumbling after him: "One pair of boots has to last three winters. If they're worn through, where will we get the money to buy another pair? Your dad won't even wear them when he goes into the city!"

When Yüeh-ying saw Mother Wang, she was so choked up with emotion that she could not utter a sound. Mother Wang put the boots on the floor next to the k'ang and wiped her nose with her hand. "Are you a little better? You seem to have a little color in your cheeks."

Yüeh-ying tried to push the comforter off, but it stayed draped around her shoulders. "I'm finished," she said. "You see, I can't even push a comforter off me."

Yüeh-ying sat in the center of the k'ang. The hushed dark room seemed to have become a shrine, and Yüeh-ying was the bodhisattva sitting in her place. Surrounded by pillows, she had sat that way for a whole year. For one whole year she had not been able to sleep lying down, for she was afflicted with paralysis. In the beginning her husband had called upon the spirits for her, had offered incense, and had gone to the temples of the local gods for medicine. Later he had even gone into the city temple to burn incense. But all the incense and prayers had done nothing to improve her condition. Finally he reasoned that he had discharged all of his responsibility. Besides, Yüeh-ying's condition deteriorated month after month. Feeling quite heartbroken, he would complain: "What rotten luck to have gotten a wife like you. It's like being married to one of my own ancestors and having to make offerings to her!"

At first, when she argued with him, he beat her. But now, no more. Despair had set in. At night when he came home from the city after selling vegetables,* he would cook his own dinner. Then after eating

---

*Green faggots in the original edition.

he would lie down and sleep till dawn. The suffering woman seated next to him would moan till daybreak. It was as if a human being and a ghost had been thrown together, each having nothing to do with the other.

When Yüeh-ying spoke only the tip of her tongue moved. As Mother Wang drew closer to her, the stench was overpowering; it came from that pile of fetid matter. Yüeh-ying pointed behind her and said: "Look. These bricks were put here by that human devil. He said that since I'm going to die soon, I don't need the comforter. So he propped me up with these bricks. I don't have a bit of flesh left on me. That heartless animal dreams of ways to torture me."

Outraged by the man's cruelty, Fifth Sister threw all of the bricks down off the k'ang. Yüeh-ying's voice began again, haltingly: "I'm finished. How can I possibly get well? I'm going to die!" The whites of her eyes had turned greenish, and so had her straight front teeth. Her frizzled hair stuck close to her scalp. She looked like a sick cat, abandoned and without hope.

Mother Wang placed a blanket around Yüeh-ying's waist.

"Look at the bottom part of my body," Yüeh-ying said. "It's so filthy!"

Mother Wang lifted up the brazier with sticks so that the heat and smoke from the fire rose up, and placed it behind Yüeh-ying. Then she uncovered the blanket and saw that the woman's tiny pelvis was soaked with excrement. Fifth Sister supported Yüeh-ying by the waist, but she uttered heartrending cries of pain: "Oh Mother! . . . oh, how it hurts!"

With her legs like two white bamboo poles stretched out before her, her skeleton formed a right angle with the k'ang. It was a human shape composed of nothing but threads. Only the head was broader; it sat on the torso like a lantern atop a pole.

Mother Wang first used some straw and then a wet cloth to wipe Yüeh-ying's body while Fifth Sister lifted her up from behind. As Mother Wang began to clean her buttocks, little white crawling things dropped onto her arms. She went closer to the fire and looked. They were maggots. She knew then that Yüeh-ying's buttocks were rotten and infested with maggots. The rest of her body, too, would soon become caves for the little maggots.

"Do you feel any pain in your legs?" Mother Wang asked her.

Yüeh-ying shook her head. Mother Wang used cold water to wash her legs. She experienced no sensation; to the paralyzed woman the lower part of her body seemed like something detached, something that did not belong to her. Mother Wang handed her a cup of water and remarked: "How did your teeth turn green?"

Fifth Sister managed to borrow a mirror from next door, and when Yüeh-ying saw her reflection she made loud crying noises. Yet not a single tear appeared on her face. Then, like a cat that had suddenly been run over, she began to make horrible gagging sounds. "I'm a ghost! Please let me die soon! Bury me alive!" She tore at her hair with her hands, twisting this way and that. She turned and twisted violently. Finally she stopped. Exhausted, her head dropped on her shoulder, and she fell into a light sleep.

Carrying the boots in her hand, Mother Wang left the little house by the hill. She saw people walking along the desolate hill, silhouetted against the sky. She was dazed by the bright light, by the paralytic's stench, by worries about birth, old age, sickness, and death. Her train of thought was blocked by all these waves of worry.

When Fifth Sister reached her door, she waved farewell to Mother Wang. The long distance still to go was thus left to this old woman who had more experience with life. Knotting the blue scarf tighter around her head, Mother Wang quickened her step. Underfoot, the snow also quickened its howl in accompaniment.

Three days later Yüeh-ying's coffin was borne swiftly over the desolate hill to be buried at the foot of the slope.

The dead were dead, and the living still had to plan how to stay alive. In winter the women made ready the summer clothes; the men started scheduling the next year's crops.

One day Chao San returned from the city carrying two goatskins over his shoulders. Mother Wang asked him: "Where did these skins come from? Did you buy them? Where did you get the money?"

Preoccupied, Chao San said nothing. He slipped past the stove, and the bright fire illuminated him for a moment. Then he went out.

It was late at night, and he was not yet home. Mother Wang sent P'ing to look for him, but since P'ing could not walk well, she herself went to Two-and-a-Half Li's house. He was not there; he had gone to the fishing village.

Chao San's loud voice came through Li Ch'ing-shan's paper window. Mother Wang could tell he had been drinking. She pushed open the door and said: "What time do you think it is? Why don't you come home to bed?"

All the men in the house clammed up immediately. Mother Wang sensed that something unusual was afoot: Ch'ing-shan's wife was not home, and neither were his children.

"What are you doing here?" Chao San asked her. "Go back home to bed. I'll . . . I'll be along soon."

Mother Wang saw the look on Chao San's face. She also saw that there was no place for her to sit, so she turned and went out. She wondered why Ch'ing-shan's wife wasn't home, and what those people inside were doing.

Another night. Chao San put on a new short jacket made of the goatskins and went out. He did not return till midnight. The moon shone on him as he knocked on the door. Mother Wang was sure that he had been drinking; yet, when he lay down to sleep, she could not smell any liquor on his breath. "Then what had he been doing? Why did he always come back in such an ugly mood?"

Second Aunt Li came with her child. "Is the land rent going to be increased?" she asked.

"I didn't hear about it," Mother Wang replied.

But Second Aunt Li was positive as she said: "Yes, didn't you know? Third Brother comes to my place daily to talk with my boy's daddy. I think there's some trouble brewing. Every night they plot. They keep secrets even from me. Last night I stood outside the window and I heard them say: 'Kill him! He's a curse!' Who do you think they're going to kill? Won't that be murder?" She touched the top of the boy's head with an air of pity. "You must talk to Third Brother. If they get into trouble, how can the likes of us carry on? The children are still young."

Fifth Sister and the other village women arrived with their little bundles at the appointed time. When they came in they were all smiles, but their expressions changed when they saw Second Aunt Li and Mother Wang sitting there in silence. When they learned what was happening, they also grew depressed. Gone were their high spirits and the sounds of their laughter. Feeling very apprehensive, they asked a few questions somewhat fearfully. Fifth Sister's elder sister was the first one to waddle out with her protruding belly. Then the rest of them left, forlornly, one after the other. They were like a school of fish: a fishhook had suddenly been lowered, and they scattered in all directions.

Second Aunt Li had not left yet. She was depending upon Mother Wang to sabotage this risky venture.

Chao San had not eaten regularly at home for several days, during which time Second Aunt Li came over three or four times a day.

"Isn't Third Brother back yet?" she would ask. "The child's daddy isn't either."

It was not until the afternoon of the second day that Chao San returned. As soon as he entered the room, he hit P'ing. Owing to P'ing's bad leg, a group of children had gathered at the house to play. In the center of the yard they had placed a few grains of rice. Then a long plank had been propped up by a short stick, to which they had attached a long piece of string. The string led back into the house. As sparrows pecked at the grains, the children crouching behind the door would keep watch, and when enough birds had assembled, they would give the string a yank. Many hungry sparrows perished beneath the long plank. The kitchen smelled of bird feathers, and the children feasted on sparrows cooked in the oven.

Chao San was in an irritable mood. When he saw a chicken that had been killed by the children, he kicked over the plank. Then he sat on the *k'ang* and lit his pipe. Mother Wang dished out breakfast rice from the pot, but he said: "I've already eaten."

So P'ing came over and finished the left-over rice.

"How's your business coming along? If everything's ready, then you'd better do it soon."

He was caught off guard. How could the news have leaked out?

"Oh, I know all about it," she said. "What's more, I can get a gun for you."

He never dreamed that his own wife was capable of such daring.

Mother Wang did in fact manage to get an old gun. However, Chao San had never used a gun before, so at night when P'ing was asleep, she taught him how to put in the gunpowder and how to load the shots. Chao San began to feel a certain respect for his woman, although the more confidential matters he still kept to himself.

Suddenly in the cow barn five new sickles were discovered, and Mother Wang knew that the day was drawing near.

When Second Aunt Li and the other village women came swarming to her door for information, Mother Wang would lower her head and say: "No such thing. They're only thinking of going hunting a hundred *li* off to bag a few skins and divide them up."

On New Year's Eve something finally happened. At the edge of the northern boundary the snow was stained crimson. But what happened was not what should have happened. Chao San, who had been acting a little odd recently, had broken a thief's leg with a wooden pole. He sought out Two-and-a-Half *Li* to help him throw the thief's body into a pit and bury it with snow. But Two-and-a-Half *Li* dissuaded him: "No, that's no good. When the snow melts in the spring and the body is discovered in the pit, then the news will spread. The charge will be murder."

The villagers heard the screams of pain and came out to investigate. They saw Chao San running around in circles dragging the crippled body, unable to hide it. In his desperation Chao San was hoping to find a well into which he could dump the body. His hands were soon covered with blood. By then the whole village was aroused, and the village chief went to report the matter to the city police. So Chao San was thrown into jail. Without him, the "Sickle Society" of Li Ch'ing-shan and the others languished and finally broke up.

By the end of the first month Chao San's master had interceded on his behalf and gotten him released from jail. His hair was long, his face pallid, and he looked somewhat older. In order to pay compensation to the crippled thief, he took his only ox to the city to be sold. He may also have sold his kidskin jacket, for no one saw him wear it anymore.

When Li Ch'ing-shan and the others came to see him that night he was penitent. "I did wrong. Maybe it was fate that brought this calamity to me. It was dark. I had been drinking, when I heard P'ing yell that someone was stealing our firewood. A couple of days before that Second Master Liu had come to say that he was going to raise the rent on our land. I protested and said that we would band together to oppose the raise. He left. After a few days he came again and said that he had to raise the rent, and if we didn't comply, he would kick us off the land. I said: 'We'll see about that!' His manager said: 'So, you want to start a riot? If you don't get out, your haystack will go up in flames!' Well, I thought it was that guy coming to burn up my firewood, so I grabbed my pole and ran out to let him have it. I couldn't have been happier about breaking his leg, until I found out that it was a thief I had hit. Ha-ha, that thief sure got his. Even if he gets well again, he'll always be a cripple."

He seemed to have forgotten all about the "Sickle Society." Li Ch'ing-shan asked him: "How do we get rid of that scoundrel Second Master Liu?"

Here are the words uttered by Chao San: "Kill him, that accursed man!"

But those were words spoken long ago. Now he had changed his tune!

"What will getting rid of him accomplish? When I was in trouble, it was Second Master Liu who interceded for me with the landlord. I acted wrongly before. Maybe that's why I'm being punished now."

When he spoke, he lacked the vigor and spirit that he had once had. His face was a mixture of contrition, embarrassment, and discomfort.

As she sat off to the side, Mother Wang was so indignant that even the curls on the back of her head were seething. "I've never seen a man like this. In the beginning he was like a piece of iron, but now he looks more and more like a lump of clay!"

Chao San merely smiled and said: "A man cannot be without a conscience."

So the conscientious Chao San daily went into the city. He would bring cabbage to the landlord one day and peanuts the next. Mother Wang got into terrible rows with him over these gifts, but he insisted on following his conscience.

One day the landlord's son came out and, standing on the doorstep, lectured Chao San: "It's lucky for you that I put in a good word for you or you could have spent the next three years in jail. That thief's luck really ran out. You just watch; I'll take care of everything for you. I'll see to it that you don't have to pay for his leg to mend. We'll just let him die, and you can save the money from the sale of the ox. We are your landlord, and we could never stand by and watch our tenants...." He paused in the middle of his speech. When he resumed he led the conversation to another topic: "But this year we'll have to increase the rent. After all, the other fields in the area all had their rents increased. We've been landlord and tenant for many years now, but we still have to ... well, we can make it a slightly smaller increase."

In a few days' time the thief was carried out from the hospital. They let him die, and the whole incident was closed. Half of the money from the sale of the ox was returned to Chao San, and the other half, according to the landlord, went for miscellaneous expenses.

It was March. The snow that had accumulated on the mountain showed signs of thawing. There were people walking on the desolate hill already. Soon people were delivering manure over the hill. The peasants, like hibernating insects, began to stir. Gradually the passage of carts delivering manure became a more frequent sight. Only Chao San's cart was not yoked to an ox. Instead, the shaft was harnessed to a sweating P'ing and his father.

And so the rent increase became effective.

5 A HERD OF GOATS

P'ing was hired as a goatherd; he chased the goats up and down the slope. On the top of the hill small flowers seemed to be blooming, first turning green, then red. P'ing played tricks on children who were out picking wild vegetables on the hill. He would drive a goat over to eat the vegetables in their baskets, and sometimes he would choose a big goat, climb on it, and charge like a horseman. The younger girls were frightened to tears when they saw him riding toward them looking like a monkey sitting atop a goat. Once his goatherd days began, P'ing's talents found an outlet. He would herd the goats into a lonely spot, then gather all the village boys to practice riding. Every day the goats, like pigs, which loathe action, dispersed over the hillside.

It was time to go home. In front of him stretched a sea of white. He rode on the back of the last goat like a general overseeing his army and played with his whip, feeling very pleased with himself.

"Have you eaten your lunch?"

Chao San was much gentler now with his son. Ever since the incident he seemed to have mellowed.

P'ing was clowning on the back of a goat. When it entered the front gate the goat, as if possessed, began to gallop, and P'ing had no chance to jump down. This time he really resembled a monkey frolicking on the back of a goat. It was a rainy day, and as the rider and mount passed through the front gate, they knocked down the master's little boy. The master picked up a rake used for gathering firewood and knocked P'ing off the goat. But even that did not stop him. He kept beating the boy as if he were pounding a piece of lifeless meat.

That night P'ing could not sleep but just tossed and turned, as his father patted him with his large hands. "You've been running around all day; aren't you sleepy yet? Go to sleep now. You have to get up early to go to work."

Under the gentle hands of his father, a feeling of being wronged came to P'ing. "I got a beating. My butt hurts."

His father got up, and from a paper packet he took out some red powder, which he put on the cuts.

The father had grown old, but his son was still so young. Chao San began to feel that life had lost its meaning. The next day P'ing reported for work but was sent home. Chao San was sitting in the kitchen weaving chicken cages with grain stalks. "Ah well," he said, "tomorrow you can come with me to sell chicken cages."

Day was breaking when he woke the child. "Get up. Come with Pa to sell the cages."

Mother Wang made rice balls, which father and son put into their pockets. These would serve as their lunch.

The first day they sold very few cages, and in the evening they came home with the rest of them on their backs. Mother Wang banged on the rice barrel. "I told you we should save some rice for ourselves, but you insisted on selling it all. What're we going to eat? Just what're we going to eat?"

The old man reached into his shirt and took out some coins.

"It's not today that we've nothing to eat," she complained. "It's tomorrow."

"Tomorrow? That's easy. I'll sell a few more cages tomorrow."

Ten cages were sold in one morning. Only three big ones remained, which were piled one upon the other. He counted the bills in his hand. P'ing was munching on a rice ball. "There must be over a hundred here," his father said. "Let's go and have some soft bean curd."

They walked over to a nearby booth and squatted beside it to eat the steaming food. P'ing was served first, while vinegar was added to the father's bowl. This food was a novelty to P'ing. How smoothly the soft bean curd coursed down to his intestines. With his eyes opened wide, he gulped down the whole bowlful.

"Shall I give the boy another bowl?" the vendor asked.

The father was surprised. "What, finished already?"

The vendor lowered his ladle into the pot. "I'll only charge you half price for the second bowl."

P'ing's eyes were glued on his father as he passed the bowl over. The boy drank noisily, but not Chao San; he fixed his eyes on the spot where he had left the cages and ate slowly; but eventually he too had downed all of his.

"P'ing, you can't possibly finish all of yours. Pour some into my bowl."

So P'ing gave a little bit to his father. After paying, his father returned to the cages, while P'ing remained at the booth, lingering over the last drop. He bent his head all the way back until the bowl covered his face.

In the vegetable section shoppers strolled by, and whenever anyone showed the slightest interest in the cages, Chao San would say: "Here, buy one. Only ten cents."

In the end, three chicken cages remained. The father took two, while he tied the other one onto P'ing's back. As they passed through the livestock section, P'ing pointed and said: "Dad, that's our ox over there!"

With the big cage swaying on his back, the boy went over to look at the ox. Chao San smiled and asked the man who was selling it: "You're reselling it?"

For no reason at all, he felt a pang in his heart. When he got home, he turned to Mother Wang and commented: "Just saw our ox in the market."

"Don't talk about it. It belongs to someone else now." Mother Wang had run out of patience.

Chao San became good at his trade and knew how to bargain. Slowly he learned how to hawk his wares while sitting at the base of the wall. Often he would buy some red and green candy balls for

P'ing. Later on, they no longer even bothered to take rice balls along with them. Every day he would hand over some coins to Mother Wang, but she was never pleased and would put them away with indifference.

Two-and-a-Half *Li* made arrangements with another family for P'ing to be taken on as an errand boy. When the boy heard about it, he was upset. "I won't go; I can't go. They'll beat me up." He was bewitched by the chicken-cage business. "I want to go with Pa into the city."

Mother Wang was adamant and insisted that the boy go to work as an errand boy. "And what do you do while your father's selling cages?"

But Chao San said: "Oh, let the boy be. If he doesn't want to go, don't make a fuss about it."

Excited by the sight of the money, Chao San stayed up nights making the cages. He said to Mother Wang: "Why don't you come and learn? It's a way to earn a living. Together we can make more."

But Mother Wang went to sleep, as if she harbored a grudge toward his work, as if she disapproved of making chicken cages.

P'ing sided with his father. He was willing and eager to carry the cages on his back. One more. He could carry one more. But his father said: "No, that's enough."

But he did carry one more, and on his way out he picked up a small one and carried it in his hand.

"Are you sure you can manage?" his father asked him. "Put two of them back. We can't sell all these."

One time they came back with a catty of meat and had a proper dinner.

The village women all envied Mother Wang.

"Third Brother is really smart. He may have sold his ox and can't do any more planting, but this is better than planting. It brings in more money."

As they passed Two-and-a-Half *Li's* place, P'ing enticed Tunnel Legs to go into the city, too. P'ing asked for a few pennies from his father and bought two fried buns for his little friend. Then they elbowed their way over to a tent from which emerged the sound of gongs, and they spent a penny each to view the "Western peep show." This was a device with a small hole covered with a lens, just big enough for one eye. Inside was a series of magnified moving pictures. Some men were fighting and brandishing their guns. The pictures moved very quickly as the man who operated the device sang and narrated stories:

"Now here is a picture of the foreigners fighting. Look at those 'hairy ones'* taking the city. Oh, what action! Look how many of them are being killed. . . ."

Tunnel Legs protested that he couldn't see.

"You have to close one eye," P'ing told him.

But it was soon over. The boys were taken away from the busy city that they loved so much. P'ing found himself back in the sleepy village. This was because the egg-hatching season had passed, and everybody had all the chicken cages they needed. Since P'ing did not want to go with his father anymore, Chao San went into the city by himself and tried to sell the cages at a reduced price. But he was unable to sell them at any price. Finally, even he stopped going. The cages piled up in the kitchen. Previously, the sight of them would have given him pleasure. Now they only served to infuriate him.

So P'ing went herding again on the back of a goat. But Chao San had suffered a setback in his fortunes.

---

*A name given to the Russians by the northeastern Chinese.

6 DAYS OF PUNISHMENT

Warm air rose from the haystack behind the house. The whole village was flooded with sunshine; stalks of grain swayed in the gentle breezes. Summer had returned and with it the leaves on the trees. If flowers could bloom on trees, then the trees would have been blossom-laden.

On the haystack behind the house a bitch was giving birth. Its limbs trembled, and its whole body shook. After a long period of time the puppies were born.

In the warmth of the season the entire village was occupied with the birth of its young. Big sows were leading their litters of piglets squealing and running, while the bellies of others were still big, nearly scraping the ground, their many teats virtually overflowing.

It was evening. Fifth Sister's elder sister could delay no longer. She went inside and spoke to her mother-in-law. "Get one of the old women. I really don't feel well."

She went into her room, let down the window shades and the bed curtain. By then she could no longer even sit properly, so she rolled up the mattress and crawled onto the straw. When the midwife arrived and saw how things were, she cocked her head to one side and said: "I've never seen anything like this. A well-to-do family like yours, and you have to give birth on the straw. 'Sit on straw and you'll never get rich.'"

Her mother-in-law gathered up the straw, stirring up clouds of dust. The naked woman squirmed on the k'ang like a fish.

Dusk had fallen, and candles glowed in the house. The woman, nearing her time, moaned softly. The midwife and an old woman from next door supported her from behind so that she could sit up and move a little on the *k'ang*. But the punishing child just would not come out. Half the night was gone, and the rooster outside had begun to crow. Suddenly the woman was in so much pain that her face turned first ashen and then yellow. Her whole family was growing uneasy, and had actually begun to prepare her shroud. In the eerie candlelight they looked around for suitable garments, the entire household under the disturbing influence of the shadow of death.

The naked woman could no longer even crawl; she was unable to muster the final burst of effort in this moment of life and death. Though the sky was getting light, fear, like a shroud, enveloped the house.

When Fifth Sister heard about her elder sister, she came to see how she was doing. "Can't she drink a mouthful of water? When did this start?"

A man stumbled in. He was drunk. Half of his face all red and swollen, he came up to the curtain and snarled: "Give me my boots!"

The woman could not reply. He tore at the curtain, moving his thick swollen lips as he said menacingly: "Feign death, will you? Let's see if you still want to feign death now!" With that he took the tobacco pouch at his side and flung it at the corpse-like figure. His mother came over and dragged him out. It was like this every year: whenever he saw his wife giving birth, this was how he showed his disapproval.

In the light of day the pain subsided a little, and she regained consciousness. Covered with sweat, she sat behind the bed curtain. Suddenly the red-faced devil rushed in again. Without saying a word, he raised his fearful hands and threw a big bucket of water through the curtain. Finally the people around pulled him out.

The pregnant woman with her still bulging abdomen sat in silence, her body drenched with cold water. She dared not move a single muscle, for like the child of a patriarchal society, she lived in dread of her man.

Once more unable to sit up, she was undergoing torment. The

midwife changed her wet outer garment. Suddenly there was a sound at the door, and the young woman was in such a nervous state that she panicked. She was not allowed even a single moan. This poor woman—had there been a hole beside her, she would have jumped in. Had there been poison beside her, she would have swallowed it. Feeling hate and contempt for everything, she nearly kicked over the window sill. She was willing to break her own legs if necessary. Her body was being torn to shreds by the heat, as though she had entered a steaming vessel.

The midwife pushed on her stomach with both hands. "Be a little stronger. Stand up and walk around, and the baby will come right out. It's about time."

After walking for a while, her legs shook and trembled horribly. Like a sick horse, she collapsed, frightening the midwife. "I'm afraid we're going to have trouble with her," she said. "Better go fetch another one of the older women."

So Fifth Sister returned home to get her mother. But while she was gone, the child came into the world. It died instantly. As the people around her helped the pregnant woman up, the baby dropped onto the k'ang with a sickening thud. The woman lay in her own blood, soaking it up with her body.

Outside, the sun was shining; inside, the woman was exhausted by childbirth.

In the green world of the fields everyone was bathed in sweat.

In May, birds were also hatching. Yellow-billed fledglings could often be seen swooping down, skipping and pecking beneath the eaves. The litters of piglets grew fatter. Only the women in the village, like horses used in farming, became skinnier in the summer.

The punishment descended upon Golden Bough. Her bloated abdomen was totally out of proportion to her short figure. She did not look like a woman yet; she still had the appearance of a young girl. But her belly had swelled up, and she soon would become a mother. The woman's punishment would soon catch up with her.

She had been married a scant four months before she learned how to curse her husband. She began to feel that men are heartless human beings, a feeling shared by the rest of the village women.

Sitting on the sandy ground beside the river, she was washing clothes. The red sun shone down on the river at an oblique angle, and gradually the reflections of the woods on the opposite bank grew fuzzy under the reddish ripples.

Ch'eng-yeh stood some distance behind her. "The sky's turned dark, and you're still washing clothes! You lazy wife, what were you doing during the day?"

In the mornings, before sunrise, Golden Bough was feeling her way in the dark to get dressed. Then in the kitchen this little woman with the big belly started to cook. When the sun came out, the workers in the field came home with their hoes on their shoulders. The whole dining room was packed with people, and a cacophony arose, produced by people gulping down their food and slurping their soup.

She had to cook at midday and again in the evening. She was so exhausted that her legs felt as if they were broken, so when the sky grew dark she lay down and rested awhile. Subconsciously she sensed that Ch'eng-yeh was home, and she sat up. With great effort she opened her sleepy eyes and asked weakly: "You just getting home?"

But there was no response, even after several moments had passed. She could see the man undressing, and she knew she was going to be tongue-lashed again. But there were no abusive words. On the contrary, Golden Bough felt a warmth on her back. The man was trying his very best to talk to her in a soft voice: "...."

Golden Bough was mesmerized by the man.

Immediately after—disaster. Suffering came close on the heels of pleasure. Golden Bough was unable to cook a meal. The village midwife arrived. Writhing in pain in a corner of the k'ang, she was taking her punishment. Mother Wang came to her assistance, and the baby was born. Mother Wang shook her head knowingly. "That was dangerous. Last night you two must have carried on. You young people, don't you know anything? When you're pregnant, you're not supposed to do it. You could easily have lost your life!"

After ten days or so Golden Bough was moving about in the yard once more, while Little Golden Bough cried for her mother in the house.

Cows or horses in their ignorance cultivate their own suffering. At night as the people sat in the cool breeze, they could hear odd noises coming from the stable or cowshed. A bull that was probably battling for its mate crashed out of the shed, breaking the fence. Ch'eng-yeh hurriedly picked up a rake to beat the crazed bull until it retreated peacefully back into the barn.

In the village men and beasts busied themselves at living and at dying.

Two-and-a-Half Li's wife and Second Aunt Li met at the edge of the field.

"Oh my, you can still bend down in your state?"

"How are you doing?"

"I can't do a thing."

"When's the date?"

"Within the next few days."

It was drizzling. Suddenly Two-and-a-Half Li's house was in an uproar. Whenever this foolish woman of his gave birth, she created a scene. She wailed and ranted loudly against her man: "I said I didn't want any more children. You heartless . . . it's all your doing. If I die, my death will be on your hands."

Mother Wang was so tickled that she turned aside and laughed through closed lips. After a while the foolish woman rolled over and cried at the top of her lungs: "My belly's killing me! Get a knife and cut it out!"

In the midst of this clamor the baby's head was visible. Just then Fifth Sister came through the door looking pale. Having seemingly lost the power of speech, she kept wringing her hands. "She's stopped breathing! Miscarriage . . . Second Aunt Li's going to die!"

Mother Wang abandoned Old Mother Pockface and hurried to

the fishing village. Another midwife arrived to find Old Mother Pockface's baby crying on the *k'ang,* so she bathed this tiny infant who could barely cry.

When Mother Wang returned, outside the window at the foot of the wall somebody's sow was also giving birth.

7 THE SINFUL SUMMER FESTIVAL

The approach of the Summer Festival in the fifth month heralded two occurrences—the self-poisoning of Mother Wang and the tragic death of Little Golden Bough.

The crescent moon, like a sickle, pierced the treetops in the woods as Mother Wang, her hair hanging loose, headed toward the wood-shed at the back of the house. There she gently opened the gate. Outside all was darkness and silence; not even the breezes dared disturb this black nocturnal picture. The cucumbers had climbed up the lattice, the cornstalks were rustling their broad leaves, no frogs were croaking; and few insects were chirping.

Her loose hair hanging about her shoulders, the phantomlike Mother Wang knelt on the hay and held the cup up to her lips. As a flood of enticing memories rushed into her mind, she dropped down in the hay and, overcome by sorrow, wept bitterly.

Chao San awoke from his dreams, totally unaware of what was going on. Once inside the woodshed he was a little harsh with her. "What's the matter? Are you crazy?" He figured she was feeling melancholy and had gone to weep in the woodshed. Then he stumbled on the cup in the hay which brought an end to his conjectures. He ran back into the house, where, in the light of the lamp he noticed a black heavy liquid at the bottom of the cup. He touched it with his finger and then tasted it with the tip of his tongue. It was bitter.

"Mother Wang has drunk poison!"

This was the cry that rang through the village the next morning. Villagers, sad and somber, came to pay their respects. Chao San was not at home, having gone out to choose a site for her in the potter's field.

In the potter's field the living were digging a grave for the dead. Two-and-a-Half *Li* was the first to jump down into the deepening pit. The wet earth piled up on the sides as the grave grew even deeper and larger. Several more people jumped down. The spades never stopped their digging. Soon the grave was up to waist level, while on the sides the earth was piled higher than a man's head.

The graveyard was a dead city; there was no fragrance of flowers, no humming of insects. Even if there had been flowers and insects, they would have been singing a song of farewell to accompany the eternal solitude of the dead.

The potter's field had been donated by the landlord as a resting place for the impoverished peasants after their deaths. But in life the peasants were constantly being hounded by the very same landlord. Shouldering their bundles and carrying their children, they were driven from ramshackle houses into even more ramshackle houses. Sometimes they were even banished to the stables. There the children cried and fretted at their mothers.

Chao San went into the city, weakened by this unexpected blow. On the road he met up with a cart from the fishing village carrying vegetables to sell in the city. The driver was in a complaining mood: "The price of vegetables has dropped and the currency is worthless. Even grains aren't worth much." He flicked his whip and continued: "Cloth is the only thing that's expensive. That and salt. Soon a family won't be able to afford salt. With the land rent going up, how can a farmer make a living?"

Chao San jumped up onto the cart and sat atop the shafts with his head bowed. His two weak and tired legs dangled over the side, swaying with the movements of the cart as it rumbled down the road.

In the city the main street was crowded, and the marketplace was terribly noisy. The people around the meat stall sounded as if they were quarreling. Young boys busily hawked their wares, carrying colorful gourds that danced in the air. It was the madness of the Summer Festival.

But Chao San saw none of this. It was as if all the pedestrians had disappeared, and the street was deserted.

"It's festival time," said a little boy who was following him. "Buy one of these to take home for your child."

Chao San did not pay him any attention, but the boy selling gourds chased after him as if he were no longer a child but an adult. "It's festival time. Buy one of these to take home for your child."

The colorful gourds that hung from the willow twig like butterflies tied together with ribbons were following Chao San.

A coffin shop. Red ones, white ones, and various others were placed at the entrance. He stopped there. The child stopped following him. Everything was in readiness. The coffin rested in front of the house; the spades had stopped their digging.

The window was opened so that the dying could take a last look at the sun. Mother Wang's heart was still beating and breath still lingered on her lips. The bright light from the window illuminated her simple shroud. They had outfitted her in a pair of black cotton pants and a light-colored jacket, and except for the purple color of her face, there was nothing unusual to be seen on her deathbed. People were beginning to clamor: "Lift her up! Lift her up!"

But she was still breathing slightly as a little froth gathered on her lips. Just as she was about to be lifted up, P'ing called urgently from outside: "The Feng girl is here! The Feng girl!"

But the meeting between mother and daughter came too late. They would never ever see each other again. Carrying a small bundle, the girl approached slowly. She took a close look, and as her face nearly touched that of her mother's, a shriek burst from her lips, and her little bundle fell to the ground.

There was not a dry eye among the people gathered around, for who could smother that unbearable sense of loss evoked by this young girl? Even people who were not related mourned with the girl. Among them was one woman newly widowed who wept the loudest, she being the most sorrowful. Imagining that she was weeping for her husband, she had deluded herself into thinking that she was seated in front of his grave.

The men clamored again: "Lift her up! We have to get this over with. After that you can weep some more."

The young woman awoke to the fact that this was not her home and there wasn't a single loved one by her side. She stopped crying.

The poisoned mother's eyes were still open, but she did not recognize her daughter. She did not recognize anything. As she lay on a plank in the kitchen, with froth on her lips, her heart continued to send out a weak pulse.

Chao San sat on the *k'ang* and lit his pipe. The women found a strip of white mourning cloth and tied it around the girl's head, while P'ing tied a white strip around his waist.

After Chao San had left the room, the women began to question the girl.

"Your father with the name of Feng, when did he die?"

"Over two years ago."

"What about your real father?"

"He went back to Shantung."

"Why didn't he take you along?"

"He was beating my mother, so she took my elder brother and me to Uncle Feng's house."

The women asked about Mother Wang's former days and were moved by what they heard.

"Why isn't your brother here?" asked the widow. "Go home and get him to come and see his mother."

The young girl with the strip of white around her head turned her face toward the wall. Her face was once again streaked with tears. With an effort she bit her lips, but they parted immediately, and she wept once more.

Emboldened by the kindness of the women, she went up to her mother and tightly grasped her icy fingers. She also wiped the froth off her mother's lips, carefully as though she didn't want to disturb her. The bundle that she had brought with her was trodden underfoot. Again the woman said: "Go home and get your brother."

The word "brother" almost started her crying again, but she managed to control herself.

"Isn't your brother home?" the widow persisted.

Finally, covering her face with the white strip, she gave rein to her grief. She could only speak of her brother in between sobs. "My brother died the day before yesterday; he was captured and shot by city officials." She tore the strip of cloth from her head. This lonely, half-crazed girl then buried her head in her mother's bosom and wept. "Mother . . . Mother." There was nothing else she could say. After all, she was still young.

The women were talking to one another: "How come her brother is dead? How come we never heard. . . ?"

Chao San's tobacco pipe appeared at the door. He could clearly hear that they were discussing Mother Wang's son, and he knew that the young man had been one of the "Red Whiskers." How had he died?

Hadn't Mother Wang taken the poison after hearing that her son had been shot? Only Chao San knew about this, and he did not want other people to learn that his wife's suicide was related to an act of banditry. He felt that it was disgraceful to be a bandit, no matter what the circumstances. His stiff voice rang out as he motioned with his pipe to the girl to leave: "Why don't you leave? She's dead. There's nothing left to see, so go back to your home."

The girl, abandoned by her father, her brother shot as a criminal, had brought her bundle along, intending to live with her mother. But now her mother was dead. And if her mother was no longer there, with whom would she stay? Stunned by this realization, she forgot her bundle, and with just the white strip around her head, she left. As she walked out the door, she seemed to be leaving her heart behind, embarking on a long journey.

Because he was old, Chao San condemned the young man in his heart: "Keeping a woman, huh? If you're rich, you can do it. But without money . . . I've never seen anything like it. When festival time came around and that whore was unable to celebrate it, she made him go out to rob. And a young man threw away his life."

When he looked on his dying wife, he hated the young man who had been shot. Yet, when he recalled how the winter before Mother Wang had come back with a borrowed gun, he could not help but feel admiration for the boy: "At least no one had dared bully him while he was a bandit."

The women kindled the firewood, and soon the pot began to emit steam. Chao San fingered his tobacco pouch as he stalked to and fro. After a time he looked at Mother Wang again; she still hung on tenaciously. As if impatient with waiting for her to die, he grew sleepy and dozed off leaning against the wall.

The prolonged threat of death began to lose its grip on the mourners. They gathered for their meal and their wine. At that moment Mother Wang made a sound at their feet. Her purple face had turned several shades lighter. They put down their cups, saying that death had been turned away.

But it was not so. Suddenly from the corner of her mouth black blood trickled out between lips that seemed to be moving. Finally she howled twice. Everybody began to whisper with wide, staring eyes that she was breathing her last. Even as they were staring, she began to move as if she wanted to get up. They grew frightened. The women ran out, and the men reached for the poles they used to carry water, saying that her body had been taken over by a spirit.

Chao San, who had downed some wine, said boldly: "If we let her get up, she'll die clasping her arms around a small child, or around a tree. She would even have the strength to do the same thing to a grown man!"

So with his large red hands he greedily pressed down hard on her with the pole as though it were a knife laid across her waist. Her stomach and chest suddenly expanded, like the bladder of a fish, and her eyes grew round as if they were about to emit sparks. Her black lips moved as though she were speaking, but no sound came out. Blood spurted from her mouth, drenching Chao San's jacket.

"Don't press so hard," he shouted to the man on the other end of the pole. "I'm getting blood all over me!"

Everyone assumed then that she had drawn her last breath, so she was put into the coffin waiting at the door.

In front of the temple in the rear village stood two homeless old men. One carried a red lantern and the other a water jug as they led P'ing to perform the initial rites at the temple. They all walked round the temple three times then came back via the narrow path, the old men reciting the usual litany. On his way home the red lantern accompanied the boy with the white strip of cloth around his waist. P'ing did not shed a single tear. After all, he recalled, he had gone through the same routine that year when his own mother had died.

But Mother Wang's daughter could not go with them.

The news of Mother Wang's death had spread throughout the village, and the women sat crying beside the coffin. They blew their noses and howled with grief. They were weeping for their children, for their husbands, for their own fates. In short, whatever tragedies they had endured they were crying for them now. Whenever one of the old villagers died, they, the village women, always acted this way.

The coffin was going to the potter's field. They would soon hammer in the nails. But Mother Wang did not die after all. She felt cold and thirsty. "I want a drink of water," she said softly. But she did not know where she was lying.

It was the Summer Festival and each family had hung a gourd over its door. From Two-and-a-Half *Li's* house came the sound of a baby wailing, but his foolish wife was crouching by the door, brushing the goat with a metal brush they used for the horse.

Two-and-a-Half *Li* limped along. The festival brought him a happy feeling. In the cabbage patch he saw several heads of cabbage that had been eaten by worms. Ordinarily he would have cursed the worms or, in a fit of temper, kicked at the cabbage. But it was festival time, and he was happy. He felt it only proper that he be happy. At the edge of the plot he saw that the tomatoes were not yet red; the thought occurred to him that maybe he should pick a few green ones for the boy. After all, it was festival time.

The whole village celebrated this holiday. The vegetable plots, the wheat fields, no matter where—every place was quiet and tranquil. Even the insects sang better than usual.

The festive feeling affected the soul of Two-and-a-Half *Li*. He passed by his house but did not go in. He just threw the tomatoes in to the boy and left, for he wanted to take advantage of the happy occasion to meet with his friends.

All the neighboring doors were festooned with paper gourds. He noticed a green gourd swaying above the door of Mother Wang's house as he passed by. Farther on was Golden Bough's house. There was no gourd outside, and there were no people inside. Two-and-a-Half *Li* stared for quite a while at the baby's diaper hanging by the stove as it billowed in the wind.

Little Golden Bough had been in the world barely a month when she was dashed to the ground by her father. Why had the baby been brought into the world? So that she could leave with resentment? It was such a very short life; it had lasted but a few days.

The little baby now slept among the dead. Wouldn't she be afraid? Her mother was getting farther and farther away, until soon the mother's weeping would be heard no more.

It was dark. Even the moon did not come out to keep the baby company.

During the few days before the Summer Festival, Ch'eng-yeh had constantly gone in and out of the city. When he came home, he had fought with his wife.

"The price of rice has gone down," he had said. "The rice bought in April now sells at a loss. The money from the sale isn't even enough to pay off our debts. But if I don't sell it, how can we celebrate the festival?"

Little by little he had lost his love for Little Golden Bough. When she woke him up at night, he would say: "Go on, scream! Scream to your heart's content!"

The day before the festival no preparations had been made at his house. Not even a catty of flour had been bought. When it was time to cook, the oil container was as dry as a bone. Ch'eng-yeh had come back angry, and when he saw the bare table, he had roared: "So! Someone like me is supposed to starve to death! Since there's nothing to eat, I'm going back to the city . . . I'm going back."

The baby had been suckling at Golden Bough's breast.

"I'll never see good days again," he had complained. "You two have become a burden to me. I can't even become a bandit."

With her head down, Golden Bough had laid out the dinner, as the baby cried off to one side. Ch'eng-yeh had looked at the pickled vegetables and the gruel on the table. He had thought for a moment and couldn't resist adding: "Go ahead and cry! You bad investment. I'll sell you to pay off our debts."

The baby had continued to cry while her mother was in the kitchen either sweeping the floor or tidying up the firewood pile. This had thrown him into a frenzy. "I'll sell the pair of you! What's the use of having you two noisy things in the house?"

In the kitchen the mother, like a struck match, had flared up: "You, what kind of father are you? You come back, and you fight. I'm not your enemy. You want to sell us? Well, go ahead!"

He threw a rice bowl; she jumped up in anger.

"I'll sell; I'm going to dash her to death . . . then, I'll show you what I'll sell. . ."

So ended a tiny life.

When Mother Wang heard about the death of Golden Bough's baby, she wanted to come and see what had happened. But though she managed to stand up with the aid of a cane, she soon had to lie down again. Her leg bones had been affected by the poison, and she could not yet move around.

After three days the young mother went to the potter's field to see her baby, but what was there to see? The wild dogs had torn everything to pieces.

Ch'eng-yeh saw a pile of blood-stained straw, which he fancied to be the straw used to wrap Little Golden Bough's body. The two wept with their backs to each other.

No one will ever know how many tears of grief had dried on this potter's field. Not even crows would land on this eternally pitiful area.

Ch'eng-yeh saw another open grave; a skull was once again exposed to the light of day. As they left the field, all the coffins, all the clusters of graves, and all the dead silent images urged them to quicken their steps.

8   BUSY MOSQUITOES

Her daughter had come. Mother Wang's daughter had come.

Mother Wang was now able to sit beside the river and fish with her fishing pole. The wrinkles on her face had neither increased nor decreased, which proved that she had not undergone any changes. She still had to go on living.

At night the croaking of the frogs by the river was deafening, while ranks of buzzing mosquitoes set out from the bushes at the edge of the river, invading every family. In the daytime the sun was scorching, burning everyone's skin. In the summer the peasants cursed the sun as they would curse an evil tyrant. That great fireball rotated in the sky above all the fields.

But Mother Wang always welcomed summer because of the plump green leaves and teeming orchards, not to mention the nocturnal gatherings that inspired poetry in her heart. This was the time for her once again to tell her stories to the summer night. But this summer she did not talk at all. She lay huddled against the window, facing the remote, far-off sky.

The sound of the frogs shattered everyone's solitude; the mosquitoes disrupted their rest.

It was the month of July, just like any other year; this time last year it had been harvest time. But Mother Wang's household hadn't done any planting this year, which made her even sadder and more silent. Whenever she passed by the waves of wheat with her fishing pole, she would occupy herself with winding up the line. Her head raised high as she looked up into the sky, she would pass right through the wheat fields without giving them so much as a glance.

Her temper grew worse, and she began to drink. She went fishing every day, no longer tending to the mending and the laundry. All she did every evening was cook the fish she had caught, drink until she was drunk, and run around the house and the yard. Gradually her wanderings even took her to the woods. Sometimes when she raised her wine cup, she would remember her former husband and would feel sorry for the lonely daughter at her side. As a rule, after she drank she would do a lot of fretting.

Now she was on the verge of becoming a laughingstock as she fell like a stone in the middle of the courtyard. She had grown accustomed to sleeping in the yard at night. When she slept there, she was pestered by throngs of mosquitoes that acted like an army of ants swarming over a rotting fly. But she had no interest in them; she had lost interest even in life.

Mother Wang was bitten by mosquitoes until her face was covered with red blotches and her skin puffy with their bites. As she gulped down her wine she remembered the day her daughter had come and how the girl had lain in her lap.

"Oh, Mother, I thought you were dead. You were frothing at the mouth, and your fingers were icy cold. Elder Brother is dead, and now Mother is dead, too. Where shall I go to beg for food? When they chased me out I left my bundle behind. I wept . . . I wept till I lost my senses. Mother, they're evil. They wouldn't even let me take one more look at you."

Finally the girl stood up and said resolutely: "I hate them all! If my brother were alive, I would have him kill them." Then she wiped her tears dry. "I must be like Elder Brother." She bit her lip.

Mother Wang wondered how the girl could have such strong feelings. Maybe she would turn out to be a sensible girl after all.

Mother Wang suddenly stopped drinking. Every evening she taught her daughter things in the woods. In the quiet woods she said solemnly: "Revenge. You must avenge your brother's death. Who killed him?"

The girl thought to herself: "The officials killed my brother." Then she heard her mother say again: "You must kill the people responsible for your brother's death."

After mulling it over for ten days or so she said to her mother hesitantly: "Who killed my brother? Mother, you take me into the city tomorrow to search out our enemy so that when I see him in the future I can kill him."

A child speaking childish words. Her mother laughed. But she laughed with an aching heart.

The evening that Mother Wang quarreled with Chao San the water of the south river overflowed its banks. Along the edge of the south river people were shouting: "Flood! Flood!"

People milled by the side of the river. Inside the house Chao San was shouting: "You tell her to leave. She's not my child, and I refuse to take care of another man's daughter. Be quick about it!"

The next day, every family took its grain to the threshing ground. At harvest time each year the peasants always feasted and drank to celebrate. This was the first year that Chao San had done no planting, and so his house was quiet. When others asked him to join in the merrymaking, he sat down at the tables, listening to the happy chatter about him and watching other people harvest. His large red hands looked conspicuously out of place. He kept wringing them, but no one really paid him any attention. They were too busy talking with one another.

After the river water receded, the mosquitoes returned in hordes. Even the croaking of the frogs at night was outmatched by the buzzing of the mosquitoes. In the daytime, too, they flew. Only Chao San kept very quiet.

9 EPIDEMIC

Corpses were strewn about in the potter's field. With no one to bury them the wild dogs were busy at their work.

The sun was blood-red. From dawn till dusk clouds of mosquitoes and fog filled the sky. Sorghum, corn, and all the vegetable crops lay abandoned in the fields and plots, for every family was a sick family. Every family was on the verge of extinction. The entire village fell silent. There were no breezes to rustle the plants. Everything was steeped in fog.

Chao San sat at the southern edge of the field trying to sell five unused sickles that were left over from the days of the "Sickle Society." As he gazed at the relics, sad memories stirred within him. An old woman from the village asked him: "I say it's a celestial sign . . . what kind of celestial sign is it though? Is the sky going to fall and the ground cave in? Does Heaven want all of us to die? Ai! . . ." She walked away from Chao San, her hunched back disappearing in the fog; but her voice floated back: "Heaven wants to destroy mankind . . . should have done it years ago. People know only how to rob and kill. Man has brought this all on himself."

As she moved farther and farther away, the faint sounds of a donkey braying in the distance could be heard. Was it braying on the slope of the hill? Or was it by the side of the ditch?

One could see nothing; one could only hear. Just then Two-and-a-Half Li's woman could be heard, muttering unhappily in her raspy voice. Chao San, worried by the sickles, sat in the fog, full of resentment against them. "I've already sold the ox," he thought, "so I can no longer work the fields."

He was not aware that the woman was speaking to him. She tripped over some rocks and got up, a little frightened. But because of the fog, it was hard to see just how frightened she was. The sound waves that emanated from her like a fine net were akin to the buzzing of mosquitoes. "Third Brother, are you still sitting here? I'm afraid the 'devils' are coming. They give injections even to little babies. You see, I've brought my child with me. I won't let them stick a needle in him; I'd rather see him die first!"

Old Mother Pockface left him and vanished in the fog, holding a baby who, though still alive, could no longer even cry.

Overhead the sun had become a big, dull red circle. Buried in the stunned village below were the seeds of a natural calamity, and slowly those seeds were germinating.

The epidemic spread like wildfire, and it flourished.

Stepping on dead toads, Chao San walked ahead. Some people bearing a coffin suddenly materialized and slipped past him. A woman with a twisted face and bound feet followed behind, sobbing quietly. Again he heard the donkey braying. Shortly afterwards, the donkey also passed, bearing a sick old man on its back.

The Westerners, called "foreign devils" by the people, came in their white smocks. The following day, after the fog had dissipated, a woman in a white smock appeared outside Chao San's window. Wearing a white mask over her mouth, she said in barely understandable Chinese: "Your . . . sick people you have? I make sickness all good again. Come, chop-chop."

The older man with her, who was on the plump side, waggled his beard and poked his head in through the window, looking around with eyes like those of a fat pig.

At first Chao San lied and said that no one in his family was sick, but in the end he allowed P'ing to be injected.

As the old "devil" spoke to the young "devil," the white mask covering his mouth moved. Then tubes, vials, and shiny knives emerged from his bag. Chao San got a pot of cold water from the well, as the "devil" began to polish his glass tube. P'ing was placed on a plank in front of the window, his eyes blindfolded with a piece of white cloth. Neighbors from across the yard gathered around to find out how the "devils" cured disease, to see what horrible methods they used.

The glass tube was inserted into a spot about one inch below the navel, leaving only half of its five-inch length shining outside. The people held the boy down firmly so that he could not thrash around. Then one of the "devils" lifted up the pot of cold water while the other one lined the spout up with the funnel on top of a longer rubber tube. It looked like they were repairing some sort of machine. The spectators collectively drew in a breath, which made it seem like they were all shrugging their shoulders. The little boy could only utter short cries, "Ah! Ah!" Soon the whole pot of water had been drained. Finally a little yellow medicine was rubbed on the bulging abdomen, and a piece of white gauze was snipped off with a small pair of scissors and put over the puncture. After that the white-clad "devils" took their bags and left nonchalantly, to go to another household.

Another sunny day. The epidemic had reached a crisis. Women held their half-dead children, still afraid of the injection and afraid that the white-clad "devils" would pump water into their children's bellies. They did not have the heart to look upon the inflated bellies.

Bad news traveled far and wide.

"The whole Li family has died!"

"They've sent people from the city to investigate. All those with symptoms are being taken into the city in carts. Even old ladies. Children, too . . . to be injected."

Gradually the sounds of mourning ceased, and quietly the corpses were wrapped in straw or placed in coffins to be quickly transported to the potter's field, one by one, endlessly . . .

After midday Two-and-a-Half Li's wife took her baby to the potter's field. She saw there the corpses of some children, their white faces covered by hair. Some had been dismembered by the wild dogs, but others were still lying there whole. At a distance the wild dogs gnawed noisily and leisurely at the bones. They were content, no longer mad with the lust for food, and no longer having to chase people.

All through the night P'ing vomited yellow and green fluid, while the whites of his eyes became covered with red lines.

Chao San went out the door, mumbling. Although the whole village had lost quite a few people, and the fields lay barren and neglected, he was still obsessed with selling his sickles. As long as they remained in the house, they were as thorns piercing his heart.

10 TEN YEARS

The hill in the village and the stream at the foot of the hill remained the same as ten years before. The water flowed gently, and the slope changed its garb with the seasons. In the village the cycle of life and death went on exactly as it had ten years before.

There were still as many sparrows congregating on the rooftops. The sun was just as warm. At the foot of the hill a young goatherd was singing a nursery rhyme, the same tune that had been sung ten years before:

> Autumn nights are long,
> Autumn winds are strong.
> Whose mommy left him when he was young?
> Whose mommy left him when he was young?
> The moon in the west window hears my song.

Everything was just as it had been ten years before. Even Mother Wang seemed unchanged. P'ing, however, had grown up. Both P'ing and Tunnel Legs had grown up.

Mother Wang, her hair blown by the wind, stood beyond the fence and listened to the nursery rhyme that drifted across the slope.

11 THE WHEEL OF TIME TURNS

One snowy day a flag never before seen by the villagers was raised and began to flutter under the open sky.

Silence reigned over the village. The only sound came from the fluttering Japanese flag raised in front of the temporary garrison set up on the hill.

The villagers were wondering: "What is happening now? Has the Chinese nation had a dynastic change?"

12 THE BLACK TONGUE

The banner proclaiming the "Kingly Order" arrived, bringing with it dust, smoke, and clamor.

Motorcars roared down the wide, tree-lined roads.

In the boundless fields the short seedlings were a light green. But this was no longer a quiet, somber village. The people had lost the equilibrium in their hearts. The motorcars whizzed across grassy fields, creating clouds of dust, after which scraps of red and green paper fell like scattered seeds. The scraps of paper covered the roofs of nearby thatched huts, they covered the branches of the trees by the wayside, and they whirled and whistled in the wind. From the city more motorcars traveled in their wake. Arrogant Japanese, Koreans, and even Chinese were standing in the cars, and as the wheels flashed by, the flags the men were holding in their hands made a flapping sound. One had the impression that the people in the cars had sprouted wings and were airborne as they passed by. The flag-waving people with their obsequious smiles vanished down the road. And the pamphlets proclaiming the "Kingly Order" fluttered over to the slope and down to the riverbank.

As Mother Wang stood in front of her doorway, Two-and-a-Half Li's goat lowered its bearded head and walked softly over underneath a luxuriant tree. The goat no longer searched for food. It was tired and so old that its entire coat had turned an earthen color. Its eyes were dim and moist. The goat looked comical yet pitiful as it walked toward the low ground, its beard swaying from side to side.

Facing the low ground and watching the goat, Mother Wang traced the sad, bygone days. She longed to recapture the past, because the present was proving to be even worse. The low ground remained uncultivated; farther up the hill the wheat fields lay fallow. She dwelled on her memories with a sad heart.

A Japanese airplane passed overhead with a great roar, and the sky was filled with dancing scraps of paper. One of them landed on a branch above Mother Wang. She took it down and, after glancing at it, threw it to the ground. The airplane flew by one more time, leaving behind even more of the pamphlets. She ignored them, crushing them underfoot as she paced back and forth.

After a time, Golden Bough's mother passed by, holding two roosters in her hand. She remarked to Mother Wang: "We can't continue like this. How can we? These are my last two roosters; I'd better sell them fast."

"Are you going into the city to sell them?"

"Where else could I find a buyer? There aren't many chickens left in the village." Then, dropping her voice, she confided to Mother Wang: "Those Japs are vicious and mean! All the young girls of the village have fled. Even the young married women. I heard that a thirteen-year-old girl in Wang Village was taken away by the Japs in the middle of the night."

"Rest awhile before you move on," Mother Wang urged her.

The two of them sat beneath the tree. Over the earth the insects made no sound. There were only the two women, talking dejectedly and worriedly. The roosters in the woman's hand occasionally flapped their wings. The sun was moving overhead, and the shadows of the trees grew round.

There were new sights in the village: Japanese flags, Japanese soldiers. And the topics of conversation turned to "The Kingly Order," "the bonds of friendship between Japan and Manchukuo," and "the coming of the true Prince of Heaven." Under the "Kingly Order" the number of abandoned plots was on the increase, and the people wandered dispiritedly in the square.

Just before leaving, the old woman said: "I've spent these past few years raising chickens. Now I don't even have a feather left. I can't even keep a rooster to announce the dawn. What kind of times are these?" She shook her sleeves a little hysterically. Then she stood up and strode across the abandoned field that stretched in front of her. The field seemed to be diseased, and under her feet the short grasses, sorry-looking and without resilience, were trodden flat.

Even after she had gone quite a distance, one could still discern that she was holding the two roosters in the hand hanging by her side, while the other hand was raised up, constantly wiping her face.

When Mother Wang lay down to rest she could vaguely hear the screams of a woman. She opened the window to listen. After listening for a while she heard shrill whistles and the sound of shooting. What kind of devils had burst into that distant house?

"Who do you have in the house?"

That night Japanese soldiers and Chinese policemen conducted a search of the entire village. They came to Mother Wang's house.

"Who do I have? Nobody."

With their hands covering their noses, they took a turn through the house and went out, the flashlights in their hands sending out crisscrossing blue rays. As they stepped over the threshold on their way out, a helmeted Japanese soldier said in Chinese: "Bring her along too."

Mother Wang heard every word he said. "Why are they taking

away the women too?" she thought. "Are they going to shoot us?"

"Who wants an old hag like her?" the Chinese policeman asked. The Chinese guffawed at this and so did the Japanese, even though they didn't understand what the words meant. Since others were laughing, they laughed right along with them.

They did, however, take one of the other women and led her away, bent over like a pig. In the faint glow of the flashlights Mother Wang could not tell who the woman was. Before they had even gone past the fence they began having fun with the woman. Mother Wang saw the hand of the helmeted Japanese soldier give the woman's buttocks a swift pat.

13   DO YOU WANT TO BE EXTERMINATED?

Mother Wang thought that it was another mock raid to cover up their search for women in the village, so she did not associate it with anything sinister and slept on soundly. Chao San was quite old, so when he came home he went right to sleep without disturbing anyone.

The next day, Japanese military policemen tapped lightly on the door. The one who came in looked like a Chinese. His high boots were damp from the dew. He took a handkerchief from his pocket, calmly sat down on the k'ang, and leisurely polished his boots. Then the interrogation began. "Did anyone come to your house last night? Don't be afraid, just tell the truth."

Chao San had just gotten up. He was still drowsy and did not know what was going on. So the military policeman gave his hat a violent shake, his manner no longer gentle or casual. "You damn fool! What do you mean you don't know! Wait till I take you in, then you'll know."

Despite his threats, he did not take anyone in. Mother Wang, buttoning her clothes, interjected: "Who is it you're asking about? Last night a few officers came around to search, but they left when they couldn't find anyone."

Directing his attention solely to Mother Wang, this man with the airs of an officer asked her cordially: "Won't you please tell me, old mother? You'll be rewarded."

But Mother Wang did not bat an eye.

"We're looking for bandits," the man continued. "You villagers are their victims too. Didn't you see the car that came yesterday to proclaim the 'Kingly Order'? The 'Kingly Order' wants you to be honest. Come on, old mother, tell us. We'll reward you for it."

Mother Wang turned toward the red glare on the window as she announced tersely: "I don't know anything about it."

The officer was on the point of screaming at her, but he managed to restrain himself, explaining to her in measured tones: "Manchukuo wants to exterminate all those bandits who do harm to the people. Anyone who has information about the bandits but refuses to divulge it will be shot." Then this man in the high boots looked at Chao San with an insulting leer. At that point he stopped speaking and waited for an answer. But none was forthcoming.

It was not yet midday when three more corpses appeared in the potter's field. Among them was that of a woman. Everyone recognized the body: it was the "girl student" who had been discovered in a widow's house in the north village.

Chao San heard others mention that the girl student had belonged to some "party," but he did not understand what a "party" was. That night, after he got drunk, he confided what he had heard to Mother Wang. He did not know what sort of secret business the girl student was involved in nor why she had died. He only sensed that this thing, which was not to be talked about, was something secret. Yet, he felt he had to talk.

Mother Wang didn't really want to listen. Since all of this had happened, she had been worrying for her daughter, afraid that she would share the same fate as the "girl student."

Chao San's beard had grown white and sparse. After a few cups of wine, his ruddy face turned even redder, and he simply flopped down in a corner of the *k'ang*.

P'ing brought home a big bundle of green grass that, when dried, would serve as firewood. He laid the grass out flat in the middle of the yard. After he entered the house, he did not eat at once but took off his sweat-drenched undershirt and put it down beside him. He looked angry, slapping hard at his own muscular shoulders and breathing deeply. After a long time his father said: "You young people should have more courage. This is no life. The country is lost. We can no longer plant in the wheat field, and even the animals have to be killed off."

When the old man spoke it sounded as if he were quarreling. Mother Wang, who was darning a big hole on P'ing's undershirt, was moved by what she heard. As she thought about the loss of the country, she made a mistake in her darning. She had sewn the two sleeve openings together.

Chao San was like an old bull who had lost all of his youthful vigor. Now he could only fall back on memories of the "Sickle Society."

"In those days you were still young," he said to P'ing. "Li Ch'ing-shan and I and the others formed a 'Sickle Society.' Oh, that was a daring move. But I suffered a real setback and ran into big trouble. Your mother had come back with a borrowed gun, but who would have thought that before I could even use the gun I would take a man's life with a mere pole! From then on my luck was all bad. Each year has been worse than the last, up to this very day."

"A dog is a dog and will never become a wolf. After your father got into trouble, he lost interest in the 'Sickle Society.' That was the year that we sold our ox."

Mother Wang's comments caused Chao San to feel humiliation and anger. He wondered how he could have been so despicable then. His heart flared up for an instant, and he spoke of things that gave him pleasure: "Well, even the master is no longer master now. With the Japanese around, even a master isn't worth anything."

Feeling flushed and lightheaded, he went out and took a walk in the woods. There the treetops traced an arc against the blue sky, a lovely, symmetrical arc that billowed like clouds. A curtain of blue sky hung straight down before him, the treetops hemming it with a scalloped border. The butterflies flitted to and fro, though the wild flowers were not yet in bloom. Spread out before him were small thatched isolated houses, some left only with sections of walls standing in the sun, and some with the roofs carried off by bombs, while the main parts of the houses remained intact.

Chao San puffed out his chest and inhaled the fresh air of the fields. Not wanting to leave, he paused at the edge of a barren field where wheat had once grown. But after a while he grew morose as he recalled his own wheat field, which had been destroyed by gunfire. Under the Japanese occupation, it would never be recultivated. He carried the sadness of the wheat field with him as he passed by a melon patch. The melon grower was absent from the patch, which was now overgrown with weeds, but the little hut where the keeper kept watch was still there. Chao San dropped down among the short grass by the little hut; he was feeling drowsy. Just before he dozed off, he saw some Koreans emerging from the woods. Viewed from his prone position, they seemed to be walking at the edge of the horizon.

Had it not been for the houses sprouting up from the ground, Chao San would have thought he was sleeping at the edge of the horizon. His eyes dazzled by the sun's glare, he could not see very far, but he could hear the village dogs barking aimlessly in the distance.

It was such a desolate wilderness that even the wild dogs stayed away. Only Chao San, whose heart was fired by wine, came prowling around, but he lacked a purpose and just wandered at will wherever his feet carried him. As he passed the countless bare fields, he experienced a sense of waste and, shaking his head and throwing up his hands, walked back home, heaving one sigh after another.

The number of widows in the village had increased. Three of them were walking ahead of him, one of them leading her child by the hand.

Just as the red-faced Chao San reached the door of his house he detoured again. He roamed aimlessly, sorrow beckoning to him. Suddenly he stepped into a big hole in the road, but he didn't seem to notice. He proceeded as if he must finish a long journey. There were more holes where bombs had exploded, but he was not deterred, for the vigor of youth, induced by wine, was urging him on.

In a dilapidated building a mother cat was suckling a litter of kittens. He could not bear to watch the scene and walked on without running into any of his acquaintances. He continued on until the western sky glowed with color and he found himself, with a heavy heart and misty eyes, in front of the graves of his youthful companions. Having brought no wine to pay his respects to the dead, he just sat silently before his friends. This Chao San, who now lived in an occupied country, missed his brave dead comrades. Those who survived them were old and could only be indignant; they could never again be adventurous. Old Chao San could not afford to be adventurous again.

It was a starry night. Li Ch'ing-shan seemed to be fired by the passion of a madman. His raspy voice added mystery and excitement to his speech. This was their first mass meeting. They gathered at Chao San's house, solemn and hushed, as if for some august ceremony. Everybody seemed to be suffering from a lack of air. No one even sniffled. The lamps in the house were not lit and everyone's eyes were like those of cats at night, shining with a phosphorescent light.

Mother Wang's pointed feet kept pacing outside the window. In her steady hand she held a broken lampshade; she was prepared to smash it at any time, for she was the mouse that kept watch during the night, looking out for the cat. She went out the gate and took a turn round the fence. Then she stood beyond the fence and listened to the rise and fall of the voices from inside the house. Was there any danger? Not for a single moment did she forget the lampshade she was holding in her hand.

Inside the house the persistent and heavy voice of Li Ch'ing-shan continued: "It's only been during the past couple of weeks that I realized that the People's Revolutionary Army was so ineffective. If you join them, you're in for trouble. They're a bunch of Western-educated students who can't even mount a horse without someone giving them a boost up. All they know is how to yell 'Retreat, retreat.' On the night of the 28th it was drizzling outside. There were ten of us comrades eating when our ricebowls exploded in our faces. Two men were dispatched to investigate the origin of the bomb. Just think about that—sending two 'Western students' out. Men, that hapless pair was chased by the enemy and, in their flight, they even lost their caps. These students often get killed by the enemy."

Tunnel Legs cut in: "Isn't the Revolutionary Army as good as the Red Whiskers?" The moonlight shining in through the window was too faint for anyone to notice the funny expression on the boy's face as he asked his question.

Li Ch'ing-shan resumed his speech: "Oh, but the discipline of the Revolutionary Army is really something. Do you understand what discipline is? Rules and regulations. Their rules are too harsh; we couldn't take it. For example, you can look at the village girls but you can't . . . ha-ha. I got into trouble once over that, and the comrades gave me ten smacks with the butt of a gun." Here he stopped and laughed, but not too loudly. Then he went on with what he was saying.

Two-and-a-Half *Li* simply could not generate any interest in these matters and dozed off to one side. Chao San nudged the politically apathetic Two-and-a-Half *Li* with the bowl of his pipe. He was very unhappy with him. "Hey you, listen. Now listen! What times are these that you can still sleep?"

They heard the irregular crunching sounds made by Mother Wang's feet, but since they did not hear the crash of the lampshade, they knew that the Japanese soldiers were not coming. Yet a grave atmosphere settled over the room. Ch'ing-shan solemnly announced his plan. Since he was a farmer, and really had no idea how to approach the issue, what he said was: "The young men of the village must come together and save our country. Those students with the

Revolutionary Army cannot do it. Only the Red Whiskers have the courage."

Old Chao San did not light his pipe but threw it down on the *k'ang* and clapped his hands with a sense of urgency. "Right, muster the young men," he said. "Call them the Revolutionary Army too."

Actually Chao San had no idea what he was talking about, for he had never heard of the Revolutionary Army. He was contented for no reason at all. In his euphoria he caressed his beard with his large hands. For him, all of this aroused the same excitement that he had experienced with the forming of the Sickle Society ten years earlier. It had also been in a dark room and there had been the same muffled speeches. He was so happy he could not sleep a wink, but kept gesturing all night long with his hands.

But anyone standing outside Two-and-a-Half *Li's* house could have counted the rhythmic snores that emerged.

In the countryside the Japanese were trying their best to poison the villagers' minds. They talked about reinstating the Manchu Dynasty and said that everyone should be loyal subjects, filial sons, and chaste wives. Meanwhile the opposing force was also gathering support.

As soon as it grew dark, a man climbed over the wall to hide in Mother Wang's house. This black-bearded man had been coming every night and had become a very familiar sight to Mother Wang. While eating a meal in her house he told her: "Your daughter was a capable woman. With a rifle on her back she could climb a hill in no time at all. But . . . she is already . . . ."

P'ing crouched beside the *k'ang*, puffing on his father's pipe. A tinge of envy crept through his heart. With deliberation, he knocked the pipe against the door, and then went out. The night was pitch-black, and he lost himself in the darkness. When he returned, still depressed, Mother Wang was already in tears.

That night old Chao San came home very late. He had been talking to everyone he met about the loss of the country, about saving the country, about volunteer armies and revolutionary armies . . . all these strange-sounding terms. That was why he came home so late. It was almost time for the rooster to crow—except there was no rooster in Chao San's house. In fact, the crow of a rooster could not be heard anywhere in the village. The fading moon shone through the windows. The "three stars" had vanished, so he knew it was close to dawn.

He roused his son from his slumber and, with pride, told him about the propaganda work he had been doing: how the widow in the east village had sent her children back to her mother's house so that she could join the volunteer army, and how the young men were gathering together. The old man was acting like an official in a magistrate's office, swaying from side to side as he spoke. His heart was also swaying, and his soul was taking giant strides. After a minute of silence, he asked P'ing: "Did that man come? The one with the black beard?"

P'ing had fallen back to sleep while his father was vibrant with energy. He slept on, his father's words like the meaningless buzzings of mosquitoes in his ear. Chao San was angry. He felt that there was no one to carry on his glorious deeds. He felt that raising such a useless son had been a waste of time. He was terribly disappointed.

Mother Wang did not make a single sound but lay there as if asleep.

The next morning the man with the black beard suddenly appeared. Mother Wang asked him again: "When the girl died, did you see her with your own eyes?"

"Old Mother, why won't you understand?" he answered her craftily. "Haven't I said from the very beginning: If you die, you die! Anyone who joins the revolution should not be afraid of dying. That is an honorable death . . . better than staying alive as a slave of the Japanese dogs!"

Mother Wang had often heard people like him talk about living and dying. Maybe it was right to die. So she calmed down and, with eyes drenched by last night's tears, studied the changing expressions on the face of this man whom she was getting to know so well. In the end she accepted. All the pamphlets that the man took from his knapsack and the sheets of paper crawling with black dot-like words, she completely accepted. He also handed a small shiny pistol over to her. The man was in a hurry to go, but Mother Wang could not keep from asking one final question: "Was she shot to death?"

He opened the door and made his exit quickly. Since he was in such a hurry, he paid no attention to Mother Wang.

Normally, Mother Wang knew no fear and often she took the pamphlets others brought her and put them in the kitchen. Some-times she would just throw them under the mattress. But today she lacked courage. She was thinking that if those things were dis-covered, she would know what it felt like to be pierced by a Jap-anese bayonet. She seemed to think that her fate would be the same as her daughter's, especially when she was holding the pistol in the palm of her hand. She grew so terrified that she began to tremble. Her daughter must have met her death by a gun like that. Finally she put a stop to such thoughts. The seriousness of the present situation began to dawn on her.

Chao San came back with a panic-stricken face. Mother Wang ignored him and went to the back where the firewood stack had been located. But it was different than during previous years, for the firewood had all been used up. Growing sparsely on the flat ground were some purslane flowers. Just as she began to dig a hole, she heard the frenzied barking of the village dogs. Flustered, she could not even muster the strength to pull out the sickle she had stuck into the ground. She felt as if she were going to fall, being subjected to some force that threatened to tear her body apart. After an unbear-able, swooning second she went to call her old man. But when she reached the door, she turned back. She remembered some advice she had been given: "Don't tell anyone anything important, not even your spouse."

The words Black Whiskers had said to her also came to mind: "Don't tell Chao San. That old man can be like a child."

After she finished her burying, a dozen or so Japanese soldiers came there, most of whom had just thrown on their helmets; they hadn't even had time to lace up their boots, and the villagers knew that they were coming for women again.

Mother Wang had lost all of her powers of observation: involuntarily, she retreated behind Chao San. She didn't even recognize the Japanese officer with the eternally smiling face who came so often to search her house. As he left, the officer said goodbye to Mother Wang, but she hesitated and said nothing in reply.

The blare of a bugle signaled the time to move out. The wives were packing clothes, shoes, and socks for their men.

Li Ch'ing-shan sent some men around to each household to look for a rooster, but they did not find any, so someone suggested killing Two-and-a-Half Li's old goat. The goat was right then in front of Li Ch'ing-shan's house, cooling itself, or perhaps it was just too tired to move. Its single horn was wedged inside the crack in the fence. The young men tried to lift the goat up, but they could not free the horn.

Yet when Two-and-a-Half Li passed by, the goat freed itself and followed him home.

"If you want to kill it, go ahead," he said. "Otherwise, sooner or later the Japs will get it."

Second Aunt Li commented from where she stood: "The Japs would never take it. It's too old."

To which Two-and-a-Half Li responded: "Even if the Japs won't take it, it's going to die of old age anyway."

The day of oath-taking arrived. Since a rooster could not be found, it was decided to use the old goat as a substitute. The young men lifted up the goat, which was suspended by its legs from a pole. It bleated pitifully. Two-and-a-Half Li, looking comical in his sorrow, walked behind the goat with a limping gait as though he were stomping holes in the ground. He traveled like an undulating wave, faster and faster. His wife tried to drag him back but could not. Thus distracted, he walked for some distance. The goat was carried along a winding path over the slope and then placed on a square table with a red cloth that stood in the center of the yard.

The widow from the east village, who had also come, knelt in front of the table and prayed for a while. Then she lit the two red candles on the table. When the candles were lit, Two-and-a-Half Li knew that they would soon be killing his goat.

Besides old Chao San, there were only young men milling around the center of the yard. They bared their chests and arms, looking strong and fierce.

Chao San kept speaking to the widow from the east village—he had begun propagandizing to her the moment he saw her. Now, whenever anything happened, he no longer puffed greedily on his pipe as he had before. And to show that he was really serious, he no longer wiggled his beard as he spoke. "The time to save our country has come. No warm-blooded person would submit to being a slave to the invaders; he would rather die by a Japanese bayonet."

Chao San knew only that he was a Chinese. No matter how many times other people explained things to him, he was still unsure as to what class of Chinese he belonged. Even so, he was considered progressive. In fact, he represented the progress made by the entire village. In prior days he had not understood what a nation was. In prior days he could even have forgotten his own nationality. He did not speak, but stood quietly in the center of the yard, waiting for the grand ceremony to begin.

More than thirty people were gathered there, forming an impressive assembly. Chao San's heart was stirred. Even his whiskers seemed to sense the solemnity of the occasion and would not bear to be touched.

The April sky streamed down the ridges of the hill. Around the house, the cluster of big trees stood bowed beneath the midday sun. The bright, clear daylight joined in the oath-taking with the human beings.

At a command from Li Ch'ing-shan, the widows and the single men who had lost their families knelt down under the sky. Daylight fell on the back of the goat, and the big red candles on the table burned before the heads of the silent crowd. Li Ch'ing-shan stood tall and erect in front of the table. "Brothers, what day is today? Do you know? Today is the day we dare to die . . . it is decided . . . even if all our heads swing from the tops of the trees throughout the village, we shall not flinch, right? Isn't that right, brothers?"

Response came first from the widows. "Yes, even if we are cut into a million pieces!"

The shrill, piercing voices stabbed painfully like an awl at the heart of everyone present. For a brief moment, intense sorrow swept through the crowd of bowed heads. The blue sky seemed about to fall.

Old Chao San stood in front of the table, and even before he spoke, his tears started to flow: "The nation . . . the nation is lost! I . . . I am old, too. You are still young, you go and save the nation! My old bones . . . are useless! I'm an old nationless slave, and I'll never see you rip up the Japanese flag with my own eyes. Wait until I'm buried . . . then plant the Chinese flag over my grave, for I am a Chinese! . . . I want a Chinese flag. I don't want to be a nationless slave. Alive I am Chinese, and when I'm dead, I'll be a Chinese ghost . . . not a nation . . . nationless slave."

The concentrated, nondiffusable grief caused even the trees to bow down. Standing before the red candles, Chao San knocked hard on the table twice. In unison, the crowd directed their supplications and tears toward the blue sky. The whole crowd fell to weeping and wailing.

And so a loaded gun was placed before the assembly. By turns, everyone walked up to the gun and knelt to take his oath.

"If I am not sincere, may Heaven slay me; may this gun end my life. The bullet has eyes, is all-knowing and sacred."

Even the widows took their oaths with the gun barrel aimed at their hearts. But Two-and-a-Half *Li* did not return until after the oath-taking, and the assembly was about to kill the goat. He had managed to find a rooster somewhere. He was the only person who did not take the oath. He did not seem particularly distressed about the fate of the nation as he led the goat home.

Everyone's eyes, especially old Chao San's, angrily followed his departure.

"You crippled old thing. Don't you want to go on living?"

14 TO THE CITY

On the eve of her departure Golden Bough sharpened a pair of scissors on the rim of the water jug. Then, using the scissors, she cut her dead baby's diapers into shreds. The young widow was now living with her mother.

"Must you go tomorrow?"

Her mother, who was sleeping beside her, was awakened by the light from the lamp. Filled with infinite tenderness, the old woman sought comfort in her already determined fate.

"No, I'll wait a couple of days more," Golden Bough replied.

After a short while the old woman woke up again. She couldn't sleep any more. When she discovered that her daughter was not beside her but was doing some laundry in the middle of the room, she sat up and asked: "Do you have to leave tomorrow? Couldn't you stay on a couple more days?"

In the night, as Golden Bough was packing her things, her mother realized that she intended to leave.

"Ma, I'll only be gone two days, then I'll come back. Ma . . . don't worry."

Seemingly groping for something, the old woman said nothing in response.

The sun was already very high in the sky, but Golden Bough was still nestling against her ailing mother, who said: "Do you have to go, Golden Bough? Well, if you must, you must. Go and earn some money; I won't hold you back." Her voice sounded subdued. "But you must behave yourself and not copy other people. Don't ever fool around with men."

The women no longer felt any enmity toward their husbands. The girl wept and spoke to her mother: "Isn't all this the doing of those little Japs? Those accursed Japs! If I stay, aren't I just asking to be killed?"

Golden Bough had heard from the old folks that it would be a good idea for a woman traveling alone to make herself up to look old, or ugly. So she girded herself with a belt, from which she hung an oil can. She also hung the little bucket that held rice from her belt. Then she stuffed the small bundle of needles, thread, and rags into the rice bucket. To make herself resemble an old beggar woman she smeared her face with dust until it was dirty and wrinkled.

Before she set out, her mother removed the pair of silver earrings from her own ears and said: "You take these with you. Put them in your bundle, and make sure that no one takes them from you. I don't have a single penny, but if you find yourself without anything to eat, you can sell them to buy some food." As the girl walked out the door, she heard her mother say: "If you run into the Japs, hide among the mugwort stalks quickly."

Even after Golden Bough had walked a very long way and was going down an incline, her mother's words still continued to ring in her ears: "Buy some food." Her mind cluttered with disconnected thoughts, she didn't notice how far she had gone. It seemed to her as if she were running away from home; she walked swiftly without ever looking back. The small path, overgrown with weeds, impeded her hurried pace.

Just then a cart carrying Japanese soldiers with cigarettes in their mouths came down the road. Golden Bough began to quake. Remembering her mother's warning, she quickly lay down among the weeds on the small path. After the Japanese soldiers had passed, she stood up with a pounding heart and looked around apprehensively. Where was her mother? Her native village was far behind her. Soon she came to an unfamiliar village and began to feel as though she had passed through countless worlds. The red sun had almost reached the edge of the sky, and the shadow she cast on the ground was long and thin like a post. After crossing the small river bridge, she wouldn't have much farther to go.

Through the haze she could see chimneys from the factories of Harbin rising up into the clouds. She drank from the river, then looked back in the direction of home. It was far away and completely out of sight. She could see only the tops of the high hills. There, at the foot of the hills, was it smoke or was it trees she was seeing? Her mother was there, amidst the smoke or the trees.

It had been terribly hard for her to leave the hills of her home. Her heart seemed to have been taken out of her breast; she felt that it had been plucked and cast away to she-knew-not-where. Not really wanting to continue on, she forced herself to cross the bridge and walk down a small path. There, in front of her, the city of Harbin beckoned, while behind her the hills of her village bade farewell.

There were no tall grasses growing on the small path, so what would she do if the Japanese soldiers came? Could she hide herself in the cracks in the ground? She searched around. But owing to her flustered state and heavily perspiring face, she was ultimately accosted by the Japanese soldiers.

"You there . . . halt!"

As if shot, Golden Bough fell down into a ditch. The Japanese soldiers approached and took a look at her dirty appearance. Then, like fat ducks, they made some noises with their mouths and waddled away without paying any attention to her. Long after they had gone, she still hadn't gotten up. Finally tears came. Her wooden bucket lay there overturned; her little bundle had rolled out. She started walking once again, her shadow on the ground growing even thinner and longer, like a fine thread.

That first night in Harbin Golden Bough slept atop the cover of a drainage ditch. The street was inhabited by workers and drivers; there were small restaurants there, and the lowest class of prostitutes, the latter appearing frequently in the doorways of the small houses, clad in red pants. Men with nothing to do had a special look about them as they chatted and joked with the girls in red pants. Then they went into the small houses and, after a while, came out again. But none of them paid any attention to the ragged-looking Golden Bough. She might as well have been a garbage can or a sick dog curled up there.

There weren't even policemen on this street where old beggar women exchanged insults with waiters from the small restaurants. The sky was covered with stars, but they seemed so remote they had absolutely nothing to do with Golden Bough. After midnight a small dog came up to her. A persecuted dog, perhaps? The stray dog crept inside the wooden bucket to sleep. When Golden Bough awoke, the sun had still not risen, and the sky was covered with stars.

A great many vagrants were still bunched up in front of the small restaurants waiting for the last leftovers. Golden Bough's legs ached so badly they felt as if they had been broken; she didn't dare stand up. But finally she squeezed herself in among the beggars where she waited for a long time, though the waiter still did not appear with any food. Having slept in the open May air, she shivered uncontrollably. The stares of the people embarrassed her, and despite her hunger, she retreated to the original spot.

What kind of a world is the street at night? Golden Bough whimpered softly for her mother, her body knocking incessantly on the drainage-ditch cover as she shivered. Despair. Tears. Yet like the small dog sleeping in the wooden bucket, she was ignored. To the rest of the world it was as though they didn't exist at all. When day dawned, she didn't feel hungry, only empty. Her head was a complete vacuum. Under a tree in the street she came face to face with an old woman who did mending. "I'm new here," she said. "I just came from the countryside."

Noticing her distressed state, the old woman paid no attention to her and walked off, her face white in the clear, cool morning. The curly-tailed little dog snuggled up against the wooden bucket as it would its own mother; the morning air was probably too chilly for it.

Gradually people began entering and leaving the small restaurant. A stack of steaming hot buns appeared in the shop window.

"Old Auntie, I'm new here from the countryside. Let me go with you to earn a few pennies."

This time Golden Bough was successful, for the old woman took her along. As they passed through some noisy and smelly streets, Golden Bough began to understand. This was not the countryside; here there were only alienation, barriers, and insensitivity. As they traveled, except for the chicken and the fish, and the aromas coming from the restaurants, she saw and heard nothing else.

"This is how you darn socks."

In front of a place that boasted a gold sign, "Exclusive Opium Shop," Golden Bough opened up her bundle and, snipping a corner off a piece of fabric, mended the socks of men whom she had never seen. The old woman counseled her again: "You have to work fast. Never mind if it's well done or not. Just sew up all the holes."

Golden Bough had no strength left. She wished she could die then and there. No matter how hard she tried, her eyes would not stay open. A motorcar whizzed past her. Then a policeman came and ordered: "Move over there! Do you think this is a place to be frequented by the likes of you?"

Golden Bough quickly looked up. "Mr. Soldier, I just got here from the countryside, and I don't know the rules yet."

In the countryside she was accustomed to using the term "Mr. Soldier," so that is how she addressed the policeman, since he looked imposing to her, and he packed a gun at his side. The passersby laughed at her. The policeman laughed too.

"Pay no attention to him," the old seamstress admonished her, and there's no need to speak, either. If he says anything to you, just move, that's all."

Golden Bough realized that she was blushing. Looking down at herself, she saw that her clothes were different from other people's. She developed an instant dislike for the broken jug she had brought from the village, and she aimed a kick at it.

The socks were mended, but the empty feeling in her stomach did not go away. If she could have managed it, she would have gone somewhere—anywhere—to steal some food. She rested her needle

for a long time as she looked intently at a boy who was eating bis-
cuits on the street corner. She was still watching him even after he
had put the last piece in his mouth.

"Hurry up. When you finish, you can have some lunch. Have
you had breakfast?"

Golden Bough experienced a feeling of such great warmth that
she felt like crying. She wanted to say: "I haven't had anything since
last night, not even a drop of water."

When noon came, they walked with the lost souls who emerged
from the "Opium Shop." The workshop had a particularly dead atmosphere, which reminded Golden Bough again that this was not
the countryside. But it was not until after lunch, when everyone
washed her face in the basin, that she noticed those lackluster eyes
and sallow faces. The entire shop was five yards long without any
dividers. The walls were smeared with the blood of bedbugs; the
surfaces of the walls were spotted here and there with black and
purple bloodstains. Dirty, moldy bundles were strewn about in
heaps. The motley group of women laid their heads down on the
bundles and talked.

"The mistress at my house treats me real nice. I eat the same food
that they eat. Why, even if they eat buns with meat stuffing, that's
what I eat, too."

The others listened to her with envy. After a while, someone said
she had been pinched on the cheeks by a messenger at her residence.
She said that she was so upset over this that she had taken sick. After
that she continued with some meaningless chatter. Golden Bough
understood none of these bits and pieces of conversation; she was
still trying to figure out what a "residence" and a "mistress" were.
She exhausted her reasoning before asking a woman with short hair
who was smoking beside her: "Doesn't mistress mean old lady?"

The woman did not answer her. Instead she put down her tobacco
pipe and vomited. Golden Bough remarked that she must have swallowed a fly when she was eating. Laughter rose from the city women
up and down the long k'ang in the room, which irritated Golden
Bough. They laughed so hard they were rocking back and forth, and

were so tickled by this countrywoman that they slapped each other on the shoulders. Some laughed till tears streamed down their cheeks. Golden Bough sat quietly off to one side. At night, when bedtime came, she spoke to the old woman who had befriended her earlier: "I don't think Harbin is as good as the countryside. The sisters in the countryside are very kind. But you saw these women. At noon they clapped their hands, they were laughing so hard at me." As she spoke she rolled her bundle tighter—inside she had secreted the two ten-cent bills that she had earned. She used her bundle as a pillow and went to sleep among the bedbugs of the city.

Golden Bough had earned a lot of money. She had sewn a little pocket into the waistband of her pants, put in the two dollar bills, and then sewn up the opening. When the woman from the workshop came to collect her fee, she said: "Can I give it to you in a few days? I haven't earned anything." She couldn't very well repeat the excuse: "Let me pay it tonight. I'm new from the countryside."

But the woman refused to be put off. She stuck her hand right under Golden Bough's eyes. The women began to gather and soon formed a circle around Golden Bough. It was almost as though she were performing tricks to attract so many spectators. Among them was a fat woman in her thirties whose hair had all fallen out and whose pink shiny scalp stood out in the crowd. Her neck was seemingly set on springs; she could rotate and shake her shiny head with ease and at will. "Come on, pay up," she said to Golden Bough. "How can you say you don't have any money? I even know where you hide it."

This made Golden Bough angry, so there in front of everyone she tore open her pocket. She was about to lose three-quarters of her earnings. When that was snatched away from her, she only had fifty cents left. "How can I give Mother fifty cents?" she thought. "How many more days will I have to work to earn another two dollars?"

She went out into the street and worked till very late. That night a good many bedbugs were squashed, giving off a nauseating smell. Golden Bough sat up, feeling itchy all over, and scratched herself until she bled. Upstairs she could hear two women quarreling. Later she heard the sound of a woman weeping. Then the children, too, began to weep.

"Has Mother recovered from her illness? Is she gathering firewood for herself? When it rains, does the roof leak?" Gradually her thoughts turned morbid: "If Mother were to die now on the k'ang, no one would ever know." Golden Bough was walking along when a bicycle, its bell ringing, sped past her. Her heart quickened as if a motorcar were about to run over her. She ceased fantasizing.

Golden Bough knew how to earn money: she went several times to the single men's dormitory to sew bedcovers.

"How old is your husband?"

"He's dead."

"How old are you?"

"Twenty-seven."

A man wearing slippers, his pants unbuttoned at the waist, glanced at Golden Bough with a strange look and moved his strange lips: "Well, well, a young widow."

She was too naive to understand the significance of his remark. When she finished her sewing, she took her money and left. On one occasion, as she was leaving, one of the men called out to her: "You come back . . . come back."

The urgent call gave Golden Bough a strange feeling, which told her she should leave immediately and not turn back. That night as she lay down to sleep, she asked Chou Ta-niang:* "After I finish sewing and am leaving with the money, why do the men call me back?"

"How much money do you take from them?" Chou Ta-niang asked.

"For a bedcover they give me fifty cents."

"No wonder they call you back. Why else would they give you so

_____

*Ta-niang, a polite salutation for an elderly woman.

much money? Usually a bedcover is only worth twenty cents."

The tired Chou Ta-niang had but one more thing to say: "No poor sewing woman can escape from their clutches."

The bald woman with the shiny head lying on the opposite *k'ang* gave an affected cry. She came up behind Golden Bough, looking as if she wanted to pull out her hair. She played with her own plump fingers as she commented: "Aiya, my fine young widow, it looks like you're in luck. You will have both money and pleasure."

Other people in the room, awakened by the talking, began to curse the bald woman: "You crafty, damned wild woman. You're not afraid of even a hundred men. In fact, a hundred men wouldn't be enough for you!"

The women cursed and talked among themselves. Some were laughing loudly as someone on the side kept repeating: "Talk about being afraid; even a hundred men wouldn't be enough!"

Finally, like a crowd of noisy bees that has calmed down, all the buzzing from the women stopped, and they drifted off to sleep.

"Talk about being afraid; even a hundred men wouldn't be enough!"

Who said it that time no one knew, for her voice fell on deaf ears. It traveled round the room once and finally dissipated on the moonlit window paper.

Golden Bough stood outside the screened window of a Russian pastry shop. Inside, displayed on the shelves, were all kinds of creamy yellow pastries, sausages, pork loins, and chicks. All these delicacies lay there glistening with oil. Eventually she noticed a whole, fat piglet crouching on a long tray, with its ears standing straight up. Around the piglet were placed some cabbages and red peppers. She felt like walking right up, grabbing the whole platter, and taking it home to show her mother. But no, she couldn't do that. Her hatred for the Japs flared up again. If it were not for the Japs creating havoc in the village, her own sow would long ago have given birth to piglets. The bundle hanging in the crook of her elbow slid slowly down her arm as she stood fidgeting in front of the shop.

The street grew more crowded, and she bumped into other pedestrians. A beautiful Russian woman came out of the pastry shop; Golden Bough noticed her painted red toenails peeking out from her sandals. The woman walked very fast, faster than a man, and she was soon out of sight.

From the pavement came loud noises: *clomp, clomp.* A troop was passing by. As soon as Golden Bough saw the helmets, she knew that they were Japanese soldiers, so she left the pastry shop and ran off quickly.

She came across Chou Ta-niang, who said to her: "I couldn't find anything to do at all. Except for this jacket that I'm wearing, I don't have another change of clothes. I couldn't even save enough to find a few feet of cloth. Every ten days I have to pay a fee to the workshop—that's a dollar-fifty each time. I'm old and my eyes are weak, and since I'm so slow at my work, no one ever askes me to go to his place to do any sewing. I'm a month behind in my board payments. Fortunately I've been here many years, because if I was a newcomer, they would already have kicked me out." She crossed a street and continued: "That newcomer, old Mrs. Chang, was sick, but they still evicted her."

They passed by a meat shop, and Golden Bough found herself lingering there. She thought that if she could only buy a catty or so of meat she would be contented. "Mother has not tasted meat for over half a year."

The Sungari River—its waters flowed on. Since it was too early for travelers, the boat operators sat around exchanging jokes and chatting with one another. Chou Ta-niang sat at the river's edge. She was silent for a second, then she wiped her eyes. As her tears flowed for the final days of her life, the river water lapped gently against the bank.

Golden Bough, however, was unmoved. That was because she had just arrived in the city; she did not yet know the city well enough.

For the sake of money, for the sake of her livelihood, she cautiously followed a single man to his room. As soon as she stepped through the door and noticed the bed, she began to feel wary. Instead of sitting on the edge of the bed, she sat on a chair to sew the bedcover. Slowly the man began to converse with her—every sentence caused her heart to beat quickly. But nothing happened, and Golden Bough felt that the man must feel sympathy toward her. Next she mended the sleeve of his shirt, which he took off right there in front of her. When the sleeve was finished, he took out a dollar from his money belt. As he passed her the money, he made a sympathetic gesture with his moustache-covered mouth and commented: "Poor little widow, who is there to take pity on you?"

Golden Bough was a peasant woman. She could not tell whether the man was sincere or not, but she was moved somewhat by the word "pity." She felt a surge of emotion welling up in her heart, and she paused at the door, trying to express her thanks. But she did not know what to say, so she left. In her ears she could hear the whistling of the big tea kettles at the roadside stalls. Cars parked at the curb in front of the bakery were loading bread. The red scarves of an old Russian lady whizzed past her.

"Hey, come back . . . you come back. I have something more for you to mend."

His neck swollen and flushed with exertion, the man came after her. But when she returned with him to his room, there was no work for her there. Like a gorilla, the man bared his hairy chest and started to lock the door with his large hands. Next he undid his pants and called to Golden Bough: "Come . . . little darling." When he saw that she was terrified, he stopped. "I'm asking you to mend my pants. What are you so afraid of?"

After she had finished, the man gave her a dollar bill. But he did not put it in her hand. Instead he threw it under the bed so that she had to stoop to pick it up. Then when she retrieved the bill, he snatched it from her so that she had to pick it up again.

Golden Bough was suddenly engulfed in his arms. She implored hoarsely: "Forgive me, Mother . . . Mother, forgive me!"

In vain she screamed, her round eyes looking at the locked door she could not open. There was no escape and what followed was inevitable.

After dinner at the workshop, Golden Bough seemed to be treading on waves of tears. Her head felt dizzy, her heart seemed to have fallen into the gutter. Her legs turned rubbery and threatened to give way as she crawled up onto the k'ang to get her old shoes and a handkerchief. She wanted to go back to the village, to lie down beside her mother and cry her heart out.

A sick woman at the end of the k'ang was being evicted even though she was on the verge of death, but the women set aside their discussion of her situation, for Golden Bough had attracted their attention.

"What happened? Why are you so troubled?" Chou Ta-niang was the first to broach the subject.

"She must have cashed in!" The second one to speak was the fat bald woman.

Chou Ta-niang, too, must have sensed that Golden Bough had earned some money, because every time a newcomer "earned money" for the first time, she felt ashamed, and shame was devouring her now. She felt as if she had contracted a contagious disease.

"You'll get used to it. It's nothing. Money is the only thing that's real. I even got these golden earrings for myself."

The fat bald woman tried to console her by showing off her ears with her hands. But the others upbraided her: "You shameless hussy. You have no shame at all!"

The women around Golden Bough were witness to her distress, for her suffering was also their suffering. Gradually they dispersed and went to bed, showing no more sign of surprise or interest in the incident.

Courage had taken Golden Bough to the city, but shame drove her back to the village. On the boughs of a tree at the entrance to the village she saw some human heads. A feeling coursed through her marrow, chilling and paralyzing her entire body. What horrible, bloody heads!

Her mother took the one dollar bill from Golden Bough. She was smiling so much her teeth were completely exposed. As she studied the pattern on the bill, she was quite beside herself with joy. "Stay here overnight, and tomorrow you can go back."

Golden Bough sat on the edge of the *k'ang* massaging her aching legs. Her mother could not see why she was so unhappy, for the bill in front of her captured her every thought. In her mind she wondered what could stop her from handling even more of these bills. She must give encouragement to her daughter. "You should wash your clothes and tidy up a bit. You take off bright and early tomorrow morning. There's no future in the village." In her own impatience she sounded as if she were reproaching her daughter, as if she did not care for her at all.

A window suddenly opened and a black-faced man with a gun jumped in, stepping on Golden Bough's left leg as he did so. He glanced up at the rafters, and with practice he climbed up. Mother Wang followed him in. She hadn't seen Golden Bough for many days, yet she did not stop to talk; she seemed oblivious to everything around her as she scrambled up into the rafters. Not knowing what was happening, Golden Bough and her mother climbed up, too. It was not until dusk fell and no bad news had come that they all crawled down like reptiles. Mother Wang said: "Harbin must be better than the countryside. If you go there again, don't come back. The Japs in the village are getting worse and worse. They're slitting open the bellies of pregnant women to counteract the Red Gun Society (one of the volunteer armies). The live fetuses slide right out of their bellies. So to avenge them Li Ch'ing-shan chopped off the heads of two Japs and hung them from a tree."

Golden Bough snorted: "I used to hate only men; now I hate the Japanese instead." She finally reached the nadir of personal grief: "Do I hate the Chinese as well? Then there is nothing else for me to hate."

It seemed that Mother Wang's knowledge was no longer the equal of Golden Bough's.

15 THE DUD

As the troops moved out and rounded the bend of Southern Hill Road, children in their mothers' arms bade farewell to their fathers. As the men marched down the tree-lined road and past the river bank, their apparel and gait did not suggest a troop of soldiers. But their clothing hid fierce and strong hearts, and it was these hearts that led them on. And so, with hearts as solid as copper, they set out. A split second before the last man disappeared beyond the slope, a little baby in his mother's arms cried out: "Daddy." The boy's cry did not elicit any response; his father's arm did not wave even once. The boy's cry seemed to have come up against solid granite.

The women returned to their houses, which now seemed empty. It was as though the houses were built in the air, yet the white sunlight shining in through the window had no real significance. They did not need for the men to come home; they needed only good news. When the news finally came, it was five days later. With his pants rolled up to expose a pair of sinewy feet, old Chao San ran to Second Aunt Li and reported: "I hear that Ch'ing-shan and the rest were beaten back." He was clearly in a state of panic. Even his whiskers seemed startled and ready to jump off his face.

"Is it true that they're coming back?" Second Aunt Li's throat had become a long, fine tube, and her voice had a shrill quality to it.

"It's true that P'ing is coming home," Chao San replied.

A night of solemnity descended from the sky. Japanese soldiers raided Fishing Village, White Banner Village, and Three-Family Village.

P'ing was at Widow Wang's house relaxing on his mistress' lap when the dogs began to bark outside. Then he heard the Japanese talking, and he climbed over the wall to escape. As he hid in a patch of mugwort stalks, toads were leaping at his feet.

"We must catch that man. He might have ties with the Volunteer Army."

Amidst the stalks, he could hear who it was who was saying: "Running dogs!" He could also hear clearly that his mistress was being beaten.

"Where did the man go? Speak up or else you'll be shot!" They kept up their cursing: "You bitches, you're all bred by pigs!"

P'ing was stark naked. After he had run quite a distance, he felt for the lapel of his coat to wipe his perspiration, but there was no lapel. He felt his legs, then realized that his shadow on the ground was as naked as a baby.

Two-and-a-Half *Li's* pockmarked wife was killed. Tunnel Legs as well. With two people slain, the village was left alone for two days. But on the third day it was time to kill again, and Japanese soldiers overran the village. P'ing went to Golden Bough's house to spend the night in the rafters, but she said: "No, they've just been here to search the rafters."

So P'ing was back in the fields, running, as a constant spray of bullets followed him. Though his eyes could not rotate, he could hear yelling close by.

"Catch him alive . . . catch him alive!"

He fancied that he could hear every sound made. He came to a door and went in, where he found an old man cooking a meal. P'ing was close to tears. "Uncle, save me. Hide me. Help me, quick!"

"What's the matter?" the old man asked.

"The Japs are after me."

P'ing's nose was bleeding. It seemed to start bleeding as soon as he mentioned the Japs. He looked around the house, but there was no place to hide. So he turned to run, but was grabbed by the old man, who took him out the back door. A long container that held manure stood beside the door. The old man lifted up the lid and said: "You just crawl in here and breathe lightly."

The old man put some rice on two strips of paper and pasted them over the back door. Then he returned to the ricepot to eat his meal. In the manure container P'ing could hear the old man talking with someone. After that he heard the sound of someone trying the door. "The door is going to open and I'm going to be caught." He was about to jump out of the container, but before long the men—the devils—left.

P'ing came out of his safe hiding place—the manure container—his face covered with traces of manure. With his white face streaked with blood and his nose still bleeding he looked a sorry sight.

Li Ch'ing-shan now believed in the effectiveness of the Revolutionary Army. When he escaped back to the village, he was not as pessimistic as the others. In Mother Wang's house he said: "What's good about the Revolutionary Army is that they don't do things rashly. They have discipline. This time I really believe in them. The Red Whiskers are finished: they fight among themselves and make a mess of things."

This time there were few who listened to him, for the people no longer trusted Ch'ing-shan. Village people are easily discouraged. Everyone very easily became discouraged; they felt that it was all over for them. Old Chao San alone did not lose faith. "Then let's re-organize and join the Revolutionary Army," he said.

Mother Wang felt that Chao San's words were as naive as those of a child, but she did not laugh at him. Sitting beside her and wearing a man's hat was a heroic young woman who had joined the bandits and had fought for her country.

"You left the dead behind, but what about the wounded?"

"Didn't those who were slightly wounded all come back? As for the seriously wounded, we couldn't take care of them. They might as well be dead."

Just then an old woman from the north village came charging in, weeping hysterically. She wanted to tear Li Ch'ing-shan to pieces. She held her head, like she would hold a rock, and dashed toward the wall, uttering disjointed phrases: "Li Ch'ing-shan . . . enemy . . . you led my son to his death!" They tried to drag her away, but she struggled mightily, like a crazed bull. "I can't go on. You might as well deliver me over to the Japs! I want to die . . . it's time for me to die."

She kept tearing at her hair. Gradually she sank down to the ground, out of breath. She patted Mother Wang's knees gently. "Old sister, you know how I feel. Widowed at nineteen, I struggled for decades, struggled for the boy . . . all those days that I had to go hungry, I went with my son to the hillside to cut grasses. But the rain came, and we were washed down the hill. My head, I thought it was broken. Who'd have thought . . . but I didn't die . . . I should have died a long time ago." Her warm tears soaked through and drenched Mother Wang's knees. She began to sob quietly. "Tell me, what is there left for me? I might as well die. With the Japs waiting, the girl Ling-hua will never live to grow up; she might as well die too."

And die they did. They were found hanging from a roofbeam, the three-year-old Ling-hua alongside her grandmother. They were swinging high like two skinny fish.

The death rate in the village began to accelerate, but the people seemed not to notice. As if caught in the throes of an epidemic the whole village struggled in delirium.

The Patriotic Army passed through Three-Family Village flying a yellow flag. On the flag spelled out in red letters were the words "Patriotic Army." Some of the men fell in behind it. They did not know how to be patriotic, nor did they know what good would come of their patriotism, but they knew they were hungry.

Li Ch'ing-shan did not go with them. He said that this army was formed by bandits too. Chao San had a fight with his son over the Patriotic Army. "I think you should go. If the word leaks out that you're here, then someone will come to get you. Go and take a look around with them. Even if you end up by killing only one Jap devil, it's still a better choice. It's a chance for revenge. You're strong and young, and it's good to have revenge."

Chao San lacked experience, and this kind of blustering talk could never convert his son. When P'ing talked with his father, he usually rolled his eyes and then glanced obliquely at him, or shrugged his shoulders a time or two. Chao San resented this kind of treatment. Sometimes he would think to himself: "Why isn't old Chao San a young Chao San?"

16 THE NUN

Golden Bough wanted to become a nun.

The red brick nunnery was on the other side of the hill. She tried to open the door, but it wouldn't budge. Flocks of sparrows were pecking in the center of the courtyard; the stone steps were overgrown with green moss. She questioned a woman next door, who told her: "After the occupation the nun disappeared. I heard that she ran off with the carpenter who was building the temple."

Golden Bough peered through the iron gate and could see that the windows had not been put up. Pieces of wood of varying lengths lay in the center of the yard. She looked into the front hall in which she saw a small clay statue of Buddha sitting despondently.

Golden Bough observed the woman's swollen belly and said: "How can you dare show your face in your condition? Haven't you heard that the Japs are using pregnant women to counteract the Red Gun Society? They slit open the women's bellies and take the fetuses with them to battle. They say that the Red Gun Society is not afraid of anything but women. The Japs even nicknamed the Red Gun Society the Iron Children."

The woman began to weep. "I said I wouldn't get married, but my mother refused to listen. She said that the Japs are interested in young maidens. Look at me now. What am I going to do? The baby's father joined the Volunteer Army and hasn't been back since."

Someone crawled out from the back of the temple. Golden Bough and the woman ran in terror.

"What's the matter with you? Am I a ghost or something?"

The beautiful young man of yesteryear came home crawling like a half-dead snake. When Fifth Sister came out and saw her man she was reminded of a stallion that had been wounded. "Has the whole Revolutionary Army disbanded?" she asked him.

"Yes, disbanded. All killed. Even I almost got killed." He waved his arm in a circle above the stalks of grass. "Well, my unfaithful little wife. Seeing me like this, don't you have some sweet words for me?"

Fifth Sister lowered her head like a sleeping sunflower. The pregnant woman went into her house. But where should Golden Bough go? The temple on which she had set her heart had long been abandoned.

17   THE UNSOUND LEG

"Where is the People's Revolutionary Army?" Two-and-a-Half *Li* asked Chao San suddenly. This set Chao San to thinking: "Has Two-and-a-Half *Li* turned traitor?" He would not answer his question, so Two-and-a-Half *Li* then asked Ch'ing-shan. "Don't ask any questions," he replied. "In a few days you just go with me."

Two-and-a-Half *Li* behaved as one who could not wait to join up with the Revolutionary Army. Ch'ing-shan raised his voice: "The Revolutionary Army is at Pan Rock. Can you get there by yourself? I don't think you have any guts at all. You can't even kill a goat." Then, as a calculated insult: "How's your goat faring?"

In his anger, Two-and-a-Half *Li* rolled his eyes so that they showed more white than black. His enthusiasm was frozen over.

Li Ch'ing-shan said nothing more but just stared out at the trees framed against the sky. He nodded his head as he began to sing a little tune. Two-and-a-Half Li was going out the door when Ch'ing-shan's wife, wet with perspiration from her work in the kitchen, said to him: "Uncle Li, have a bite with us before you go."

Ch'ing-shan, who had begun to feel sorry for him, smiled and said: "What's the point of going home? You don't have a wife anymore. We'll eat first and talk about all this later."

Having lost his own family, he felt a longing for the company of other people's families. So he picked up the chopsticks and quickly downed a bowl of rice. Then he ate two more bowls, and, before the others had finished, he was puffing on his pipe. Rather than drink any soup, he began to smoke right after dinner.

"Have some soup. The cabbage soup is good."

"No. It's been three days since my wife died, and three days since I had a bowl of rice," he said as he shook his head.

Ch'ing-shan cut in: "How about your goat; did it eat?"

With a full stomach, everything looked brighter to Two-and-a-Half Li; so instead of getting angry, he laughed as he normally would. He left Ch'ing-shan's house feeling contented, and as he walked along the small path, he smoked his pipe. The boundless sky did not evoke any sadness in him. Frogs were croaking beside the stream; the small trees on the bank were rustling in the wind. He trod on land that had once been his own vegetable plot, and memories stirred his heart. Not a single vegetable was growing in the plot.

In the dusk an old woman and some children were bending low in the field. They met at the edge of the field where Two-and-a-Half Li asked them: "Are you digging for something? Is there buried treasure under the ground? If so, I'll get down and help you dig."

A little child replied in a clear voice: "We're scrounging for grains of wheat." The child seemed to be enjoying himself.

"Treasure? Good heavens, no," his old grandmother replied with a sigh. "The children were so hungry they were clamoring, so I brought them here to glean some grains to take home for food."

Two-and-a-Half *Li* passed his pipe over to the old woman, who took it and, without even wiping it off, stuck it into her mouth. Obviously she was accustomed to smoking a pipe, and in desperate need of it. She hunched her shoulders and closed her eyes tightly, as thick smoke poured from her mouth and issued from her nostrils. He sensed danger, for she looked as if her nose were on fire. "It's been more than a month since I touched a pipe."

She was reluctant to relinquish the pipe, but common sense won out. Two-and-a-Half *Li* took it and knocked the bowl against the ground.

The world was so lonely: no birds were flying at the crimson edge of the sky, and no dogs were barking beneath the people's fences.

The old woman slowly took a rolled-up piece of paper from her waistband, which she deliberately smoothed out and then refolded neatly. "Read this at home," she said. "Your wife and son are both dead. Who can save you? You go home and read this, then you'll understand." She pointed at the piece of paper as if a spell had been cast on it.

The sky was getting darker, so dark that it seemed as if a curtain had been thrown around everyone's face. After a few steps the youngest boy clasped his grandmother's thigh and cried: "Grandma, my basket is full. It's too heavy for me to carry."

So his grandmother picked up the basket and held his hand as they walked. The older children ran on ahead like troopers. When they arrived home, the grandmother lit a lamp and checked over what they had gotten. The basket was chock-full of mugwort stalks. It was overflowing with them, and there were no grains at all. The grandmother hit him on the head and laughed: "Are these the grains you've gleaned?" The smile on her face turned into a look of sadness. She was thinking: "The child can't even recognize grains yet. Poor little one."

The Fifth Moon Festival. Even though it was summer, an autumn wind was blowing. Two-and-a-Half *Li* snuffed out the lamp and, with a stern heart, emerged from beneath the eaves, holding a cleaver in his hand. He looked in the corner of the yard, in the goat's pen, and under the poplar tree beyond the courtyard. In order to free himself from all worries and ties, it seemed to him that he must kill the goat at once.

This was the eve of Two-and-a-Half Li's departure.

The goat returned, bleating, with weeds stuck in its whiskers. It scratched itself noisily at the fence. Two-and-a-Half Li raised the cleaver above his head and walked toward the fence. The cleaver flew through the air and chopped down a sapling.

The old animal came up to him and scratched itself against his legs. For a long time, Two-and-a-Half Li stroked its head. He was overcome with shame, and like a Christian, he prayed to the goat.

In the morning he seemed to be talking to the goat again. He muttered for a while in the goat pen, then he fastened the gate. The goat grazed in the pen.

The Fifth Moon Festival under sunny blue skies—to old Chao San, it did not feel like the Fifth Moon Festival at all. The wheat had not sprouted, so he could not smell its fragrance, and no paper gourds were hanging above the doors. Everything had changed, he thought, and so swiftly. He could remember last year's Fifth Moon Festival, clearly and in detail, as if it were happening right before his eyes. Hadn't the children been catching butterflies? Hadn't he been drinking? He sat on a fallen tree trunk in front of his house, paying homage to all of this, which was now lost to him.

Li Ch'ing-shan passed by him, made up like a laborer, barefooted and with his pantlegs rolled up. "I'm leaving," he said to Chao San. "There's someone waiting for me in the city, so I have to go." Ch'ing-shan made no mention of the Fifth Moon Festival.

From a distance, Two-and-a-Half Li came limping up. His pale equine face seemed to carry a smile. "Look at you sitting here," he said to Chao San. "I think you're going to rot there on top of that piece of wood."

Two-and-a-Half Li turned and saw the goat, which he had locked up in its pen, following him. Instantly his face grew even longer. "This old goat . . . keep it for me, Third Brother Chao. As long as you're alive, take care of it for me." He rested his hands on the goat's hair, saying goodbye. His weeping hands caressed the goat's hair for the last time. He ran quickly to catch up with Li Ch'ing-shan. Behind him the goat bleated continuously, its whiskers swaying slowly.

Two-and-a-Half *Li* hobbled along on his unsound leg. Soon he became just a blur. Past the hill and the forest. Farther and farther away. The goat, bleating in ignorant bliss, kept Chao San company.

September 9, 1934*

---

*This is the date the novel was completed. It is customary in Chinese works to place the date at the end.

Hsiao Hung

Tales of
Hulan River

Translated by Howard Goldblatt

1 HULAN RIVER

I

After the harsh winter has sealed up the land, the earth's crust begins to crack and split. From south to north, from east to west; from a few feet to several yards in length; anywhere, anytime, the cracks run in every direction. As soon as harsh winter is upon the land, the earth's crust opens up.

The severe winter weather splits the frozen earth.

Old men use whisk brooms to brush the ice off their beards the moment they enter their homes. "Oh, it's cold out today!" they say. "The frozen ground has split open."

A carter twirls his long whip as he drives his cart sixty or seventy *li* under the stars, then at the crack of dawn he strides into an inn, and the first thing he says to the innkeeper is: "What terrible weather. The cold is like a dagger."

After he has gone into his room at the inn, removed his dogskin cap with earflaps, and smoked a pipeful of tobacco, he reaches out for a steamed bun; the back of his hand is a mass of cracked, chapped skin.

The skin on people's hands is split open by the freezing cold. The man who sells cakes of bean curd is up at dawn to go out among the people's homes and sell his product. If he carelessly sets down his square wooden tray full of bean curd it sticks to the ground, and he is unable to free it. It will have quickly frozen to the spot.

The old steamed-bun peddler lifts his wooden box filled with the steaming buns up onto his back, and at the first light of day he is out hawking on the street. After emerging from his house he walks along at a brisk pace shouting at the top of his voice. But before too long, layers of ice have formed on the bottoms of his shoes, and he walks as though he were treading on rolling and shifting eggs. The snow and ice have encrusted the soles of his shoes. He walks with an unsure step, and if he is not altogether careful he will slip and fall. In fact, he slips and falls despite all his caution. Falling down is the worst thing that can happen to him, for his wooden box crashes to the ground, and the buns come rolling out of the box, one on top of the other. A witness to the incident takes advantage of the old man's inability to pick himself up and scoops up several of the buns, which he eats as he leaves the scene. By the time the old man has struggled to his feet, gathered up his steamed buns—ice, snow, and all—and put them back in the box, he counts them and discovers that some are missing. He understands at once and shouts to the man who is eating the buns, but has still not left the scene: "Hey, the weather's icy cold, the frozen ground's all cracked, and my buns are all gone!"

Passersby laugh when they hear him say this. He then lifts the box up onto his back and walks off again, but the layers of ice on the soles of his shoes seem to have grown even thicker, and he finds the going more difficult than before. Drops of sweat begin to form on his back, his eyes become clouded with the frost, ice gathers in even greater quantity on his beard, and the earflaps and front of his tattered cap are frosting up with the vapor from his breath. The old man walks more and more slowly, his worries and fears causing him to tremble in alarm; he resembles someone on iceskates for the first time who has just been pushed out onto the rink by a friend.

A puppy is so freezing cold it yelps and cries night after night, whimpering as though its claws were being singed by flames.

The days grow even colder:

Water vats freeze and crack;

Wells are frozen solid;

Night snowstorms seal the people's homes; they lie down at night to sleep, and when they get up in the morning they find they cannot open their doors.

Once the harsh winter season comes to the land everything undergoes a change: the skies turn ashen gray, as though a strong wind has blown through, leaving in its aftermath a turbid climate accompanied by a constant flurry of snowflakes whirling in the air. People on the road walk at a brisk pace as their breath turns to vapor in the wintry cold. Big carts pulled by teams of seven horses form a caravan in the open country, one following closely upon the other, lanterns flying, whips circling in the air under the starry night. After running two *li* the horses begin to sweat. They run a bit farther, and in the midst of all that snow and ice the men and horses are hot and lathered. The horses stop sweating only after the sun emerges and they are finally turned into their stalls. But the moment they stop sweating a layer of frost forms on their coats.

After the men and horses have eaten their fill they are off and running again. Here in the frigid zones there are few people; unlike the southern regions, where you need not travel far from one village to another, and where each township is near the next, here there is nothing but a blanket of snow as far as the eye can see. There is no neighboring village within the range of sight, and only by relying on the memories of those familiar with the roads can one know the direction to travel. The big carts with their seven-horse teams transport their loads of foodstuffs to one of the neighboring towns. Some have brought in soybeans to sell, others have brought sorghum. Then when they set out on their return trip they carry back with them oil, salt, and dry goods.

Hulan River is one of these small towns, not a very prosperous place at all. It has only two major streets, one running north and south and one running east and west, but the best-known place in town is The Crossroads, for it is the heart of the whole town. At The Crossroads there is a jewelry store, a yardage shop, an oil store, a salt store, a teashop, a pharmacy, and the office of a foreign dentist. Above this dentist's door there hangs a large shingle about the

size of a rice-measuring basket, on which is painted a row of oversized teeth. The advertisement is hopelessly out of place in this small
town, and the people who look at it cannot figure out just what it's
supposed to represent. That is because neither the oil store, the yardage shop, nor the salt store displays any kind of advertisement;
above the door of the salt store, for example, only the word "salt" is
written, and hanging above the door of the yardage shop are two
curtains which are as old as the hills. The remainder of the signs are
like the one at the pharmacy, which gives nothing more than the
name of the bespectacled physician whose job it is to feel women's
pulses as they drape their arms across a small pillow. To illustrate:
the physician's name is Li Yung-ch'un, and the name of his pharmacy is simply "Li Yung-ch'un." People rely on their memories, and
even if Li Yung-ch'un were to take down his sign, the people would
still know that he was there. Not only the townsfolk, but even the
people from the countryside are more or less familiar with the streets
of the town and what can be found there. No advertisement, no pub-
licity is necessary. If people are in need of something, like cooking
oil, some salt, or a piece of fabric, then they go inside and buy it. If
they don't need anything, then no matter how large a sign is hung
outside, they won't buy anything.

That dentist is a good case in point. When the people from the
countryside spot those oversized teeth they stare at them in be-
wilderment, and there are often many people standing in front of
the large sign looking up at it, unable to fathom its reason for being
there. Even if one of them were standing there with a toothache,
under no circumstances would he let that dentist, with her foreign
methods, pull his tooth for him. Instead he would go over to the Li
Yung-ch'un Pharmacy, buy two ounces of bitter herbs, take them
home and hold them in his mouth, and let that be the end of that!
The teeth on that advertisement are simply too big; they are hard
to figure out, and just a little bit frightening.

As a consequence, although that dentist hung her shingle out for
two or three years, precious few people ever went to her to have
their teeth pulled. Eventually, most likely owing to her inability to

make a living, the woman dentist had no recourse but to engage in midwifery on the side.

In addition to The Crossroads, there are two other streets, one called Road Two East and the other called Road Two West. Both streets run from north to south, probably for five or six *li*. There is nothing much on these two streets worth noting—a few temples, several stands where flatcakes are sold, and a number of grain store-houses.

On Road Two East there is a fire mill standing in a spacious court-yard, a large chimney made of fine red brick rising high above it. I have heard that no one is allowed to enter the fire mill, for there are a great many knobs and gadgets inside which must not be touched. If someone did touch them, he might burn himself to death. Other-wise, why would it be called a fire mill? Because of the flames in-side, the mill is reportedly run neither by horses nor donkeys—it is run by fire. Most folk wonder why the mill itself doesn't go up in flames since only fire is used. They ponder this over and over, but are unable to come up with an answer, and the more they ponder it, the more confused they become, especially since they are not allowed to go inside and check things out for themselves. I've heard they even have a watchman at the door.

There are also two schools on Road Two East, one each at the southern and northern ends. They are both located in temples—one in the Dragon King Temple and one in the Temple of the Patriarch—and both are elementary schools.

The school located in the Dragon King Temple is for the study of raising silkworms, and is called the Agricultural School, while the one in the Temple of the Patriarch is just a regular elementary school with one advanced section added, and is called the Higher Elemen-tary School.

Although the names used for these two schools vary, in fact the only real difference between them is that in the one they call the Agricultural School the silkworm pupae are fried in oil in the au-tumn, and the teachers there enjoy several sumptuous meals.

There are no silkworms to be eaten in the Higher Elementary School, where the students are definitely taller than those in the Agricultural School. The students in the Agricultural School begin their schoolwork by learning the characters for "man," "hand," "foot," "knife," and "yardstick," and the oldest among them cannot be more than sixteen or seventeen years of age. But not so in the Higher Elementary School; there is a student there already twenty-four years old who is learning to play the foreign bugle and who has already taught in private schools out in the countryside for four or five years, but is only now himself attending the Higher Elementary School. Even the man who has been manager of a grain store for two years is a student at the school.

When this elementary school student writes a letter to his family he asks questions like: "Has Little Baldy's eye infection gotten better?" Litle Baldy is the nickname of his eldest son, who is eight. He doesn't mention his second son or his daughters, because if he were to include all of them the letter would be much too long. Since he is already the father of a whole brood of children—the head of a family—whenever he sends a letter home he is mainly concerned with household matters: "Has the tenant Wang sent over his rent yet?" "Have the soybeans been sold?" "What is the present market situation?" and the like.

Students like him occupy a favored position in the class; the teacher must treat them with due respect, for if he drops his guard, this kind of student will often stand up, classical dictionary in hand, and stump the teacher with one of his questions. He will smugly point out that the teacher has used the wrong character in a phrase he has written on the board.

As for Road Two West, not only is it without a fire mill, it has but one school, a Moslem school situated in the Temple of the City God. With this exception, it is precisely like Road Two East, dusty and barren. When carts and horses pass over these roads they raise up clouds of dust, and whenever it rains the roads are covered with a layer of mud. There is an added feature on Road Two East: a five-

or six-foot-deep quagmire. During dry periods the consistency of the mud inside is about that of gruel, but once it starts to rain the quagmire turns into a river. The people who live nearby suffer because of it: When they are splashed with its water, they come away covered with mud; and when the waters subside as the sun reappears in the clearing sky, hordes of mosquitos emerge and fly around their homes. The longer the sun shines, the more homogenized the quagmire becomes, as though something were being refined in it; it's just as though someone were trying to refine something inside it. If more than a month goes by without any rain, that big quagmire becomes even more homogenized in makeup. All the water having evaporated, the mud has turned black and has become stickier than the gummy residue on a gruel pot, stickier even than paste. It takes on the appearance of a big melting vat, gummy black with an oily glisten to it, and even flies and mosquitos that swarm around stick to it as they land.

Swallows love water, and sometimes they imprudently fly down to the quagmire to skim their wings over the water. It is a dangerous maneuver, as they nearly fall victim to the quagmire, coming perilously close to being mired down in it. Quickly they fly away without a backward glance.

In the case of horses, however, the outcome is different: they invariably bog down in it, and even worse, they tumble down into the middle of the quagmire, where they roll about, struggling to free themselves. After a period of floundering they lie down, their energy exhausted, and the moment they do so they are in real danger of losing their lives. But this does not happen often, for few people are willing to run the risk of leading their horses or pulling their carts near this dangerous spot.

Most of the accidents occur during drought years or after two or three months without any rainfall, when the big quagmire is at its most dangerous. On the surface it would seem that the more rain there is, the worse the situation, for with the rain a veritable river of water is formed, nearly ten feet in depth. One would think this would make it especially perilous, since anyone who fell in would surely drown. But such is not the case. The people of this small town of Hulan River aren't so stupid that they don't know how brutal this pit can be, and no one would be so foolhardy as to try leading a horse past the quagmire at such times.

But if it hasn't rained for three months the quagmire begins to dry up, until it is no more than two or three feet deep, and there will always be those hardy souls who will attempt to brave the dangers of driving a cart around it, or those with somewhat less courage who will watch others make their way past, then follow across themselves. One here, two there, and soon there are deep ruts along both sides of the quagmire formed by the passage of several carts. A late arrival spots the signs of previous passings, and this erstwhile coward, feeling more courageous than his intrepid predecessors, drives his cart straight ahead. How could he have known that the ground below him is uneven? Others had safely passed by, but his cart flips over.

The carter climbs out of the quagmire, looking like a mud-spattered apparition, then begins digging to free his horse from the mud, quickly making the sad discovery that it is mired down in the middle of the quagmire. There are people out on the road during all of this, and they come over to lend a helping hand.

These passersby can be divided into two types. Some are attired in traditional long gowns and short overjackets and are spotlessly clean. Apparently none of them will move a finger to assist in this drama because their hands are much too clean. Needless to say, they are members of the gentry class. They stand off to the side and observe the goings-on. When they see the horse trying to stand up they applaud and shout, "Oh! Oh!" several times. But then they see that the horse is unable to stand and falls back down; again they clap their hands and again they shout several times, "Oh! Oh!" But this time they are registering their displeasure. The excitement surrounding the horse's attempts to stand and its inability to do so continues for some time, but in the end it cannot get to its feet and just lies there pitifully. By this time those who have only been watching the feverish activity conclude that this is about all that will happen, that nothing new will materialize, and they begin to disperse, each heading off to his home.

But let us return to the plight of the horse lying there. The passersby who are trying to free it are all common folk, some of the town's onion peddlers, food sellers, tile masons, carters, and other workers. They roll up their trouser cuffs, remove their shoes, and seeing no alternative, walk down into the quagmire with the hope that by pooling their strength they will be able to hoist the horse out. But they fail in their attempts, and by this time the horse's breathing has become very faint. Growing frantic, they hasten to free the horse from its harness, releasing it from the cart on the assumption that the horse will be able to get up more easily once it is freed from that burden. But contrary to their expectations, the horse still cannot stand up. Its head is sticking up out of the mire, ears twitching, eyes shut, snorts of air coming from its nostrils.

Seeing this sad state of affairs, people from the neighborhood run over with ropes and levers. They use the ropes to secure the horse and the levers to pry it free. They bark out orders as though they were building a house or constructing a bridge, and finally they manage to lift the animal out. The horse is still alive, lying at the side of the road. While some individuals are pouring water over it and washing the mud off its face, there is a constant flow of people coming and going at the scene of the spectacle.

On the following day everyone is saying: "Another horse has drowned in the big quagmire!" As the story makes its rounds, although the horse is actually still alive, it is said to have died, for if the people didn't say so, the awe in which they held that big quagmire would suffer.

It's hard to say just how many carts flip over because of that big quagmire. Throughout the year, with the exception of the winter season when it is sealed up by the freezing weather, this big quagmire looks as though it has acquired a life of its own—it is alive. Its waters rise, then subside; now it has grown larger, in a few days it recedes again. An intimate bond between it and the people begins to form.

When the water is high, not only are horses and carts impeded, it is an obstacle even to pedestrians. Old men pass along its edge on trembling legs, children are scared out of their wits as they skirt around it.

Once the rain begins to fall, the water quickly fills the now glistening quagmire, then overflows and covers the bases of neighboring walls. For people out on the street who approach this place, it is like being dealt a setback on the road of life. They are in for a struggle: sleeves are rolled up, teeth are ground tightly, all their energy is called forth; hands clutch at a wooden wall, hearts pound rapidly; keep your head clear, your eyes in focus . . . the battle is joined.

Why is it that this, of all walls, has to be so smooth and neatly built, as though its owners have every intention of not coming to anyone's aid in this moment of distress? Regardless of how skillfully these pedestrians reach out, the wall offers them no succor; clawing here and groping there, they grab nothing but handfuls of air. Where in the world is there a mountain on which wood like this grows, so perfectly smooth and devoid of blemishes or knots?

After five or six minutes of struggling, the quagmire has been crossed. Needless to say, the person is by then covered with sweat and hot all over. Then comes the next individual, who must prepare himself for a dose of the same medicine. There are few choices available to him—about all he can do is grab hold here and clutch there, till after five or six minutes he too has crossed over. Then, once he is on the other side he feels revitalized, bursts out laughing, and looks back to the next person to cross, saying to him in the midst of his difficult struggle: "What's the big deal? You can't call yourself a hero unless you've faced a few dangers in your life!"

But that isn't how it always goes—not all are revitalized; in fact, most people are so frightened that their faces are drained of color. There are some whose trembling legs are so rubbery after they have crossed the quagmire that they cannot walk for some time. For timid souls like this, even the successful negotiating of this dangerous stretch of road cannot dispel the mood of distress that has involuntarily settled upon them; their fluttering hearts seemingly put into motion by this big quagmire, they invariably cast a look behind them and size it up for a moment, looking as though they have something they want to say. But in the end they say nothing, and simply walk off.

One very rainy day a young child fell into the quagmire and was rescued by a bean-curd peddler. Once they got him out they discovered he was the son of the principal of the Agricultural School. A lively discussion ensued. Someone said that it happened because the Agricultural School was located in the Dragon King Temple, which angered the venerable Dragon King. He claimed it was the Dragon King who caused the heavy downpour in order to drown the child.

Someone disagreed with him completely, saying that the cause of the incident rested with the father, for during his highly animated lectures in the classroom he had once said that the venerable Dragon King was not responsible for any rainfall, and for that matter, did not even exist. "Knowing how furious this would make the venerable Dragon King, you can imagine how he would find some way to vent his anger! So he grabbed hold of the son as a means of gaining retribution."

Someone else said that the students at the school were so incorrigible that one had even climbed up onto the old Dragon King's head and capped him with a straw hat. "What are the times coming to when a child who isn't even dry behind the ears would dare to invite such tremendous calamities down upon himself? How could the old Dragon King not seek retribution? Mark my word, it's not finished yet; don't you get the idea that the venerable Dragon King is some kind of moron! Do you think he'd just let you off once you've provoked his anger? It's not like dealing with a ricksha boy or a vegetable peddler whom you can kick at will, then let him be on his way. This is the venerable Dragon King we're talking about! Do you think that the venerable Dragon King is someone who can easily be pushed around?"

Then there was someone who said that the students at that school were truly undisciplined, and that with his own eyes he had once seen some of them in the main hall putting silkworms into the old Dragon King's hands. "Now just how do you think the old Dragon King could stand for something like that?"

Another person said that the schools were no good at all, and that anyone with children should on no account allow them to go to school, since they immediately lose respect for everyone and everything.

Someone remarked that he was going to the school to get his son and take him home—there would be no more school for him.

Someone else commented that the more the children study, the worse they become. "Take, for example, when their souls are frightened out of their bodies; the minute their mothers call for the souls to return, what do you think they say? They announce that this is nothing but superstition! Now what in the world do you think they'll be saying if they continue going to school?"

And so they talked, drifting further and further away from the original topic.

Before many days had passed, the big quagmire receded once again and pedestrians were soon passing along either side unimpeded. More days passed without any new rainfall, and the quagmire began to dry up, at which time carts and horses recommenced their crossings; then more overturned carts, more horses falling into it and thrashing around; again the ropes and levers appeared, again they were used to lift and drag the horses out. As the righted carts drove off, more followed: into the quagmire, and the lifting began anew.

How many carts and horses are extricated from this quagmire every year may never be known. But, you ask, does no one ever think of solving the problem by filling it in with dirt? No, not a single one.

An elderly member of the gentry once fell into the quagmire at high water. As soon as he crawled out he said: "This street is too narrow. When you have to pass by this water hazard there isn't even room to walk. Why don't the two families whose gardens are on either side take down their walls and open up some paths?"

As he was saying this, an old woman sitting in her garden on the other side of the wall chimed in with the comment that the walls could not be taken down, and that the best course of action would be to plant some trees; if a row of trees were planted alongside the wall, then when it rained the people could cross over by holding on to the trees.

Some advise taking down walls and some advise planting trees, but as for filling up the quagmire with dirt, there isn't a single person who advocates that.

Many pigs meet their end by drowning in this quagmire; dogs are suffocated in the mud, cats too; chickens and ducks often lose their lives there as well. This is because the quagmire is covered with a layer of husks; the animals are unaware that there is a trap lying below, and once they realize that fact it is already too late. Whether they come on foot or by air, the instant they alight on the husk-covered mire they cannot free themselves. If it happens in the day-time there is still a chance that someone passing by might save them, but once night falls they are doomed. They struggle all alone until they exhaust their strength, then begin to sink gradually into the mire. If, on the contrary, they continue to struggle, they might sink even faster. Some even die there without sinking below the surface, but that's the sort of thing that happens when the mud is gummier than usual.

What might happen then is that some cheap pork will suddenly appear in the marketplace, and everyone's thoughts turn to the quag-mire. "Has another pig drowned in that quagmire?" they ask.

Once the word is out, those who are fast on their feet lose no time in running to their neighbors with the news: "Hurry over and get some cheap pork. Hurry, hurry, before it's all gone."

After it is bought and brought home, a closer look reveals that there seems to be something wrong with it. Why is the meat all dark and discolored? Maybe this pork is infected. But on second thought, how could it really be infected? No, it must have been a pig that drowned in the quagmire. So then family after family sautés, fries, steams, boils, and then eats this cheap pork. But though they eat it, they feel always that it doesn't have a fragrant enough aroma, and they fear that it might have been infected after all. But then they think: "Infected pork would be unpalatable, so this must be from a pig that drowned in the quagmire!"

Actually, only one or two pigs drown each year in the quagmire, perhaps three, and some years not a single one. How the residents manage to eat the meat of a drowned pig so often is hard to imagine, and I'm afraid only the Dragon King knows the answer.

Though the people who eat the meat say it is from a pig drowned in the quagmire, there are still those who get sick from it, and those unfortunates are ready with their opinions: "Even if the pork was from a drowned pig, it still shouldn't have been sold in the market-place; meat from animals that have died isn't fresh, and the rev-enue office isn't doing its job if it allows meat like this to be sold on the street in broad daylight!"

Those who do not become ill are of a different opinion: "That's what you say, but you're letting your suspicions get the best of you. If you'd just eat it and not give it another thought, everything would be all right. Look at the rest of us; we ate it too, so how come we're not sick?"

Now and then a child lacking in common sense will tell people that his mother wouldn't allow him to eat the pork since it was in-fected. No one likes this kind of child. Everyone gives him hard looks and accuses him of speaking nonsense.

For example, a child says that the pork is definitely infected—this he tells a neighbor right in front of his mother. There is little reac-tion from the neighbor who hears him say this, but the mother's face immediately turns beet-red. She reaches out and smacks him.

But he is a stubborn child, and he keeps saying: "The pork is in-fected! The pork is infected!"

His mother, feeling terribly embarrassed, picks up a poker that is lying by the door and strikes him on the shoulder, sending him crying into the house. As he enters the room he sees his maternal grandmother sitting on the edge of the k'ang, so he runs into her arms. "Grannie," he sobs, "wasn't that pork you ate infected? Mama just hit me."

Now this maternal grandmother wants to comfort the poor abused child, but just then she looks up to see the wet nurse of the Li family who shares the compound standing in the doorway looking at her. So she lifts up the back of the child's shirttail and begins spanking him loudly on the behind. "Whoever saw a child as small as you speaking such utter nonsense!" she exclaims. She continues spanking him until the wet nurse walks away with the Li's child in her arms. The spanked child is by then screaming and crying uncontrollably, so hard that no one can make heads or tails of his shouts of "infected pork this" and "infected pork that."

In all, this quagmire brings two benefits to the residents of the area: The first is that the overturned carts and horses and the drowned chickens and ducks always produce a lot of excitement, which keeps the inhabitants buzzing for some time and gives them something to while away the hours.

The second is in relation to the matter of pork. Were there no quagmire, how could they have their infected pork? Naturally, they might still eat it, but how are they to explain it away? If they simply admit they are eating infected pork, it would be too unsanitary for words, but with the presence of the quagmire their problem is solved: infected pork becomes the meat of drowned pigs, which means that when they buy the meat, not only is it economical, but there are no sanitation problems either.

II

Besides the special attraction of the big quagmire, there is little else to be seen on Road Two East: one or two grainmills, a few bean-curd shops, a weaving mill or two, and perhaps one or two dyeing establishments. These are all operated by people who quietly do their own work there, bringing no enjoyment to the local inhabitants, and are thus unworthy of any discussion. When the sun sets these people go to bed, and when the sun rises they get up and begin their work. Throughout the year—warm spring with its blooming flowers, autumn with its rains, and winter with its snows—they simply follow the seasonal changes as they go from padded coats to unlined jackets. The cycle of birth, old age, sickness, and death governs their lives as they silently manage their affairs.

Take, for example, Widow Wang, who sells bean sprouts at the southern end of Road Two East. She erected a long pole above her house on top of which she hangs a battered old basket. The pole is so tall it is nearly on a level with the iron bell at the top of the Dragon King Temple. On windy days the *clang-clang* of the bell above the temple can be heard, and although Widow Wang's battered basket does not ring, it nonetheless makes its presence known by waving back and forth in the wind.

Year in and year out that is how it goes, and year in and year out Widow Wang sells her bean sprouts, passing her days tranquilly and uneventfully at an unhurried pace.

But one summer day her only son went down to the river to bathe, and he fell in and drowned. This incident caused a sensation and was the talk of the town for a while, but before many days had passed the talk died away. Not only Widow Wang's neighbors and others who lived nearby, but even her friends and relatives soon forgot all about it.

As for Widow Wang herself, even though this caused her to lose her mind, she still retained her ability to sell bean sprouts, and she continued as before to live an uneventful and quiet life. Occasionally someone would steal her bean sprouts, at which time she was overcome by a fit of wailing on the street or on the steps of the temple, though it soon passed, and she returned to her uneventful existence.

Whenever neighbors or other passersby witnessed the scene of her crying on the temple steps, their hearts were momentarily touched by a slight feeling of compassion, but only for a brief moment.

There are some people who are given to lumping together misfits of all kinds, such as the insane and the slow-witted, and treating them identically.

There are unfortunates in every district, in every county, and in every village: the tumorous, the blind, the insane, the slow-witted. There are many such people in our little town of Hulan River, but the local inhabitants have apparently heard and seen so much of them that their presence does not seem the least bit unusual. If, unhappily, they encounter one of them on the temple steps or inside a gateway alcove, they feel a momentary pang of compassion for that particular individual, but it is quickly supplanted by the rationalization that mankind has untold numbers of such people. They then turn their glances away and walk rapidly past the person. Once in a while someone stops there, but he is just one of those who, like children with short memories, would throw stones at the insane or willfully lead the blind into the water-filled ditch nearby.

The unfortunates are beggars, one and all. At least that's the way it is in the town of Hulan River. The people there treat the beggars in a most ordinary fashion. A pack of dogs are barking at something outside the door; the master of the house shouts out: "What are those animals barking at?"

"They're barking at a beggar," the servant answers.

Once said, the affair is ended. It is obvious that the life of a beggar is not worth a second thought.

The madwoman who sells bean sprouts cannot forget her grief even in her madness, and every few days she goes to wail at the steps of the temple; but once her crying has ended, she invariably returns home to eat, to sleep, and to sell her bean sprouts. As ever, she returns to her quiet existence.

III

A calamity also struck the dyer's shop: Two young apprentices were fighting over a woman on the street, when one of them pushed the other into the dyeing vat and drowned him. We need not concern ourselves here with the one who died, but as for the survivor, he was sent to jail with a life sentence.

Yet this affair too was disposed of silently and without a ripple. Two or three years later, whenever people mentioned the incident they discussed it as they would the famous confrontation between the heroic general Yüeh Fei and the evil prime minister Ch'in K'uai, as something that had occurred in the long distant past.

Meanwhile the dyer's shop remains at its original location, and even the big vat in which the young man drowned is quite possibly still in use to this day. The bolts of cloth that come from that dye shop still turn up in villages and towns far and near. The blue cloth is used to make padded cotton pants and jackets, which the men wear in the winter to ward off the severe cold, while the red cloth is used to make bright red gowns for the eighteen- and nineteen-year-old girls for their wedding days.

In short, though someone had drowned in the dyer's shop on such and such a day during such and such a month and year, the rest of the world goes on just as before without the slightest change.

Then there was the calamity that struck the bean-curd shop: During a fight between two of the employees the donkey that turned the mill suffered a broken leg. Since it was only a donkey, there wasn't much to be said on that score, but a woman lost her sight as a result of crying over the donkey (it turned out to be the mother of the one who had struck the donkey), so the episode could not simply be overlooked.

Then there was the paper mill in which a bastard child was starved to death. But since it was a newborn baby, the incident didn't amount to much, and nothing more need be said about it.

IV

Then, too, on Road Two East there are a few ornament shops, which are there to serve the dead.

After a person dies his soul goes down to the nether world, and the living, fearing that in that other world the dear departed will have no domicile to live in, no clothes to wear, and no horse to ride, have these things made of paper, then burn them for his benefit; the townspeople believe that all manner of things exist in the nether world.

On display are grand objects like money-spewing animals, treasure-gathering basins, and great gold and silver mountains; smaller things like slave girls, maidservants, cooks in the kitchen, and attendants who care for the pigs; and even smaller things like flower vases, tea services, chickens, ducks, geese, and dogs. There are even parrots on the window ledges.

These things are enormously pleasing to the eye. There is a court-yard surrounded by a garden wall, the top of which is covered with gold-colored glazed tiles. Just inside the courtyard is the principal house with five main rooms and three side rooms, all topped with green- and red-brick tiles; the windows are bright, the furniture spotless, and the air fresh and clean as can be. Flower pots are ar-ranged one after another on the flower racks; there are cassias, pure-white lilies, purslanes, September chrysanthemums, and all are in bloom. No one can tell what season it is—is it summer or is it autumn?—since inexplicably the flowers of the purslanes and the chrysanthemums are standing side by side; perhaps there is no di-vision into spring, summer, autumn, and winter in the nether world. But this need not concern us.

Then there is the cook in his kitchen, vivid and lifelike; he is a thousand times cleaner than a true-to-life cook. He has a white cap on his head and a white apron girding his body as he stands there preparing noodles. No sooner has lunchtime arrived than the noodles have been cooked, and lunch is about to be served.

In the courtyard a groom stands beside a big white horse, which is so large and so tall that it looks to be an Arabian; it stands erect and majestic, and if there were to be a rider seated upon it, there is every reason to believe it could outrun a train. I'm sure that not even the general here in the town of Hulan River has ever ridden such a steed.

Off to one side there is a carriage and a big mule. The mule is black and shiny, and its eyes, which have been made out of egg-shells, remain stationary. There is a particularly fetching little mule with eyeballs as large as the big mule's standing alongside it.

The carriage, with its silver-colored wheels, is decorated in es-pecially beautiful colors. The curtain across the front is rolled half-way up so that people can see the interior of the carriage, which is all red and sports a bright red cushion. The driver perched on the running board, his face beaming with proud smiles, is dressed in magnificent attire, with a purple sash girding his waist over a blue embroidered fancy gown, and black satin shoes with snow-white soles on his feet. (After putting on these shoes he probably drove the carriage over without taking a single step on the ground.) The cap he is wearing is red with a black brim. His head is raised as though he were disdainful of everything, and the more the people look at him, the less he resembles a carriage driver—he looks more like a bridegroom.

Two or three roosters and seven or eight hens are in the courtyard peacefully eating grain without making a sound, and even the ducks are not making those quacking noises that so annoy people. A dog is crouching next to the door of the master's quarters maintaining a motionless vigil.

All of the bystanders looking on comment favorably, every one of them voicing his praise. The poor look at it and experience a feel-ing that it must be better to be dead than alive.

The main room is furnished with window curtains, four-poster bed frames, tables, chairs, and benches. Everything is complete to the last detail.

There is also a steward of the house who is figuring accounts on his abacus; beside him is an open ledger in which is written:

"Twenty-two catties of wine owed by the northern distillery.

"Wang Family of East Village yesterday borrowed 2,000 catties of rice.

"Ni Jen-tzu of White Flag Hamlet yesterday sent land rent of 4,300 coppers."

Below these lines is written the date: "April twenty-eighth."

This page constitutes the running accounts for the twenty-seventh of April; the accounts for the twenty-eighth have evidently not yet been entered. A look at this ledger shows that there is no haphazard accounting of debts in the nether world, and that there is a special type of individual whose job it is to manage these accounts. It also goes without saying that the master of this grand house is a landlord.

Everything in the compound is complete to the last detail and is very fine. The only thing missing is the master of the compound, a discovery which seems puzzling: could there be no master of such a fine compound? This is certainly bewildering.

When they have looked more closely the people sense that there is something unusual about the compound: how is it that the slave girls and maidservants, the carriage drivers and the groom all have a piece of white paper across their chests on which their names are written? The name of the carriage driver whose good looks give him the appearance of a bridegroom is:

"Long Whip."

The groom's name is:

"Fleet of Foot."

The name of the slave girl who is holding a water pipe in her left hand and an embroidered napkin in her right is:

"Virtuous Obedience."

The other's name is:

"Fortuitous Peace."

The man who is figuring accounts is named:

"Wizard of Reckoning."

The name of the maid who is spraying the flowers with water is:

"Flower Sister."

A closer look reveals that even the big white horse has a name; the name tag on his rump shows that he is called:

"Thousand-Li Steed."

As for the others—the mules, the dogs, the chickens, and the ducks—they are nameless.

The cook who is making noodles in the kitchen is called "Old

Wang," and the strip of paper on which his name is written flaps to and fro with each gust of wind.

This is all rather strange: the master of the compound doesn't even recognize his own servants and has to hang name tags around their necks! This point cannot but confuse and bewilder people; maybe this world of ours is better than the nether world after all!

But though that is the opinion of some, there are still many others who are envious of this grand house, which is so indisputably fine, elegant, peaceful and quiet (complete silence reigns), neat and tidy, with no trace of disorder. The slave girls and maidservants are fashioned exactly like those in this world; the chickens, dogs, pigs, and horses, too, are just like those in this world. Everything in this world can also be found in the nether world: people eat noodles in this world, and in the nether world they eat them too; people have carriages to ride in this world, and in the nether world they also ride them; the nether world is just like this world—the two are exactly alike.

That is, of course, except for the big quagmire on Road Two East. Everything desirable is there; undesirable things are simply not necessary.

V

These are the objects that the ornament shops on Road Two East produce. The displayed handiwork is both dignified-looking and eye-catching, but the inside of the shop is a mass of confusion. Shredded paper is everywhere; there are rods and sticks all in a heap; crushed boxes and a welter of cans, paint jars, paste dishes, thin string, and heavy cord abound. A person could easily trip just walking through the shop, with its constant activity of chopping and tying as flies dart back and forth in the air.

When making paper human figures, the first to be fashioned is the head; once it has been pasted together it is hung on a wall along with other heads—men's and women's—until it is taken down to be used. All that is needed then is to put it atop a torso made of rods and sticks on which some clothes have been added, and you have the figure of a human being. By cutting out white paper hair and pasting it all over a sticklike papier-mâché horse, you have a handsome steed.

The people who make their living this way are all extremely coarse and ugly men. They may know how to fashion a groom or a carriage driver, and how to make up women and young girls, but they pay not the slightest attention to their own appearance. Long scraggly hair, short bristly hair, twisted mouths, crooked eyes, bare feet and legs; it is hard to believe that such splendid and dazzlingly beautiful lifelike human figures could have been created by those hands.

Their daily fare is coarse vegetables and coarse rice, they are dressed in tattered clothes, and they make their beds among piles of carriages, horses, human figures, and heads. Their lives seemingly are bitter ones, though they actually just muddle their way through, day by day, the year round, exchanging their unlined jackets for padded coats with each seasonal change.

Birth, old age, sickness, death—each is met with a stoic absence of expression. They are born and grow in accordance with nature's dictates. If they are meant not to grow old, then so be it.

Old age—getting old has no effect on them at all: when their eyesight fails they stop looking at things, when their hearing fades they stop listening, when their teeth fall out they swallow things whole, and when they can no longer move about they lie flat on their backs. What else can they do? Anyone who grows old deserves exactly what he gets!

Sickness—among people whose diet consists of a random assortment of grains, who is there who does not fall prey to illness?

Death—this, on the other hand, is a sad and mournful affair. When a father dies, his sons weep; when a son dies, his mother weeps; when a brother dies, the whole family weeps; and when a son's wife dies, her family comes to weep.

After crying for one, or perhaps even three days, they must then go to the outskirts of town, dig a hole, and bury the person. After the burial the surviving family members still have to make their way back home and carry on their daily routine. When it's time to eat, they eat; when it's time to sleep, they sleep. Outsiders are unable to tell that this family is now bereft of a father or has just lost an elder brother. The members of that particular family even fail to lock themselves in their home each day and wail. The only expression of the grief they feel in their hearts is joining the stream of people who go to visit the graves on the various festivals each year as prescribed by local custom. During the Ch'ing-ming Festival—the time for visiting ancestral graves—each family prepares incense and candles and sets out for the family grave site. At the heads of some of the graves the earth has settled and formed a small pit, while others have several small holes in them. The people cast glances at one another, are moved to sighing, then light the incense and pour the wine. If the survivor is a close relative, such as a son, a daughter, or a parent, then they will let forth a fit of wailing, the broken rhythm of which makes it sound as though they were reading a written composition or chanting a long poem. When their incantation is finished they rise to their feet, brush the dirt from their behinds, and join the procession of returning people as they leave the grave sites and re-enter the town.

When they return to their homes in the town they must carry on life as before; all year round there is firewood, rice, oil, and salt to worry about, and there is clothing to starch and mend. From morning till evening they are busy without respite. Nighttime finds them exhausted, and they are asleep as soon as they lie down on the *k'ang*. They dream neither of mournful nor of happy events as they sleep, but merely grind their teeth and snore, passing the night like every other night.

If someone were to ask them what man lives for, they would not be confounded by the question, but would state unhesitatingly, directly, and unequivocally: "Man lives to eat food and wear clothes."

If they were then asked about death, they would say: "When a man dies that's the end of it."

Consequently, no one has ever seen one of those ornament crafts-men fashion an underworld home for himself during his lifetime; more than likely he doesn't much believe in the nether world. And even if there were such a place, he would probably open an ornament shop when he got there; worse luck, he'd doubtless have to rent a place to open the shop.

VI

In the town of Hulan River, besides Road Two East, Road Two West, and The Crossroads, there remain only a number of small lanes. There is even less worth noting on these small byways; one finds precious few of the little stalls where flatcakes and dough twists are made and sold, and even the tiny stands that sell red and green candy balls are mainly located where the lanes give out onto the road—few find their way into the lanes themselves. The people who live on these small lanes seldom see a casual stroller. They hear and see less than other people, and as a result they pass their lonely days behind closed doors. They live in broken-down huts, buy two pecks of beans, which they salt and cook to go with their rice, and there goes another year. The people who live on these small lanes are isolated and lonely.

A peddler carrying a basket of flatcakes hawking his product at the eastern end of the lane can be heard at the western end. Although the people inside the houses don't care to buy, whenever he stops at their gates they poke their heads out to take a look, and may on occasion even ask a price or ask whether or not the glazed or fried dough twists still sell for the same price as before.

Every once in a while someone will walk over and lift up the piece of cloth that covers the basket, as though she were a potential custo-mer, then pick one out and feel to see if it's still hot. After she has felt it she puts it right back, and the peddler is not the least bit angry. He simply picks up his basket and carries it to the next house.

The lady of this second house has nothing in particular to do, so she too opens up the basket and feels around for a while. But she also touches them without buying any.

When the peddler reaches the third house, a potential customer is there waiting for him. Out from the house comes a woman in her thirties who has just gotten up from a nap. Her hair is done up in a bun on top of her head, and probably because it isn't particularly neat, she has covered it with a black hairnet and fastened it on with several hairpins. But having just slept on it, not only is her hair all disheveled, even the hairpins have worked their way out, so that the bun atop her head looks as though it has been shot full of darts.

She walks out of her house in high spirits, throwing the door open and virtually bursting through the doorway. Five children follow in her wake, each one of them in high spirits; as they emerge they look every bit like a platoon marching in a column.

The first one, a girl of twelve or thirteen, reaches in and picks out one of the dough twists. It is about the length of a bamboo chopstick, and sells for fifty coppers. Having the quickest eye among them, she has selected not only the biggest one in the basket, but the only one in that size category.

The second child, a boy, chooses one that sells for twenty coppers.

The third child also chooses one that sells for twenty coppers; he, too, is a boy.

After looking them all over, the fourth child has no alternative but to choose one that sells for twenty coppers; and he, too, is a boy.

Then it is the fifth child's turn. There is no way of telling if this one is a boy or a girl—no hair on the head, an earring hanging from one ear, skinny as a dry willow branch, but with a large, protruding belly, it looks to be about five years old. The child sticks out its hands, which are far blacker than any of the other four children's— the hands of the other four are filthy black, all right, but at least they still look like human hands and not some other strange objects. Only this child's hands are indistinguishable. Shall we call them hands?

Or what shall we call them? I guess we can call them anything we like. They are a mottled mixture of blacks and grays, darks and lights, so that looking at them, like viewing layers of floating clouds, can be a most interesting pastime.

The child sticks its hands into the basket to choose one of the fried dough twists, nearly each of which is touched and felt in the process, until the entire basket is soon a jumble. Although the basket is fairly large, not many dough twists had been put inside it to begin with: besides the single big one, there were only ten or so of the smaller ones. After this child has turned them all over, the ones that remain are strewn throughout the basket, while the child's black hands are now covered with oil as well as being filthy, and virtually glisten like shiny ebony.

Finally the child cries out: "I want a big one."

A fight then erupts by the front door.

The child is a fast runner, and takes out after its elder sister. Its two elder brothers also take off running, both of them easily outdistancing this smallest child. The elder sister, holding the largest dough twist in her hand, is unimaginably faster on her feet than the small child, and in an instant she has already found a spot where there is a break in the wall and has jumped through; the others follow her and disappear on the other side. By the time all the others have followed her past the wall, she has already jumped back across and is running around the courtyard like a whirlwind.

The smallest child—the one of indeterminate sex—cannot catch up with the others and has long since fallen behind, screaming and crying. Now and then, while the elder sister is being held fast by her two brothers, the child runs over and tries to snatch the dough twist out of her hand, but after several misses falls behind again, screaming and crying.

As for their mother, though she looks imposing, actually she cannot control the children without using her hands, and so seeing how things are going, with no end in sight, she enters the house, picks up a steel poker, and chases after her children. But unhappily for her, there is a small mud puddle in her yard where the pigs wallow, and she falls smack into the middle of it, the poker flying from her hand and sailing some five feet or so away.

With that this little drama has reached its climax and every person watching the commotion is in stitches, delighted with the whole affair. Even the peddler is completely engrossed in what is going on, and when the woman plops down into the mud puddle and splashes muck all over, he nearly lets his basket fall to the ground. He is so tickled he has forgotten all about the basket in his hands.

The children, naturally, have long since disappeared from sight. By the time the mother gets them all rounded up she has regained her imposing parental airs. She has each of them kneel on the ground facing the sun so that they form a line, then has them surrender up their dough twists.

Little remains of the eldest child's dough twist—it was broken up in all the commotion.

The third child has eaten all of his.

The second one has a tiny bit left.

Only the fourth one still has his clenched in his hand.

As for the fifth child, well, it never had one to begin with.

The whole chaotic episode ends with a shouting match between the peddler and the woman, after which he picks up his basket and walks over to the next house to try to make another sale. The argument between the two of them is over the woman's wanting to return the dough twist that the fourth child had been holding onto all that time. The peddler flatly refuses to take it back, and the woman is just as determined to return it to him. The end result is that she pays for three dough twists and drives the peddler with his basket out of her yard.

Nothing more need be said about the five children who were forced to kneel on the ground because of those dough twists, and as for the remainder of the dough twists that had been taken into the lane to be handled and felt by nearly everyone, they are then carried over into the next lane and eventually sold.

A toothless old woman buys one of them and carries it back wrapped in a piece of paper, saying: "This dough twist is certainly clean, all nice and oily." Then she calls out to her grandchild to hurry on over.

The peddler, seeing how pleased the old lady is, says to her: "It's just come from the pan, still nice and warm!"

VII

In the afternoon, after the dough-twist peddler has passed by, a seller of rice pudding may come by, and like the other peddlers, his shouts from one end of the lane can be heard at the other end. People who want to buy his product bring along a small ceramic bowl, while others who are not interested in buying just sit inside their homes; as soon as they hear his shouts they know it is time to begin cooking dinner, since throughout the summer this peddler comes when the sun is setting in the west. He comes at the same time every day, like clockwork, between the hours of four and five. One would think that his sole occupation is bringing rice pudding to sell in this particular lane, and that he is not about to jeopardize his punctual appearance there in order to sell to one or two additional homes in another lane. By the time the rice-pudding peddler has gone, the sky is nearly dark.

Once the sun begins to set in the west the peddler of odds and ends, who announces his presence with a wooden rattle, no longer enters the lanes to peddle his wares. In fact, he does no more business on the quieter roadways either, but merely shoulders his load and makes his way home along the main streets.

Th pottery seller has by then closed shop for the day.

The scavengers and rag collectors also head for home.

The only one to come out at this time is the bean-curd peddler.

At dinnertime some scallions and bean paste make for a tasty meal, but a piece of bean curd to go along with it adds a pleasant finishing touch, requiring at least two additional bowlfuls of corn-and-bean gruel. The people eat a lot at each sitting, and that is only natural; add a little hot-pepper oil and a touch of bean sauce to the bean curd and the meal is greatly enhanced. Just a little piece of bean curd on the end of the chopsticks can last a half bowlful of gruel, and soon after the chopsticks have broken off another chunk of bean curd, a full bowlful of gruel has disappeared. Two extra bowlfuls are consumed because of the addition of the bean curd, but that doesn't mean the person has overeaten; someone who has never tasted bean curd cannot know what a delightful flavor it has.

It is for this reason that the arrival of the bean-curd peddler is so warmly welcomed by everyone—men, women, young, and old alike. When they open their doors, there are smiles everywhere, and though nothing is said, a sort of mutual affinity quietly develops between buyer and seller. It is as though the bean-curd peddler were saying: "I have some fine bean curd here."

And it is as though the customer were answering: "Your bean curd doesn't seem half bad."

Those who cannot afford to buy the bean curd are particularly envious of the bean-curd peddler. The moment they hear the sound of his shouts down the lane drawing near they are sorely tempted; wouldn't it be nice to be able to have a piece of bean curd with a little green pepper and some scallions!

But though they think the same thought day in and day out, they never quite manage to buy a piece, and each time the bean-curd peddler comes, all his presence does for these people is confront them with an unrealizable temptation. These people, for whom temptation calls, just cannot make the decision to buy, so they merely eat a few extra mouthfuls of hot peppers, after which their foreheads are bathed in perspiration. Wouldn't it be wonderful, they dream, if a person could just open his own bean-curd shop? Then he could eat bean curd anytime he felt like it!

And sure enough, when one of their sons gets to be about five years of age, if he is asked: "What do you want to do when you grow up?"

He will answer: "I want to open a bean-curd shop." It is obvious that he has hopes of realizing his father's unfulfilled ambition.

The fondness these people have for this marvelous dish called bean curd sometimes goes even beyond this; there are those who would even lead their families into bankruptcy over it. There is a story about the head of a household who came to just such a decision, saying: "I'm going for broke; I'll buy myself a piece of bean curd!" In the classical language, the words "going for broke" would be the equivalent of giving up one's all for charity, but in modern speech most people would just say: "I'm wiped out!"

VIII

Once the bean-curd peddler packs up and heads for home, the affairs of another day have come to an end.

Every family sits down to its evening meal, then after they have finished, some stay up to watch the sunset, while the others simply lie down on their *k'angs* and go to sleep.

The sunsets in this place are beautiful to behold. There is a local expression here, "fire clouds"; if you say "sunset," no one will understand you, but if you say "fire clouds," even a three-year-old child will point up to the western sky with a shout of delight.

Right after the evening meal the "fire clouds" come. The children's faces all reflect a red glow, while the big white dog turns red, red roosters become golden ones, and black hens become a dark purple. An old man feeding his pigs leans against the base of a wall and chuckles as he sees his two white pigs turn into little golden ones. He is about to say: "I'll be damned, even you have changed," when a man out for a refreshing evening stroll walks by him and comments: "Old man, you are sure to live to a ripe old age, with your golden beard!"

The clouds burn their way in the sky from the west to the east, a glowing red, as though the sky had caught fire.

The variations of the "fire clouds" here are many: one moment they are a glowing red, a moment later they become a clear gold, then half purple-half yellow, and then a blend of gray and white. Grape gray, pear yellow, eggplant purple—all of these colors appear in the sky. Every imaginable color is there, some that words cannot describe and others that you would swear you have never seen before.

Within the space of five seconds a horse is formed in the sky with its head facing south and its tail pointing west; the horse is kneeling, looking as though it is waiting for someone to climb up onto its back before it will stand up. Nothing much changes within the next second, but two or three seconds later the horse has gotten bigger, its legs have spread out, and its neck has elongated . . . but there is no longer any tail to be seen. And then, just when the people watching from below are trying to locate the tail, the horse disappears from sight.

Suddenly a big dog appears, a ferocious animal that is running ahead of what looks like several little puppies. They run and they run, and before long the puppies have run from sight; then the big dog disappears.

A great lion is then formed, looking exactly like one of the stone lions in front of the Temple of the Immortal Matron. It is about the same size, and it, too, is crouching, looking very powerful and dominant as it calmly crouches there. It appears contemptuous of all around it, not deigning to look at anything. The people search the sky, and before they know it something else has caught their eye. Now they are in a predicament—since they cannot be looking at something to the east and something to the west at the same time— and so they watch the lion come to ruin. A shift of the eyes, a lowering of the head, and the objects in the sky undergo a transformation. But now as you search for yet something else, you could look until you go blind before finding a single thing. The great lion can no longer be seen, nor is there anything else to be found—not even, for example, a monkey, which is certainly no match for the glimpse of a great lion.

For a brief moment the sky gives the illusion of forming this object or that, but in fact there are no distinguishable shapes; there is nothing anymore. It is then that the people lower their heads and rub their eyes, or perhaps just rest them for a moment before taking another look. But the "fire clouds" in the sky do not often wait around to satisfy the children below who are so fond of them, and in this short space of time they are gone.

The drowsy children return home to their rooms and go to sleep. Some are so tired they cannot make it to their beds, but fall asleep lying across their elder sister's legs or in the arms of their grandmother. The grandmother has a horsehair fly swatter, which she flicks in the air to keep the bugs and mosquitoes away. She does not know that her grandchild has fallen asleep, but thinks he is still awake.

"You get down and play; Grandma's legs are falling asleep." She gives the child a push, but he is fast asleep.

By this time the "fire clouds" have disappeared without a trace. All the people in every family get up and go to their rooms to sleep for the night after closing the windows and doors.

Even in July it is not particularly hot in Hulan River, and at night the people cover themselves with thin quilts as they sleep.

As night falls and crows fly by, the voices of the few children who are not yet asleep can be heard through the windows as they call out:

> Raven, raven, working the grain-threshing floor;
> Two pecks for you, not a tiny bit more.

. . . .

The flocks of crows that cover the sky with their shouts of *caw-caw* fly over this town from one end to the other. It is said that after they have flown over the southern bank of the Hulan River they roost in a big wooded area. The following morning they are up in the air flying again.

As summer leads into autumn the crows fly by every evening, but just where these large flocks of birds fly to, the children don't really know, and the adults have little to say to them on the subject. All the children know about them is embodied in their little ditty:

> Raven, raven, working the grain-threshing floor;
> Two pecks for you, not a tiny bit more.

Just why they want to give the crows two pecks of grain doesn't seem to make much sense.

IX

After the crows have flown over, the day has truly come to an end.

The evening star climbs in the sky, shining brightly there like a little brass nugget.

The Milky Way and the moon also make their appearance.

Bats fly into the night.

All things that come out with the sun have now turned in for the night. The people are all asleep, as are the pigs, horses, cows, and sheep; the swallows and butterflies have gone to roost. Not a single blossom on the morning glories at the bases of the houses remains open—there are the closed buds of new blossoms, and the curled up petals of the old. The closed buds are preparing to greet the morning sun of the following day, while the curled petals that have already greeted yesterday's sun are about to fall.

Most stars follow the moon's ascent in the sky, while the evening star is like her advance foot soldier, preceding her by a few steps.

As night falls the croaking of frogs begins to emerge from rivers, streams, and marshes. The sounds of chirping insects come from foliage in the courtyards, from the large fields outside the city, from potted flowers, and from the graveyard.

This is what the summer nights are like when there is no rain or wind, night after night.

Summer passes very quickly, and autumn has arrived. There are few changes as summer leads into autumn, except that the nights turn cooler and everyone must sleep under a quilt at night. Farmers are busy during the day with the harvest, and at night their more frequent dreams are of gathering in the sorghum.

During the month of September the women are kept busy starching clothes, and removing the covers and fluffing the matted cotton of their quilts. From morning till night every street and lane resounds with the hollow twang of their mallets on the fluffing bows. When their fluffing work is finished, the quilts are re-covered, just in time for the arrival of winter.

Winter brings the snows.

Throughout the seasons the people must put up with wind, frost, rain, and snow; they are beset by the frost and soaked by the rain. When the big winds come they fill the air with swirling sand and pebbles, almost arrogantly. In winter the ground freezes and cracks, rivers are frozen over, and as the weather turns even colder the ice on the river splits with resounding cracks. The winter cold freezes off people's ears, splits open their noses, chaps their hands and feet. But this is just nature's way of putting on airs of importance, and the common folk can't do a thing about it.

This is how the people of Hulan River are: when winter comes they put on their padded clothes, and when summer arrives they change into their unlined jackets, as mechanically as getting up when the sun rises and going to bed when it sets.

Their fingers, which are chapped and cracked in the winter, heal naturally by the time summer arrives. For those that don't heal by themselves, there is always the Li Yung-ch'un Pharmacy, where the people can buy two ounces of saffron, steep it, and rub the solution on their hands. Sometimes they rub it on until their fingers turn blood red without any sign of healing, or the swelling may even get progressively worse. In such cases they go back to the Li Yung-ch'un Pharmacy, though this time rather than purchasing saffron, they buy a plaster instead. They take it home, heat it over a fire until it becomes gummy, then stick it on the frostbite sore. This plaster is really wonderful, since it doesn't cause the least bit of inconvenience when it is stuck on. Carters can still drive their carts, housewives can still prepare food.

It is really terrific that this plaster is sticky and gummy; it will not wash off in water, thereby allowing women to wash clothes with it on if they have to. And even if it does rub off, they can always heat it once more over a fire and stick it back on. Once applied it stays on for half a month.

The people of Hulan River value things in terms of strength and durability, so that something as durable as this plaster is perfectly suited to their nature. Even if it is applied for two weeks and the hand remains unhealed, the plaster is, after all, durable, and the money paid for it has not been spent in vain.

They go back and buy another, and another, and yet another, but the swelling on the hand grows worse and worse. For people who cannot afford the plasters, they can pick up the ones others have used and discarded and stick them on their own sores. Since the final outcome is always unpredictable, why not just muddle through the best one can!

Spring, summer, autumn, winter—the seasonal cycle continues inexorably, and always has since the beginning of time. Wind, frost, rain, snow; those who can bear up under these forces manage to get by; those who cannot must seek a natural solution. This natural solution is not so very good, for these people are quietly and wordlessly taken from this life and this world.

Those who have not yet been taken away are left at the mercy of the wind, the frost, the rain, and the snow . . . as always.

2   FESTIVALS AND SUCH   I

In Hulan River, besides these inconsequential and common realities of daily life, there are several special events that are not immediately related to the villagers' hand-to-mouth existence, such as:

The dance of the sorceress;
The harvest dances;

Releasing river lanterns;
Outdoor opera performances; and
The festival at the Temple of the Immortal Matron on the eighteenth day of the fourth lunar month.

We'll begin with the sorceress. The sorceress can cure diseases, and she dresses herself in peculiar clothing of a type that ordinary people do not wear. She is all in red—a red skirt—and the moment she puts this skirt around her waist she undergoes a transformation. Rather than starting by beating her drum, she wraps her embroidered red skirt around her and begins to tremble. Every part of her body, from her head down to her toes, trembles at once, then begins to quake violently. With her eyes closed, she mumbles constantly. Whenever her body begins to quake, she looks as though she is about to collapse to the ground, which throws a scare into the people watching her; but somehow she always manages to sit down properly.

The sorceress seats herself on a stool directly opposite a spirit tablet on which black letters are written on a piece of red paper. The older the spirit tablet, the better, for it gives evidence of the many occasions she has had during the course of a year to perform her dance, and the more dances she performs, the further her reputation will spread, causing her business to prosper. Lighted incense is placed in front of the spirit tablet, from which smoke curls slowly upward.

Usually the spirit enters the sorceress' body when the incense has burned halfway down. As soon as she is possessed by the spirit her imposing airs undergo a change. It is as though she were in command of a huge army of soldiers and horses; invigorated, she rises to her feet and begins to cavort and jump around.

An assistant—a man—stands off to the sorceress' side. Unlike the woman, he presents a picture of orderliness, and is as organized and composed as the next man. He hurriedly places a round drum in the sorceress' hand, which she holds as she cavorts and begins to narrate the story of the descent from the mountain of the spirit that has possessed her: how it has ridden on the clouds, flown with the winds, and been carried by the mist on its journey. It is a most impressive story. Whatever the sorceress asks the assistant standing alongside her, he answers. Appropriate answers will flow from the mouth of a good assistant, while the occasional careless response from a less competent one will throw the sorceress into a fit. She is then driven to beating on her drum and letting loose a volley of epithets. She will curse the afflicted person, saying that he will die before the night is out; that his ghost will not depart, but will wander endlessly; and that his immediate family, relatives, and neighbors will all be visited by fiery calamities. Members of the terror-stricken family that has requested the services of the sorceress frantically light incense and offer libations. But if these offerings fail to placate her, they must hurriedly make a presentation of red cloth, which they drape over the spirit tablet. If this too fails, they must then sacrifice a chicken. Once the tumult has reached the stage of sacrificing a chicken, it seldom goes any further, for there would be nothing more to be gained from continuing along this course.

The chicken and the cloth become the sorceress' property; after she has finished her dance she takes the chicken home to cook and eat; the red cloth she dyes a dark blue and makes into a pair of pants for her own use.

But no matter what some sorceresses do, the spirits fail to make an appearance. The family that has requested her services must then quickly sacrifice a chicken, for if they are even a little slow in doing so, the sorceress will come to a halt in middance and begin haranguing them. Now since the sorceress has been invited to cure an illness, it is an unlucky omen if she begins to shout curses. As a result, she is both greatly respected and greatly feared.

The dance of the sorceress normally commences at dusk. At the sound of her drum, men, women, and children dash over to the house where she is engaged; on summer evenings crowds of people fill the rooms and the yard outside. Excited, shouting women drag or carry their children along as they clamber over walls to watch the dance of the sorceress, which continues late into the night until at last the spirit is sent back up the mountain. That moment is signaled by fiercely resounding drumbeats and the sorceress' enthralling chants, sounds which reach all the neighboring homes and produce in everyone within earshot a sense of desolation. The assistant begins to chant: "Return to your mountain, Great Fairy; proceed with care and deliberation."

The sorceress responds: "Assistant Fairy of mine . . . Green Dragon Mountain, White Tiger Peak . . . three thousand *li* in a single night is an easy task when riding on the winds."

The lyrics and melody of her incantation merge with the beat of the drum and carry a great distance; it is an eerie and depressing sound, which adds to the desolation of those who hear it. Often there are people who cannot sleep at night after hearing these pulsating sounds.

The sorceress has been requested by a family to drive away an illness, but has the patient been cured or not? This only produces anguished sighs throughout the neighborhood, and there are often those who lie awake all night troubled by this thought.

A star-filled sky, moonlight flooding the rooms; what is human existence and why must it be so desolate?

Ten days or two weeks later the thudding drumbeat of the sorceress' dance is heard again, and once more the people are aroused. They come over the walls and through the gate to take a look at the sorceress who has been summoned: What are her special talents? What is she wearing? Listen to hear what chants she is singing; look to see how beautiful her clothing is.

She dances into the still of the night, then the spirit is sent back up the mountain, escorted by a tantalizing cadence on the drum.

The feelings of desolation are particularly strong on rainy nights: widows are moved to tears, widowers wander aimlessly about. The beat of the drum seems designed to torment the unfortunates. Alternating between a rapid and a languid cadence, it calls forth the image of a lost traveler who is giving voice to his confusion, or of an unfortunate old man recalling the happier days of his all-too-short childhood. It is also reminiscent of a loving mother sending her son off on a long journey, or of someone at the point of death who is unwilling to part with this world.

What is human existence all about? Why must there be nights of such desolation?

Seemingly, the next time the sound of drums is heard no one would be willing to even listen, but such is not the case: at the first beat of the drum, people again clamber over the walls, straining their ears to the sound with more enthusiasm than foreigners from the West going to a concert.

II

On the fifteenth day of the seventh month—during the Festival of the Hungry Ghosts—river lanterns are set adrift on the Hulan River. There are river lanterns shaped like cabbages, watermelons, and also lotuses.

Buddhist monks and Taoist priests, dressed in bright red satin robes with gold designs, play their reed organs, flutes, and panpipes along the riverbank, calling the people together to an open-air ritual. The music from their instruments can be heard at a distance of two *li* from the river. At dusk, before the sky has completely darkened, a continuous stream of people rushes to watch the river lanterns. Even people who never leave their homes at any other time fill the streets and lanes as they join the procession to the riverbank. The first arrivals squat at the edge of the river, until both banks are crowded with people resting on their haunches, while an unbroken line of people continues to emerge. Even the blind and the crippled come to see the river lanterns (no, I am wrong; the blind, of course, do not come to *see* the river lanterns), and a cloud of dust is raised over the roadway by the running people. There is no need to ask the maidens and the young married women who emerge from their gates in groups of twos and threes where they are headed. For they are all going to see the river lanterns.

By dusk during the seventh lunar month the "fire clouds" have just disappeared and a pale glow illuminates the streets; the noise of activity disturbs the silence of the preceding days, as each roadway comes alive. It is as though a huge fire had broken out in the town and everyone was rushing to put it out. There is a sense of great urgency among the people surging forward on flying feet. The first to arrive at the river's edge squat down, and those who follow wedge themselves in and squat down on their haunches beside the others. Everyone waits; they are waiting for the moon to climb into the sky, at which time the river lanterns will be set adrift on the water.

The fifteenth day of the seventh lunar month, which is a festival devoted to spirits, is for the ghosts of the wronged who are denied transmigration and cannot extricate themselves from their bitter existence in the nether world; they are unable to find the road that will release them. On this night each of them able to rest a river lantern on the palm of the hand can gain release—apparently the road leading from the nether world to this world is so dark that it cannot be seen without the aid of a lantern. Therefore the releasing of river lanterns is a charitable act. It is to show that the living—shall we call them the gentlefolk?—have not forgotten the ghosts of those who have been wronged.

But the day is not without its contradictions, for a child born on the fifteenth day of the seventh lunar month is held in low esteem, since it is thought that his soul is a wild ghost that has come to him on a lotus lantern. These children will grow up without the love of their parents. Now when boys and girls reach marrying age, their families must exchange and compare the children's horoscopes to determine their suitability before the nuptials can take place. If it is a girl who was born on the fifteenth day of the seventh lunar month, it will be difficult to arrange a marriage for her, and she must deceive the boy's family by altering her birth date. If it is a boy who was born on this day, the outlook is not much better, but if his family is a wealthy one, this shortcoming can be overlooked and he is still considered marriageable. Possessed though he may be by an evil spirit, the fact that he is wealthy proves that it cannot be all that evil. But if it is the girl in this position, the situation is hopeless. That is, unless she is the only child of a wealthy widow; that is another matter altogether, for marrying one of those girls means that her wealth hangs in the balance. Even if she does not bring her entire fortune with her in the marriage, the dowry alone will be of considerable size, and the fact that she is the reincarnation of an evil spirit will lose its importance. The people have a saying that "Money can make even a ghost put his shoulder to the grindstone!" It would seem that they don't really believe in ghosts and feel that the reports of their existence are not altogether true.

And yet the monks beat their drums resoundingly as the river lanterns are released, urgently reciting their charmlike sutras in celebration of the ghosts' transmigration. They therefore give witness to the belief of the critical nature of this fleeting moment; it is an opportunity that cannot be missed, one in which each ghost—male or female—must quickly raise a river lantern on the palm of its hand in order to achieve reincarnation. After they have finished reciting the sutras the monks begin to play their reed organs, flutes, and panpipes again, producing beautiful sounds that are heard far and wide.

It is at this time that the river lanterns begin floating downstream in bunches. They drift slowly, calmly, and steadily, and there are no visible signs that there are ghosts in the river waiting to snatch them away. As the lanterns drift downstream they give off golden flashes of light that combine with the masses of spectators to give a sense of real activity. There are more river lanterns than can be counted, perhaps hundreds or even thousands. The children on the riverbank clap their hands, stomp their feet, and shout continuously in appreciative delight. The adults, on the other hand, are so completely absorbed in the sight that they utter not a sound and act as though they are mesmerized by the light of the lanterns glistening on the river. The water glimmers under the rays of the lanterns, and moonlight dances on the surface. When in the history of man has there ever been such a magnificent spectacle!

The clamor continues until the moon is directly overhead and the evening star and its followers fill the sky, at which time the grand spectacle gradually begins to abate.

The river lanterns have begun their voyage several *li* upstream, and after a long, long while start passing in front of the people. They continue to drift for a long, long while before they have all passed by. During this process some are extinguished in the middle of their voyage, others are dashed against the riverbank where they are snagged in the wild grass growing there. Then, too, when the river lanterns get to the lower reaches children use poles to snatch them out of the water, and fishermen lift out a couple that drift near their boats, so that as time goes by the number of lanterns diminishes.

As they approach the lower reaches they have thinned out to the point that they present a desolate and lonely sight. They drift to the farthest part of the river, which appears pitch black, and one after another they disappear.

As the river lanterns pass by, though many fall behind and many others sink below the surface, nonetheless one still does not have the feeling that they are disappearing on the palms of ghosts. As the river lanterns begin their voyage far upstream the people's hearts are light and gay, and they experience little emotion as the lanterns pass in front of them; it is only at the end, when they have drifted to the farthest point of the lower reaches, that an involuntary emptiness grips the hearts of the river-lantern watchers.

"Where do those river lanterns float to, after all?"

When things have reached this point most people pick themselves up and leave the riverbank to return to their homes. By then not only have the waters grown desolate, but the riverbank, too, is deserted and quiet. If you should then gaze far downstream, with each successive glance still another river lantern is extinguished, or perhaps two die out simultaneously, and at this time it truly looks as though they are being carried away on the palms of ghosts.

By the third watch the banks are completely deserted and the river is totally devoid of lanterns. The river waters are as calm as ever, though gusts of wind now and then raise slight ripples on the surface. The moon's rays do not strike the river as they do the ocean, where splinters of gold flash about on the surface; here the reflection of the moon sinks to the bottom of the river, making it seem as though a fisherman could simply reach out and lift it into his boat.

The southern bank of the river is lined with willow groves; the northern bank of the river is where the town of Hulan River is located. The people who have returned home after watching the river lanterns are probably all fast asleep, but the moon continues to cast its rays down onto the river.

III

The open-air opera is also performed on the bank of the river, and also in the autumn. If, for example, the autumn harvest is good, there will be an opera performance to thank the gods. If there is a summer drought, people wearing willow headdresses will call for rain; dozens of them will dash back and forth in the streets for days, singing and beating drums. These rain dancers are not permitted to wear shoes, so that the venerable Dragon King will take pity on them, as their feet are being scalded on the sun-drenched ground, and reward them with rain. Then if the rains do in fact come, there will be an opera performance in the autumn as fulfillment of a vow taken during the rain dance. All vows must be fulfilled, and since the vow was the offering of an opera, then that opera must be performed.

A performance lasts for three days.

A stage is put up on a sandbar alongside the river. It is erected on poles that are tied together and covered with an awning, so that it will not matter if it drizzles, and the stage will be protected from the sun's rays.

After the stage has been finished bleachers are erected on both sides, which include gallery seats. Sitting in the gallery seats is very desirable, for not only is it cool there, it also affords one the opportunity to look all around the area. But gallery seats are not easy to come by, as they are reserved for local officials and members of the gentry; most people seldom get the chance to use them, and since tickets are not sold, even money won't buy them.

The construction of the stage alone takes nearly a week. When the stage framework has been put in place the townspeople say: "The stage framework is up." Then when the awning is in place they say: "The stage awning is in place."

Once the stage is completed a row of bleacher seats is placed to the left and to the right of it, parallel and facing each other. They extend for a distance of perhaps fifty yards.

Seeing that the structure is nearly completed, the people go to fetch their families and call their friends. For example, when a young married woman who is visiting the home of her parents is about to return to her husband's home, her mother will see her just beyond the front gate, wave to her, and say: "When the opera is performed in the autumn I'll come and fetch you."

Then as the cart bearing her daughter moves off into the distance, the mother says again with tears in her eyes: "I'll come and fetch you when it's time to watch the opera."

And so the opera entails more than just the simple entertainment of watching a performance; it is an occasion to summon daughters and sons-in-law, a time of great festivity.

The daughter of a family to the east has grown up, and it is time for the son of a family to the west to take a wife; whereupon the matchmaker begins to make her calls on the two families. Arrangements are made for the parents of both children to look them over below the opera stage on the first or second day of the performance. Sometimes these arrangements are made only with the boy's family, without telling the girl's, something known as "stealing a look." This way it matters not whether the match is made, and it offers more freedom; for, after all, the girl is unaware of what is going on.

With this in mind, all the young maidens who go to watch the opera make themselves up as nicely as they can: they wear new clothes, apply rouge and powder to their faces, trim their bangs neatly, and comb their braids so that not a hair is out of place. Then they tie their braids with red bands at the top and green at the bottom, or perhaps with bands of pink and light blue. They carry themselves with the airs of honored guests, and as they nibble on melon seeds they hold their heads high and keep their eyes fixed straight ahead in a cultured and refined manner, as though they have become the daughters of highly respected families. Some are dressed in long robin's-egg-blue gowns, some in purplish blue, and others in silvery gray. Some of them have added borders to their gowns: there are robin's-egg-blue gowns with black borders, and there are pink gowns made of muslin adorned with dark blue borders. On their feet they wear shoes of blue satin or embroidered black satin. The shoes are embroidered with all manner of designs: butterflies, dragonflies, lotus flowers, and peonies.

The girls carry embroidered hankies in their hands and wear long earrings, which the local people call "grain-tassel earrings." These grain-tassel earrings come in two types: one is made of gold and jadeite, the other of copper and glass. Girls from wealthy families wear gold ones, those from less-well-off families wear glass ones. At any rate, they are all attractive as they dangle beneath the girls' ears. Dazzling yellows and deep greens, set off by very correct smiles on their faces; who can all these respectable young ladies be?

Young women who have already married also make themselves up and gather to meet their sisters of the neighborhood below the stage, where they examine and compare each other. So-and-so looks very comely, the curls of temple hair on so-and-so are shiny black; so-and-so's bracelet is the newest thing at the Fu-t'ai Jewelry Shop, so-and-so's hair ornaments are dainty and lovely; the embroidery on so-and-so's dark purple satin shoes is exquisitely done.

The old women shy away from colorful clothes, though every one of them is neat as a pin. They carry long pipes in their hands and arrange their hair in buns atop their heads, looking very kindly and gentle.

Before the opera performances have even begun, the town of Hulan River is all a-bustle, as the people scurry about fetching the young married daughters and summoning sons-in-law; the children have a delightful little ditty they sing:

> Pull the long saw,
> Drag the long saw;
> By Grandpa's gate they sing an opera song.
> The daughters are brought,
> The sons-in-law too;
> Even the grandchildren all go along.

By then young nephews, third aunts, second aunts by marriage—the reunions all start taking place.

Every family performs the same tasks: they kill chickens, buy wine, greet visitors with smiles, and talk among themselves of family affairs. They discuss matters of interest deep into the night, wasting more lamp oil than anyone knows.

An old woman in such-and-such a village is mistreating her daughter-in-law. The old grandfather of such-and-such a family makes a scene whenever he drinks. And how about the girl who married into such-and-such a family just barely a year before giving birth to twins! Did you hear about so-and-so's thirteen-year-old son who has been betrothed to an eighteen-year-old girl? The people nearly talk the night away under the light of candles and lanterns amidst a warm and cheery atmosphere of intimacy.

In families where there are many daughters who have already married it sometimes happens that as many as two or three years pass without an opportunity for the sisters to be reunited, since they usually live far apart. Separated by rivers or mountains and encumbered with many children and household duties, it is fruitless for them to even think of calling on one another.

And so when their mother summons them all home at the same time, their meeting truly seems as though it follows a separation of decades. At their family reunion they are at a loss for words and terribly shy; wanting desperately to say something, they hold back, overcome by embarrassment the moment they begin to speak, and before long their faces are flushed. They greet each other with silence, their hearts torn between happiness and sadness. But after the time it takes to smoke a pipeful, when the blood that had rushed to their faces has receded and the dizzying effects of their meeting have abated, they finally manage a few short comments of little relevance, such as: "When did you arrive?" or: "Did you bring the children?" They dare not utter a single word regarding their long separation of several years.

On the surface they don't seem the least bit like sisters, since there isn't the slightest trace of an expression of affection; as they face each other it is impossible to determine their relationship. It looks as though they were complete strangers, that they had never met before, and were seeing one another for the first time today, so coolly formal do their attitudes seem. But this is only the exterior; a mutual understanding has long filled their hearts. For that matter, as many as ten days or two weeks earlier their hearts had already begun to stir, starting from the day they had received their mother's letters. The letters had said that she wanted to summon the sisters home to watch the opera, and from that moment on each of them began deciding upon the gifts she was going to take home to give her sisters.

It might be a pair of black velvet cloud-slippers that she made with her own hands. Or perhaps in the town or village where one of them is living there is a famous dyer's shop that produces beautifully hued cotton goods, so she will supply the shop with a couple of bolts of white cotton fabric and instructions to dye them as delicately as possible. One bolt is to have blue designs over a white background, the other white designs on a blue background. The design on the blue material is to be a little boy with bangs playing with a gold coin, that on the white material is to be butterflies frolicking amongst lotus flowers. One bolt will be given to elder sister, the other to younger sister.

All these things are packed in a hamper and brought along, then after a day or two, during a quiet evening, she will gently remove them from the bottom of her hamper and place her elder sister's gift in front of her, saying: "Why don't you take this dyed cotton quilt cover back home with you!"

That is all she says, not at all the sort of thing one would expect from someone giving a gift. Her way is quite different from that of modern times, where a person gives some little present and, afraid that the neighbors might miss the event, shouts and carries on, boasting that it comes from a certain mountain somewhere, or that it was taken from the ocean. Even if it has only been gotten from a little stream somewhere, the glories of that particular stream have to be sung—how uncommon and unique it is, not at all like your average stream.

These countryfolk with their muddling ways don't know how to express what they feel, and so they say nothing, but simply hand the thing over and are done with it.

The recipient of the gift says nothing either—not a single word of thanks—and merely takes it from her. Some will briefly decline to accept the gift, saying: "Why don't you just keep it for your own use!" Naturally the giver refuses to do so, at which time the gift is accepted.

Every young woman who returns to her mother's home to watch the opera brings a great many different items along with her—gifts for her parents, her brothers and their wives, nieces, nephews, and other members of the family. Whoever brings the most and can produce a little something for each of her elders and all of the young children is the one who is judged to be the warmest and most affectionate.

Talk of these things, however, must await the completion of the opera performances and the dismantling of the stage; then they gradually work their way into each family's conversations.

Every young woman who then returns to her husband's home from the home of her parents takes back with her a wealth of objects that have been given to her as gifts. There is an abundance of things to use and things to eat: salted meat that her mother had prepared herself, fish that her elder sister had personally dried and cured, and the pickled drumstick of a wild goose that her brother had shot on a hunting trip in the mountains (this has been given to the young woman who had come home for the opera to take back for her father-in-law to enjoy with his wine).

With one thing and another to keep them busy on the night before their departure, the sisters don't even have a free moment to talk to each other, and when they finish there is a pile of packages of all sizes.

During the period of the opera performances, besides family reunions and gatherings of friends, there are many other happy events taking place, specifically the engagements of young couples and the announcements of their forthcoming weddings in March or April of the following year. After the drinking of the betrothal wine comes the exchanging of the "engagement gifts," which constitutes a legally binding commitment; once it has been completed, the girl is considered a daughter-in-law in the boy's family.

Families with marriageable children from neighboring villages also come to town for the opera, leaving the young boys and girls at home and making arrangements for the nuptials through a matchmaker. Sometimes during the drinking and festivities some families will casually promise their daughters to someone, and there are even those who betroth their unborn sons and daughters. This is called a "marriage made in the womb," and it generally only occurs between families of substantial means.

Both families are very wealthy: one operates the local distillery, the other is a big landowner from White Flag Village. One of the two families plants sorghum, the other distills wine. The distiller needs sorghum, and the sorghum farmer needs a distiller to buy his harvest; a distillery cannot get by without sorghum, and sorghum must have its distillery. By a happy coincidence, the wives of both families are pregnant, and so they arrange a "marriage made in the womb." It makes no difference who has a boy and who has a girl, for as long as there is one of each, they are proclaimed husband and wife. Now if both give birth to boys, there is no need to force the issue of their marriage, and the same holds true if both give birth to girls.

The drawbacks of these "marriages made in the womb," however, greatly outnumber the advantages. If along the way the fortunes of one of the families should decline—if the distillery should go out of business or the landowner lose his land—then the remaining family would be unwilling to gain a poverty-stricken daughter-in-law or lose its daughter to a family of no means. If it is the girl's family that has suffered reverses, then the matter is easily disposed of, for if the marriage agreement is not honored, there is nothing they can do about it. But in cases where the boy's family has fallen on bad times, inasmuch as a boy must take a wife, if the marriage is then canceled, the girl's reputation is ruined; people will say that she "brought injury" to so-and-so's family, and then would not marry into it. The superstition surrounding these words "brought injury" is that a certain family has been reduced to poverty owing to the harshness of the girl's horoscope. From that time on it will be extremely difficult to find a family that will accept her as a daughter-in-law, and she will be labeled an "unwanted spinster." With this unhappy prospect before it, her family will reluctantly allow the marriage to take place. But as time goes on, her sisters-in-law will accuse her of being a woman who cares only for luxury, and they will insult her in every conceivable manner. Eventually even her husband will grow to dislike her, and she will be mistreated by her parents-in-law; unable to withstand so much abuse, this unworldly young woman returns to her parents' home, but there is nothing that can be done there either. The mother who years before had been a party to the "marriage made in the womb" will say to her: "This is all part of your 'fate,' and you must accept it as best you can!"

The young women, bewildered, cannot understand why they must suffer such a fate, and so tragedy is often the result; some jump down wells, others hang themselves.

An old saying goes: "A battlefield is no place for a woman." Actually, that's not a fair statement; those wells are terribly deep, and if you were to casually ask a man whether or not he would dare to jump down one, I'm afraid the answer would be "no." But a young woman, on the other hand, would certainly do so. Now while an appearance on a battlefield doesn't necessarily lead to death, and in fact might even result in an official position later, there's not much chance of someone emerging alive after jumping down a well—most never do.

Then why is it that no words of praise for the courage of these women who jump down wells are included in the memorial arches for a chaste woman? That is because they have all been intentionally omitted by the compilers of such memorials, nearly all of whom are men, each with a wife at home. They are afraid that if they write such things, then one day when they beat their own wife, she too may jump down a well; if she did she would leave behind a brood of children, and what would these men do then? So with unanimity they avoid writing such things, and concern themselves only with "the refined, the cultured, and the filial. . . ."

These are some of the things that happen before the staging of the first opera. Once the performances actually begin, throngs of people swarm around the foot of the stage, pushing and shoving insufferably. The people who erect the stage certainly know what they are doing: they select a large level sandbar beside the river that is both smooth and clean, so that even if someone were to fall down his clothing wouldn't get the least bit soiled. The sandbar is about a half *li* in length.

The people are laughing and carrying on as they watch the opera performance, making such a loud commotion it would undoubtedly drown out the chorus of gongs and drums. On the stage someone dressed in red walks on as someone in green walks off, and this parade of people walking on and off is about all the spectators notice; naturally they cannot tell you if the singing is of high quality or not, since they cannot even hear it. Those closer to the stage can see that the beardless actor's mouth is open; those farther away can't even tell clearly whether the actor on stage is a male or female.

One might think it would be preferable to watch a puppet theater. But supposing a puppeteer were to come around then and begin singing; if you asked these people if they would prefer to watch him, their answer would be emphatically negative, and even those who are so far away they cannot even make out the edge of the stage, or, for that matter, those as much as two *li* distant, still would not choose to watch the puppet show. For even if all they do is take a little snooze beneath the big stage and then go home, what counts is that they have returned from a spot beneath the big opera stage, and not from some other place. Since there isn't much of anything else to see during the year, how could they lightly let this opera performance pass them by? And so whether they watch it or not, they must at least put in an appearance at the foot of the opera stage.

They come from the countryside, riding in great wagons with teams of horses, in carts pulled by old oxen, in fancily decorated carriages, and in small drays pulled by big mules. In a word, they arrive in whatever vehicles they happen to own, and those who don't raise horses or other beasts of burden hook up a young donkey to a carriage that they have decorated and come in it.

After they have arrived they leave their vehicles and their animals on the sandbar, where the horses feed on the grass and the mules go down to the river to drink. Awnings are put up over their carts, which then become little bleachers standing in a line some distance from the stage. The carts and wagons have brought entire families, from grandmothers to the wives of their grandsons—three generations of family—and have deposited them a considerable distance from the stage. They can hear nothing and can see only figures in red and green wearing strange hats and clothing who are running around in circles on the stage. Who can tell what they are doing up there on the stage? Some people attend all three days of the performances, yet cannot tell you the name of a single opera performed. They return to their villages and relate to others their experiences, and if by chance someone should ask them what opera they are talking about, their sole answer is a long, hard stare.

The children at the foot of the stage are even less aware of what is going on. About all they know is that there is someone with a beard and someone else with a painted face up there, but they haven't the slightest idea what they are doing; just a confusion of movements and a flurry of swords, spears, clubs, and staffs. At any rate, there are peddlers of rice pudding and candy balls beneath the stage, so the children can always go and eat what they like. There are all kinds of things like rice cakes, pan-fried buns, and fermented bean curd, and since these things are not filling, they can always sample a little of everything. Watermelons are sold there, and muskmelons, and there are swarms of flies buzzing to and fro.

The heavens reverberate with the clanging of gongs and the beating of drums at the foot of the stage. Apparently concerned that the people in the rear cannot hear them, the actors shout their songs for all they are worth, but they could never drown out the chorus of gongs and drums even if they destroyed their vocal cords in the process. People beneath the stage have long since forgotten that they are there to watch the opera, as they talk interminably about this or that. Men and women alike spend their time discussing domestic affairs. Then there are the distant relatives who never see each other throughout the year; meeting here today, how could they not greet one another? Therefore maternal and paternal aunties shout to each other amidst the crowds of people gathered there. Suddenly an old woman sitting in the bleachers beneath one of the awnings jumps to her feet and shouts out: "Second Maternal Auntie, when did you get here?"

She is answered by the person she has called to. Now the people in the gallery seats are relatively near the stage, close enough to actually hear the singing, so it is generally less noisy there. Young women—married and unmarried—sit there nibbling melon seeds and sipping tea. People are naturally annoyed by the shouts of this old woman, but they dare not try to stop her, for the minute they asked her to speak a little more softly, she would begin cursing them: "This open-air opera isn't being performed just for your family, you know! If you want to hear some opera then invite the troupe of actors to come to your house to sing it!"

Then the other woman would chime in with: "Well, I'll be! I've never seen anything like this. Once they start watching the opera they don't even give a damn about their own kin. Why, a person can't even talk. . . ."

These are some of the nicer things; there are worse. Out of their mouths might come such comments as: "You husband-stealing slut . . . screw your grandmother! Never in my life have I heard a harsh or angry word from anyone, and now you expect me to let you tell me what to do . . . up your mother's. . . ."

If the abused party lets this pass without notice, the whole incident is soon forgotten, but if there is a reply, naturally it will not be one that is very pleasing to the ear. What ensues is a brawl between the two parties, with watermelon rinds and other objects flying back and forth.

Here we have people who have come to watch an opera performance, but who have unexpectedly begun putting on their own show beneath the stage. Like a swarm of bees, people rush over to watch this real-life, knock-down-drag-out performance. Several ruffians and good-for-nothings in the crowd shout their approval, causing all present to roar with laughter. If one of the combatants is a young woman, then those irksome ruffians, with their lewd comments, provoke her into more volatile and viciously abusive language.

Naturally the old woman has been guilty of shouting abuses at the other without any regard for propriety or reason, but after a while it is impossible to tell who is in the right and who is in the wrong.

Fortunately, the actors on the stage remain cool and collected, not wavering from their singing in the face of this disruption, so that in the end the slugfest and all its attendant commotion gradually die down.

Another activity at the foot of the stage is the flirting that goes on, primarily by people like the married woman from the bean-curd shop on Avenue South, or the wife of the miller who runs the grain mill. The miller's wife has her eye on one of the carters, or a bean-curd maker casts amorous looks at the daughter of a grain shop owner. With some, furtive glances pass back and forth between both of them, but on other occasions one of the parties is eagerly attentive, while the other demonstrates total indifference. The latter situation usually involves one member of the upper class and one from a lower class, two people with a great disparity in family wealth.

Members of the gentry also have their flirtations as they sit in the gallery seats casting glances here and there. They cannot help but eye members of their own families—in-laws, cousins, and the rest—especially since every one of them is made up so beautifully and is so eye-catching.

Normally when members of the gentry call upon one another in the guest halls of their homes they absolutely will not allow themselves to ogle their host's daughter; this would be terribly ungentrylike behavior, not to mention immoral. And if one of these young girls were to tell her parents, they would immediately sever their relationship with the friend in question. Actually, a severed relationship isn't all that serious; what is important is that once this information has leaked out, the person's reputation is quite ruined, and since the gentry are supposed to be noble, how could they let their names be besmirched? How could they permit themselves to desire the daughter of a friend without respect to the difference in ages, like the lower classes do?

When members of the gentry come calling they are ushered into the guest hall, where they seat themselves very correctly, drink a little tea, and smoke a pipe. Well-mannered and ceremoniously courteous, they give one another the respect due a peer. The wife and children come out to pay their respects, treating the guest as their elder, and in such a situation the guest can inquire only about how many books the young master has read and how many more characters he has learned to write. He cannot speak more than a few words even to his friend's wife, to say nothing of the daughter; he cannot even raise his head to face her, let alone give her the once-over.

But here in the gallery seats it makes no difference, for if someone asks what he is doing, he can say he is just looking around to see if some of his friends are in any of the other rows. Besides, with all those people casting glances here and there, most likely no one is even paying attention. A look here and a look there, and even though he doesn't fall for any of his friends' daughters, he has an infatuation for a woman he has seen somewhere or other before. This woman is holding a small goosefeather fan over which she looks his way. She might be a married woman, but she is certainly young and pretty.

Logically, this particular member of the gentry ought to stand up right then and whistle to show how pleased he is, but the older Chinese gentry don't operate that way. They have a different way of acting; he just looks straight ahead, his eyes half-open in that style of his that shows the limitless affection he feels for the woman. But unhappily, she is so far away she probably cannot see him clearly, and his efforts may all be in vain.

Some of the young people beneath the stage refuse to heed the admonitions of their parents and the counsel of matchmakers, and pledge their lives to one another on their own, though these activities are generally restricted to cousins who are the sons and daughters of fairly respectable families. They vow on the spot to share their lives forever. For some of these young couples their parents' obstruction will produce a great many frustrations. But these frustrations will be beautiful ones, as talk of them will engender more interest than a reading of the romance Dream of the Red Chamber, and during the opera performances of years to come, the young girls' reminiscenses will be greatly enhanced by talk of such delightful things.

The countryfolk who have come to town in carts for the opera pitch camp on the sandbar beside the river. In the evening after the day's performance has ended, the townspeople return to their homes, leaving only those with their carts and horses to spend the night on the sandbar. The scene is reminiscent of a military bivouac with the ground beneath and the sky above. Some just stay over for the night and return home the next day, while others stay for all three nights, until the performances are concluded, before they drive their carts back to the country. Needless to say, the sandbar presents a fairly impressive sight at nighttime, as each family sits and drinks tea or chats among itself around a campfire, though, in point of fact, their number is rather too small—no more than twenty or thirty carts. Since the campfires they build aren't numerous enough to really light up the sky, there is a certain air of forlornness there. In the deep of night the river water turns especially cold, chilling the people sleeping on the riverbank. It is even worse for the carters and others who tend the animals, as they cannot sleep for fear that bandits may come and steal their horses, and must sit there waiting for the coming day.

Sitting beneath paper lanterns in groups of twos and threes, they gamble until the first light of day appears, at which time they lead their horses down to the river to drink. There they are met by an old fisherman in a crab boat who says to them: "Yesterday's performance of *A Fisherman's Revenge* wasn't bad. I hear they're going to do *Fen-ho Bay* today."

The fellow who has led his animal to the water knows nothing at all about opera. He listens only to the lapping noises of the drinking animals, having no response for any comments made to him.

IV

The festival at the Temple of the Immortal Matron, which falls on the eighteenth day of the fourth lunar month, is for spirits and ghosts, not people. This festival, which the local people call a "temple stroll," is attended by men and women of all ages, although most are young women.

The young women get up in the morning and begin combing their hair, bathing, and preparing themselves as soon as breakfast is over. Then after they have finished getting themselves ready, they arrange with neighbor girls to go and join the temple stroll. Some begin making themselves up the moment they get out of bed, even before breakfast, then leave the house as soon as they have eaten. In any event, on the day of the temple stroll there is a mad rush to get there early, so that before noon the temple grounds are already so crowded there is barely room to breathe.

Women who have lost their children in the crush stand there shouting, while the children who cannot find their mothers cry in the midst of all those people. Three-year-olds, five-year-olds, and even some two-year-olds who have just learned to walk are separated from their mothers in the crowds.

Consequently there are policemen at the festival each year whose job it is to locate such children and stand on the temple steps until their parents come to claim them. Since these children are always the more timorous ones, they wail loudly and pitifully until their faces are bathed in tears and sweat. Even twelve- and thirteen-year-olds get lost, and when one of them is asked where he lives, he is invariably stumped for an answer. Pointing first to the east, then to the west, he says that there is a small river running past his gate, which is called "Shrimp Canal" because it is full of tiny shrimp. It is possible that the place where the child lives is itself called "Shrimp Canal," a name that means nothing to the people who hear it. When asked how far from town this Shrimp Canal is, the child answers that it is about a meal's ride on horseback or three meals' ride in a cart. But this doesn't tell you how far from town the place is. Asked his family name, he answers that his grandfather is called Shih Erh and his father, Shih Ch'eng, and no one dares pursue the matter any further. If he is asked whether or not he has eaten, he answers: "I've already had a nap." There's nothing anyone can do at this point, and it's best to just let him go; and so children of all ages gather at the temple gate under the watchful eyes of policemen, crying and shouting, and sounding like a pack of small animals.

The Temple of the Immortal Matron is on Avenue North, not far from the Temple of the Patriarch.

Even though the people who go to light incense at the temple are doing so to ask for sons and grandsons, and by rights should first light their incense in front of the Immortal Matron, still they believe that men are considered superior to women in the nether world, just as they are here, and they dare not upset the cosmic order. Consequently they always go first to the Temple of the Patriarch, where they strike the gong and kowtow to the deity, as though they were kneeling there to report for duty; then and only then do they proceed to the Temple of the Immortal Matron.

In the Temple of the Patriarch there are more than ten clay images, and it is hard to tell just which one is the Patriarch, as they are all so imposing and stern, truly looking as though they rise above the world. The fingertips of some of the clay idols have been broken off, and they stand there with their fingerless hands raised in the air; some have had their eyes gouged out and look like blind people; some even have written characters scribbled all over their toes, characters with rather inelegant meanings that are not at all suited to deities. There are comments that say that the clay idol should take a wife or else it will be jealous when it sees the monks chasing after the little nuns. Actually, the characters themselves no longer remain, but this is what people say used to be written there.

Because of this the County Magistrate once sent down an order that the doors of all temples were to be closed and locked on days other than the first and fifteenth day of each month, and no loiterers were to be allowed entrance.

This County Magistrate is a man particularly concerned with the Confucian concepts of humanity, justice, and morality. The story has it that his fifth concubine was taken from the nunnery, so he has always been convinced that no nun would ever try to tempt a monk. From earliest times nuns have been ranked together with monks, and inasmuch as the common people do not personally investigate the situation, they simply parrot what others before them have said. Take the County Magistrate's number five concubine, for example: she herself was a nun, and can it be possible that she too had been sought out by some monk? There isn't the slightest chance of that. And so the order was sent to close all temple doors.

The Temple of the Immortal Matron is generally more serene

than the others. There are clay idols there too, mostly female, and they are for the most part devoid of harsh, malignant stares. People are simply not frightened by them when they enter the main hall, since the idols look pretty much like common people. Obviously these are the Matrons, and of course they are good and obedient females. Why, even the female ghosts are not particularly malevolent; their hair is a little mussed up and that's about all. There isn't one that even barely resembles the clay idols in the Temple of the Patriarch, with their flaming eyes or tigerlike mouths.

Children are not the only ones who are frightened to tears when they walk into the Temple of the Patriarch; even a young man in his prime becomes very respectful when he enters, as if to show that even though he is in the prime of his life, if that clay idol were to take it into its head to walk over and begin fighting with him, the man would certainly come out on the short end. And so whoever kowtows in the Temple of the Patriarch, where the clay idols are so tall and powerful, does so with greater piety.

When they go to the Temple of the Immortal Matron the people also kowtow, though they have the feeling that there is nothing very spectacular about the Matron.

The people who cast the clay idols were men, and they fashioned the female figures with an obedient appearance, as though out of respect to women. The male figures they fashioned with a savage, malignant appearance, as though in condemnation of men's dispositions. That, however, is not the case. Throughout the world, no matter how fiercely savage, there has probably never been even one man who had flaming eyes. Take Occidentals, for instance: though their eyes are unlike those of the Chinese, it is simply that theirs are a limpid blue, somewhat resembling those of cats, but by no means are they flaming. The race of people with flaming eyes has never appeared on the face of the earth. Then why have the people who cast the clay idols made them look that way? For the simple reason that a single glance will strike fear into someone, and not only will he kowtow, he will do so with absolute conviction. Upon completing his kowtows, when he rises and takes another look, there will never be the slightest regret; the thought that he has just prostrated himself before an ordinary or unremarkable individual would simply not occur to him. And why have the idol-makers cast the female figures with such obedient appearances? That is in order to tell everyone that obedience indicates a trusting nature, and that the trusting are easily taken advantage of; they are telling everyone to hurry and take advantage of them!

If someone is trusting, not only do members of the opposite sex take advantage of her, but even members of the same sex show no compassion. To illustrate: when a woman goes to worship at the Temple of the Immortal Matron all she does is ask for some sons and grandsons. Her prayers ended, she rises and leaves, and no manifestations of respect are apparent. She has the feeling that the Matrons of Sons and Grandsons is nothing but a common, ordinary woman who just happens to have a surplus of children.

Then when men hit their wives they can say: "The Immortal Matron is supposed to be in constant fear of being beaten by the Patriarch, so what makes a gossipy woman like you any different?"

It is obvious that for a man to beat a woman is a Heaven-ordained right, which also holds true for gods and demons alike. No wonder the idols in the Temple of the Immortal Matron have such obedient looks about them—this comes from having been beaten so often. It becomes apparent that obedience is not the exceptionally fine natural trait it has been thought to be, but rather the result of being beaten, or perhaps an invitation to receive beatings.

After they have worshiped at the two temples the people come out and crowd into the streets, where there are peddlers of all types of toys, most of which are suited for the smaller children. There are clay roosters with two red chicken feathers stuck on to make a tail, causing the toys to look better by far than the real thing. Anyone with children will be forced to buy one, especially since it will make a loud whistling noise when put to the mouth and blown. After they have bought the clay rooster the children spy some little clay men with holes in their backs in which reeds can be inserted to make whistles. The sound they make is not very pleasing to the ear—almost like a cry of grievance—but the children like it, so their mothers have to buy them.

Of the remaining toys—the whistles, reed flutes, metal butterflies, and tumbler dolls—it is the tumbler dolls that are the most popular and the ones made with the greatest care. Every family buys one—bigger dolls for the well-to-do families, smaller ones for poorer families. The big ones are nearly two feet in height and the small ones can be as tiny as a duck's egg. But big or small, they are all very lively. They right themselves the moment they are pushed over, quickly and without fail. They are tested on the spot by every prospective buyer; occasionally, if a doll has been made by an inexperienced hand, the bottom will be too large and the doll will not fall over, while others will fall over and not right themselves. So before they buy the tumbler dolls, the people invariably reach out and push them all over together, then buy whichever one rights itself first. This process of knocking them down and watching them right themselves produces a great deal of hilarity among the children who surround the peddler's stand to laugh at the goings-on.

A tumbler doll is very attractive, so white and plump, and though it is called "the old man who won't fall down," this is just a name, and the toy looks nothing like an old man. In fact, it is a fat little child, and the ones that have been made with a little more care even have a few strands of hair that represent the child's hair. The ones with hair sell for ten coppers more than those without, and many of the children are adamant in wanting a doll with hair. Not wishing to make this additional expense, the child's mother offers to take it home and add a few hairs she can cut off the family dog. But the child insists on having one with hair already on it, so he picks one of them up and refuses to put it back. Seeing that there is nothing she can do, the mother buys it for him. The child carries the doll with him on the road back home, happy as can be, but by the time he arrives home he discovers that the tuft of hair has already fallen off somewhere along the way, and he begins to cry loudly. His mother quickly cuts a few hairs from the family dog and sticks them onto the doll, but the child cannot help but feel that this hair is not the real thing and doesn't look nearly as good as the original. Now the original hair may very well have been dog hair too, for that matter, and worse looking than what is on the doll now, but the child is not content with it, and is dejected for the rest of the day.

By the afternoon the festival is concluded, but the temple doors remain open, and there are still some people inside burning incense and worshiping the Buddha. Women who have no sons remain inside the Temple of the Immortal Matron to play some little tricks: they stick buttons onto the back of the Matron of Sons and Grandsons, tie red sashes around her feet, and hang earrings on her ears. They fit her with a pair of eyeglasses, then steal off with one of the clay infants that have been placed beside her, in the belief that they themselves will then produce sons the following year.

There are a great many peddlers of sashes at the gate to the Temple of the Immortal Matron, and the women flock to buy them, believing that this purchase will bring a son into the family. If an unmarried girl should inadvertently buy one she becomes the object of a great deal of raucous laughter.

Once the temple festival is over, each family is in possession of a tumbler doll, even those who live as far away from the city as eighteen *li*. When they get home they place the doll just inside the front door so that other people can see it at a glance and know that this family now has a tumbler doll of its very own. This is incontrovertible evidence that the family was not left behind during the time of the festival, but clearly had participated in the "stroll."

There is a local song that goes:

> Dear young woman, take your temple stroll.
> A graceful walk, a charming gait;
> And don't forget to buy a tumbler doll.

V

All these special occasions are designed for ghosts, certainly not for people. Although the people do get to watch some opera and take their temple strolls, these are really only the incidental benefits they receive.

The dance of the sorceress is all about ghosts; the great opera is sung for the benefit of the venerable Dragon King; the river lanterns are released on the fifteenth day of the seventh lunar month to be used by ghosts, so that they can light the road to transmigration by carrying these lanterns over their heads; the lighting of incense and kowtowing on the eighteenth day of the fourth lunar month is also to honor ghosts.

Only the harvest dances are performed for the benefit of the living and not for ghosts. These dances are performed on the fifteenth day of the new year, during the season of rest for those who work the land. They take advantage of the New Year's festivities to masquerade themselves, with men making themselves up as women, presenting a comical scene that delights everyone.

Lion dances, dragon-lantern dances, land-boat dances, and the like, also seem to be in honor of ghosts, though there are so many different kinds it is difficult to give a clear account of them all.

3 GRANDDAD AND ME   I

The town of Hulan River is where my granddad lived. When I was born Granddad was already past sixty, and by the time I was four or five he was approaching seventy.

The house where we lived had a large garden that was populated by insects of all types—bees, butterflies, dragonflies, and grasshoppers. There were white butterflies and yellow ones, but these varieties were quite small and not very pretty. The really attractive butterflies were the scarlet ones whose entire bodies were covered with a fine golden powder.

The dragonflies were gold in color, the grasshoppers green. The bees buzzed everywhere, their bodies covered with a fine layer of down, and when they landed on flowers their plump little round bodies appeared to be motionless tiny balls of fur.

The garden was bright and cheerful, deriving its freshness and beauty from all the reds and the greens. It had once been a fruit orchard that was planted because of Grandmother's fondness for fruit. But Grandmother had also been fond of raising goats, and they had stripped all the bark from her fruit trees, killing them. From the time of my earliest recollection the garden had only a single cherry tree and a single plum tree, and since neither bore much fruit, I was not very aware of their existence. When I was a child I was conscious only of the garden's big elm tree. This tree, which was in the northwest corner of the garden, was the first to rustle in the wind and the first to give off clouds of mist when it rained. Then when the sun came out, the leaves of this big elm tree shone radiantly, sparkling just like the mother-of-pearl found on a sandbar.

Granddad spent most of the day in the rear garden, and I spent my time there with him. Granddad wore a large straw hat, I wore a small one; when Grandad planted flowers, so did I; and when Granddad pulled weeds, that's what I did too. When he planted cabbage seeds, I tagged along behind him filling in each of the little holes with my foot. But with my random and careless footwork, there was no way in the world I could have made a neat job of it. Some of the time not only did I fail to cover the seeds with soil, I even sent the seeds themselves flying with my foot.

The Chinese cabbages grew so quickly that sprouts began appearing within just a few days, and in no time at all they were ready to be picked and eaten.

When Granddad hoed the ground, so did I, but since I was too small to manage the long handle on my hoe, Granddad removed it and let me do my hoeing using only the head. Actually, there wasn't much hoeing involved in it, as I really just crawled along on the ground chopping and digging at will with the head of my hoe, not bothering to differentiate between the sprouts and the grass. Invariably I mistook leeks for weeds and pulled them all out together by their roots, leaving the foxtails, which I had mistaken for grain stalks, in the ground. When Granddad discovered that the plot of ground I had been hoeing was covered only with foxtails, he asked me: "What is all that?"

"Grain," I answered.

He started to laugh, and when he had finished he pulled up a foxtail and asked me: "Is this what you've been eating every day?"

"Yes."

Seeing that he was still laughing, I added: "If you don't believe me, I'll go inside and get some to show you."

So I ran inside and got a handful of grain from the birdcage, which I threw to Granddad from a distance, saying: "Isn't this the same thing?"

Granddad called me over and explained to me patiently that the grain stalks have beards, while the foxtails have only clusters that look very much like real foxes' tails. But although Granddad was teaching me something new, I wasn't really paying any attention, and I only made a cursory acknowledgment of what he was saying. Then, raising my head, I spotted a ripe cucumber and ran over, picked it, and began to eat. But before I had even finished, a large dragonfly darting past me caught my eye, so I threw down the cucumber and started chasing after it. But how could I ever expect to catch a dragonfly that flew that fast? The nice part about it was that I never really had any intention of catching it, and only got to my feet, ran a few steps, then started doing something else.

At such times I would pluck a pumpkin flower or catch a big green grasshopper and tie one of its legs with a piece of thread; after a while the leg might even snap off, so that there would be a leg dangling from the piece of thread, while the grasshopper from which it had come was nowhere to be found.

After I grew tired of playing I would run back over to where Grandad was and dash about noisily for a while. If he was watering the plants, I would grab the watering gourd away from him and do it myself, though in a peculiar fashion: instead of sprinkling water on the vegetables themselves, I would splash the water upward with all my might and shout: "It's raining, it's raining!"

The sun was particularly strong in the garden and there was a very high sky above. The sun's rays beat down in all directions so brightly I could barely keep my eyes open; it was so bright that worms dared not bore up through the ground, and bats dared not emerge from their dark hiding places. Everything that was touched by the sunlight was healthy and beautiful, and when I smacked the trunk of the big elm tree with my hands, it resounded; when I shouted it seemed as though even the earthen wall standing opposite me was answering my shouts.

When the flowers bloomed it was as though they were awakening from a slumber. When the birds flew it was as though they were climbing up to the heavens. When the insects chirped it was as though they were talking to each other. All these things were alive. There was no limit to their abilities, and whatever they wanted to do, they had the power to do it. They did as they willed in complete freedom.

If the pumpkins felt like climbing up the trellis they did so, and if they felt like climbing up the side of the house they did so. If the cucumber plant wanted to bring forth an abortive flower it did so; if it wanted to bear a cucumber it did so; if it wanted none of these, then not a single cucumber nor a single flower appeared, and no one would question its decision. The cornstalks grew as tall as they wished, and if they felt like reaching up to the heavens, no one would give it a second thought. Butterflies flew wherever they desired; one moment there would be a pair of yellow butterflies flying over from the other side of the wall, the next moment a solitary white butterfly flying over from this side of the wall. Whose house had they just left? Whose house were they flying to? Even the sun didn't know the answers to such questions.

There was only the deep blue sky, lofty and far, far away.

But when white clouds drew near they looked like great etched silver ingots, and as they passed over Granddad's head they were so low they seemed about to press down and touch his straw hat.

When I had grown tired from all my playing I searched for a cool, shady place near the house and went to sleep. I didn't need a pillow or a grass mat, but simply covered my face with my straw hat and fell asleep.

II

Granddad had smiling eyes and the hearty laugh of a child. He was a very tall man of robust health who liked to carry a cane when he walked. Never without a pipe in his mouth, whenever he met children he loved to tease them by saying: "Look at that sparrow up in the sky."

Then, when the child was looking skyward, he would snatch the child's cap off his head. Sometimes he stuck it up under his long gown, other times he hid it up his wide sleeve; then he would say: "The sparrow has flown away with your cap."

The children all knew this trick of Granddad's and were never fooled by it; they would wrap their arms around his legs and try to get their caps back by feeling around inside his sleeve or by opening up the inner lapel of his gown until they found what they were looking for.

Granddad often did this, and he always hid the caps in the same places—either up his sleeve or inside the lapel of his gown, and there wasn't a single child who didn't find his cap inside Granddad's clothing. It was as though he had made an agreement with the children: "Now I'll just put it in here and you try to find it."

I don't know how many times he did this, but it was a lot like an old woman who is forever telling the story of "Going Tiger Hunting on the Mountain" to the children; even if they have already heard it five hundred times, they still clap their hands and shout appreciatively each and every time. Whenever Granddad played this little trick both he and the children laughed loud and long, as though it were the very first time.

Other people who saw Granddad do this usually laughed too, but not in appreciation of his sleight-of-hand; rather they laughed because he used the same method each and every day to snatch away the children's caps, and this was a very comical thing as far as they were concerned.

Granddad wasn't much good at financial matters, and all the household affairs were handled by my grandmother. He simply passed his day relaxing to his heart's content, and I felt it was a good thing I had grown up—I was three—otherwise, how lonely he would have been. I could walk . . . I could run. When I was too tired to walk Granddad carried me, and then when I felt like walking again he pulled me along. Day in and day out, inside or out-of-doors, I never left his side; for the most part, Granddad was in the rear garden, and so that's where I was too.

When I was little I had no playmates to speak of, and I was my mother's first-born child. I can remember things from my very early childhood, including a time when I was three years old when my grandmother used a needle to prick my finger. I disliked her a great deal as a result of this.

The windows in our house had paper stuck up on all four borders, with an inlay of glass in the center. Grandmother had an obsession with cleanliness, and the paper in the window of her room was always the cleanest in the house. Whenever anyone carried me into her room and put me down on the edge of the k'ang, I would dash over to the window beside the k'ang almost automatically, reach out to touch the white paper with the floral decoration in her window, and poke some small holes in it with my finger; if no one interfered, there would soon be a whole line of little holes, but if they did try to stop me, I would hurriedly poke one or two final holes before stopping. That paper was as tight as a drumhead, so it made a popping noise each time my finger poked through. The more holes I made, the more pleased I was with myself, and I was even happier when

Grandmother came and tried to chase me away—I would laugh, clap my hands, and stomp my feet.

One day when Grandmother saw me coming she picked up a large needle and went around to the outside of the window to wait for me. The moment I poked my finger through, it began to hurt like the dickens, and I shouted out in pain. Grandmother had pricked my finger with the needle. From that time on I never forgot what she had done, and I disliked her because of it.

She sometimes gave me candy and shared her pork kidney with me when she prepared kidney and Szechwan fritillary for her cough, but after I had finished the kidney I still didn't like her.

Once, when her illness was at its worst and her days were numbered, I gave her a real scare. She was sitting by herself on the edge of the *k'ang*, mixing some medicine in a medicine kettle that rested on a charcoal brazier beside her. The room was so quiet I could hear the medicine bubbling in the kettle. Grandmother lived in two rooms, one inner and one outer, and by a happy coincidence, that day there was no one else in either the outer or the inner room—she was all alone. She didn't hear me open the door, so I rapped loudly with my fist on the wooden partition: *Bang, bang!* I heard her blurt out "Oh!" and the steel fire tongs crashed to the floor. As I looked inside, she saw me and began cursing at me. She looked like she was going to climb down and chase after me, so I ran off laughing.

Frightening Grandmother like that wasn't something I had done for revenge; I was just an ignorant little five-year-old, and I probably just thought it would be fun.

All day long Granddad was idle, as Grandmother was unwilling to give him any jobs to do. There was just one thing: on a casket on the floor there were some pewter ornaments, and Granddad regularly polished them. I'm not sure if he was given this assignment by her or if it was something he undertook to do on his own. But whenever he began to polish them, I became unhappy, partly because this meant he couldn't take me out to play in the rear garden, and also because he would often be yelled at; Grandmother would scold him for being lazy and scold him for not doing a good job of polishing. And whenever she began to scold him, somehow or other even I got yelled at.

When Grandmother started to scold Granddad I took him by the hand and started walking out with him. "Let's go out into the rear garden," I would say.

Maybe that's the reason Grandmother started scolding me too. She would curse at Granddad, calling him a "useless old bag of bones," and then call me a "useless little bag of bones."

I would lead Granddad out into the rear garden, and the minute we got there we were in a different world altogether. We were no longer in the confined and cramped environment of the room, but in a spacious world where we were at one with heaven and earth. The sky above and the ground below were vast, stretching far, far into the distance; try though we might, we could not touch the sky with our outstretched hands. And the earth around us was so luxuriant with growing things that we could not take it all in at a single glance, which made us feel that we were surrounded by a vast layer of fresh greenery.

As soon as I stepped into the rear garden I began aimlessly running to and fro. It may have looked as though I was running after something that had caught my eye, or that there was something just waiting for my arrival, but I actually seldom had any objective in mind at all; I simply felt that absolutely everything in the garden was so alive that I was powerless to keep my legs from jumping. When Granddad called to me to stop before I wore myself out, if I hadn't yet exhausted my energy I would have none of it, and in fact, the more he called for me to stop, the worse I behaved.

I would sit down to rest only when I was too tired to even move, but my respites were very brief ones: I would sit down right in the middle of a vegetable bed, pick a cucumber, and eat it. Then after this brief rest I would be up and running again.

Obvious though it might have been that there was no fruit on the cherry tree, I would still climb up the tree to look for some cherries.

The plum tree was already half dead, and had long since stopped bearing fruit, but still I went over to look for plums. As I searched for them I shouted out questions to Granddad: "Grandpa, why aren't there any cherries on the cherry tree?"

"There aren't any cherries because there are no flowers on the tree," Granddad would answer from afar.

"Why aren't there any flowers on the cherry tree?"

"There aren't any flowers on the tree because you have such a greedy mouth."

As soon as I heard this I knew he was teasing me, and I would virtually fly over to where he was standing, pretending I was mad at him. But when he raised his eyes to look at me, I could see that there was no trace of malice in the look he gave me, and I would break out laughing. I would laugh for the longest time before I could stop. Just where all this happiness came from, I simply couldn't say. I don't know how loud my laughter was during such hell-raising in the rear garden, but it seemed even to me to be earsplitting.

There was a rosebush in our rear garden that bloomed every June and stayed in bloom until July. Each blossom was as big as a soy-sauce plate, and they were in such great profusion that the entire bush was covered with them. The fragrance of the flowers attracted tremendous numbers of bees to the rosebush, around which they swarmed with a great buzzing noise. When I had tired of playing with everything else I would be reminded of this rosebush and its flowers, and I would pick a great many of them and put them into the overturned crown of my straw hat. There were two things that frightened me about picking the roses: first I was afraid that I might be stung by a bee, and second that I might prick my fingers on a thorn. One time I picked a large bunch of the flowers, which was no easy task for me, but then I found I didn't know what to do with them after having picked them. Suddenly a brilliant idea came to me: Wouldn't Granddad look terrific wearing these flowers!

He was kneeling on the ground picking weeds, so I began adorning him with flowers, and though he was aware that I was playing

around with his hat, he didn't know for sure just what I was up to.
I decorated his straw hat with a wreath of twenty or thirty bright
red flowers, laughing all the while.

"The spring rains have been heavy this year," he said. "The flowers on that rosebush of ours are so fragrant you can smell them a
couple of *li* away."

I was so convulsed with laughter when I heard him say this that I
was barely able to continue sticking the flowers in, and even after
I had finished, Granddad was still blissfully unaware of what was
happening. He just kept pulling up the weeds from a little mound
of earth. I ran off some distance and stood there, not daring to even
look over where he was in order to keep from laughing. I took the
opportunity to go inside the house to get something to eat, and even
before I returned to the garden, Granddad followed me into the
house.

The moment he stepped inside, Grandmother noticed the bright
red flowers that covered his head. She didn't say a word when she
saw them, but just broke out laughing. My father and mother
started to laugh too, though I was laughing the hardest of anyone
and rolling around on the *k'ang*.

Then Granddad took off his hat, looked at it, and found that the
source of the fragrance of the roses wasn't a result of heavy spring
rains this year, but rather because his head was covered with a
wreath of flowers. He put his hat down and laughed for a full ten
minutes or more without stopping; after a while he thought about
it again and broke out laughing. Then just when he seemed to have
forgotten the incident, I reminded him of it again: "Grandpa, the
spring rains this year have sure been heavy."

With this reminder Granddad's laughter returned, and I started
rolling around on the *k'ang* again.

This is how it went, day in and day out: Granddad, the garden,
and me—the inseparable trio. I don't know how windy or rainy days
affected Granddad, but I always felt extremely lonesome. With no
place to go and nothing to do, such a day seemed to me to last several days.

Hard though I may have wished it otherwise, the rear garden was sealed off once every year. Following the autumn rains it would begin to languish; the flowers would yellow and fall, and it seemed that they would very soon wither and die, almost as though there were someone crushing and destroying them. None of them appeared as hardy as before—it was as though they were worn out and needed rest, and were thus putting their affairs in order before returning to the place from which they had come.

The big elm tree was also shedding its leaves, and on those occasions when Granddad and I sat beneath the tree, its leaves fell upon my face. Soon the rear garden was blanketed with the fallen leaves.

Before too long heavy snows would begin to fall, burying the garden. The rear door leading into the garden was sealed with a thick layer of mud, and frost and icicles hung from it throughout the winter.

There were five rooms in our house, two for my grandparents and two for my parents. My grandparents occupied the rooms to the west, my parents the ones to the east. The five rooms of the main house were arranged in a line, the middle one being the kitchen; the rooms all had glass windows, dark green walls, and tile roofs.

My grandparents had an outer and an inner room. The former was furnished with a large oblong chest, a rectangular table, and an armchair. There was a red cushion on the armchair, a vermilion vase atop the oblong chest, and a desk clock on the rectangular table. Hat stands were placed on either side of the clock, though instead of being used for hats, they were decorated with a number of peacock feathers. As a child I was intrigued by those peacock feathers; I used to say that there were gold-colored eyes on them, and I was forever wanting to play with them. But Grandmother refused to let me touch them—Grandmother had an obsession with cleanliness.

The desk clock atop the oblong chest was a strange-looking timepiece on which was painted the very lifelike figure of a young maiden dressed in ancient costume. Whenever I was in Grandmother's room alone, this young maiden glowered at me, and I told Granddad about this several times; but he always said: "She's just a painted figure; she can't stare at you."

But I was convinced that she could, and I told him that as far as I was concerned her eyeballs moved.

The large oblong chest in Grandmother's room was also decorated from one end to the other with carved human figures, each of them wearing ancient costume—wide-sleeved gowns, officials' caps, and peacock feathers. The chest was virtually covered with the figures— there must have been twenty or thirty of them; some were drinking wine, others were eating, and still others were in the act of bowing.

I was forever trying to get a closer look at the figures, but Grandmother wouldn't let me get within arm's length of the chest, saying to me as I stood off at a distance: "Don't you dare touch it with your filthy hands!"

On the wall of Grandmother's inner room hung a strange, strange clock that had two metal cornhusks suspended by chains beneath it. The metal cornhusks were a lot bigger than real ones, and looked to be so heavy that you could kill a person if you hit him with one. The inside of the clock was even stranger and more curious; there was a figure of a little blue-eyed girl inside, and every second those eyes of hers moved in concert with the ticking noise of the clock.

The differences between that little girl with her yellow hair and blue eyes and me were too great, and even though Granddad told me that it was the figure of a *mao-tzu-jen* or "hairy one," I wouldn't accept the notion that she was supposed to be a real person. Every time I looked at that wall clock I stared at it so long I began to look dazed. I thought to myself: "Doesn't that *mao-tzu-jen* do anything else but stay inside that clock? Won't she ever come down and play?"

In the slang of Hulan River, Caucasian foreigners were called *mao-tzu-jen*. When I was four or five I had yet to see my first *mao-tzu-jen*, and I thought this girl was called "hairy one" because she had such curly hair.

There were a lot of other things besides these in Grandmother's room, but since none of them really interested me in those days, I can only remember these few items.

In my mother's rooms there were none of these kinds of unusual curios; there were only commonplace things like a gold-bordered wardrobe and a variety of hat stands and flower vases—nothing remarkable enough to linger in my memory.

In addition to these five rooms—four serving as living quarters plus a kitchen—there were two incredibly small and dark rooms in the rear of the house, one for my grandparents and one for my parents. These rooms were filled with things of all kinds, since they served as storerooms. Earthen jugs and pitchers, chests and wardrobes, baskets and hampers—besides the things that belonged to our family, there were objects that other people had left there for safekeeping.

It was so dark inside the rooms that I could see only if I carried a lantern in with me. The air inside these rat- and cobweb-infested rooms was pretty bad, and there was always a sort of medicinal odor that assailed my nose. I loved playing in those storerooms, since any chest that I opened was invariably filled with a number of good-looking things like colorful silk thread, strips of silk of all colors, perfume satchels, waistband pouches, trouser legs, detachable oversleeves, and embroidered collars, all of them antique-looking, their colors blending together beautifully. Often I would also find jadeite earrings or rings in the chests, and when I did I was so insistent about wanting one to play with that Mother would usually toss one over to me.

Then there were the drawers in a desk that yielded up even more interesting items: copper rings, a wooden knife, bamboo measuring sticks, and the white material we called Kuan-yin powder. These were all things I had never seen anywhere else, and the best part of all was that these drawers were never locked. So I opened them pretty much whenever I felt like it, digging out whatever was inside without being the slightest bit selective. Holding the wooden knife in my left hand and some Kuan-yin powder in my right, I chopped here and daubed there. Then I came across a little saw, and I began destroying things right and left with it, sawing on objects like chair legs and the edges of our *k'angs*. I even ruined my little wooden knife by sawing on it. I carried these things with me whether I was eating or sleeping. At meals I used my little saw to cut open steamed buns, and when I dreamed at night I would shout out: "Where did my little saw go?"

The storerooms became in a way the scenes of my explorations. Often, when Mother was not in her room, I would grab the opportunity to open the door and go inside. There was a window at the rear of the storeroom through which a little light filtered in during the afternoons. I used to take advantage of this light to open the drawers, all of which I eventually rummaged through completely, until there was nothing new to be found inside them. I would go through them again until I lost interest, then emerge from the room. In the end I even dug out a lump of resin and a little piece of string, at which time I had picked all five desk drawers absolutely clean.

In addition to these drawers there were some baskets and trunks, but I didn't have the nerve to touch them, since they were all so dark and covered with who knows how much dust and how many layers of cobwebs that I never even gave a thought to touching them.

I remember that once when I went to the farthest and darkest recess of this unlighted room, my foot bumped into something with a thud. I picked it up and carried it over to the light, where I discovered that it was a lantern. I scraped off some of the dust with my finger, revealing that it was made of red glass. The chances are that when I was one or two years old I had seen this lantern before, but by the time I had reached four or five I no longer recognized it and didn't really know what to call this thing I was holding in my hand. I carried it out with me to ask Granddad what it was. After he had cleaned it all up for me he stuck a piece of candle inside. I was so delighted with it that I carried it all around the room with me, and, in fact, ran around with it in my hand for several days until I finally dropped it, breaking it into little pieces.

Once I also bumped into a piece of wood in the unlighted room. The top part of the wood had carvings on it and was very rough to the touch. I took it outside and began sawing on it with my little saw, until Granddad spotted me: "That's an engraving block for printing currency certificates," he said.

I had no idea what a currency certificate was, so he smeared a little ink on it and printed one to show me. I could only see that there were a few human figures on it, plus some motley designs and some written characters.

"When we operated the distillery we used this to make the currency certificates we issued," he told me. "This one is for a thousand coppers; we also had them for five hundred and one hundred." He printed up a bunch of them for me, and even printed some using red ink.

I also found and tried on a tasseled hat worn during the Ch'ing dynasty, and I fanned myself with a great big goose-feather fan that had been around for many years. During my rummaging I came across a little *sha-jen*, which was a medicine for stomach ailments. Mother took some, and I took some right along with her.

Before too long I had brought all these ancient relics out into the open; some had been put there for safekeeping by my grandmother, while others had been stored by aunts of mine who had married and left home. They had lain in that storeroom for years, touched by no one. Some of the things were falling apart, and others were infested by bugs, owing to the fact that they had long been neglected by their owners. It was as though they no longer existed on the face of the earth. Suddenly here they all were, right in front of everyone's eyes, and the memories of these things came rushing back to them with a start.

Each time I brought out some new item, Grandmother would say to me: "This goes back a lot of years! Your eldest aunt played with this when she was living at home."

If Granddad saw something he might say: "Your second aunt used this when she was living at home," or: "This was your eldest

aunt's fan; those embroidered shoes belonged to your third aunt. . . ."
Everything had a history of its own. The problem was, I didn't
know who my third aunt and my eldest aunt were. Perhaps I had
seen them when I was one or two years old, but I had forgotten them
by the time I was four or five.

My grandmother had three daughters, though by the time I was
old enough to know about such things, they had all married and left
home. Obviously, for some twenty or thirty years there had been no
children around, and now there was only one—me. Actually, I had
a younger brother, but at the time he was no more than a year old,
so he didn't count. All these things had been put away in the house
years before and left untouched. The people led their lives, looking
neither ahead nor behind; that which was in their past was forgotten,
while they held out no great hope for the future. They simply passed
their days in their stolid fashion, uncomplainingly accepting the lot
handed down to them by their ancestors.

My birth had proved a source of inestimable joy to my Granddad,
and as I grew up I was the apple of his eye. As for me, I felt that all I
needed in this world was Granddad, and with him by my side I had
nothing to fear. Even the cold attitude of my father, my mother's
mean words and nasty looks, and the incident in which my Grandmother pricked my finger with a needle faded into insignificance.
And if that weren't enough, there was also the rear garden! And even
though the garden was sealed off by ice and snow some of the time,
I had discovered the storerooms. Just about everything conceivable
could be found inside, and the treasures they held were often things
I had never imagined could even exist. I was struck by the thought
of how many, many things there must be in this world! And all of
them fun and unique.

For example, once I dug up a package of dye—Chinese dark green—
and although it gave off a gold sheen when I looked at it, the moment
I dabbed some on my fingernail, the fingernail turned green; then
when I rubbed a little on my arm, the spot appeared a leafy green.
It was both highly attractive and highly confusing, and I was se-

cretly delighted to think that I might have stumbled onto a real treasure.

I came across a chunk of Kuan-yin powder. When I rubbed this powder on the door, a white streak appeared on it, and when I rubbed it across the window, it left a white streak there too. This was very strange to me; probably what Granddad used when he wrote was black ink, I thought, and what I had here was white ink.

I also discovered a round piece of glass that Granddad called a "magnifying glass." Holding it under the sun, I found that it could light the tobacco in his pipe.

How happy things like this could make me, as each and every one of them underwent some kind of change. Someone might call a certain thing a piece of scrap metal, but who was to say it might not prove useful? To illustrate: once I picked up a square piece of metal that had a small hole on the top, into which Granddad placed a hazelnut, cracked it, then gave it to me to eat. Breaking the hazelnut open in that hole was unbelievably faster than using his teeth to open it. Besides, Granddad was an old man, and most of his teeth weren't much good anyway.

Every day I moved objects out of that dark room, and every day there was something new. I would carry out a load of things and play with them till I broke them or grew tired of them, then go and get some more. All of this caused a lot of sighing on the part of my grandparents. They told me how old a certain thing was, that it had been in our home before my third aunt was even born. They they told me how old something else was, that it had been brought to our home when my great-grandfather's inheritance was divided up. Then there was this thing or that, given to us by someone whose family had by this time completely died off without a trace, and yet this object was still around.

I remember the wicker bracelet that I used to play with; Grandmother told me that she had worn this bracelet, and that one summer she was riding to her mother's home in a small carriage, carrying my eldest aunt in her arms, when she encountered some bandits

on the road. They took her gold earrings from her, but not this bracelet. Had it been made of gold or silver, there was the danger it too
would have been taken by them.

After hearing this story I asked her: "Where is my eldest aunt
now?"

Granddad chuckled as Grandmother answered me: "Your eldest
aunt's children are all older than you."

So this incident had happened some forty years earlier; no wonder
I wasn't aware of it! Yet here I was, wearing that very same wicker
bracelet, so I raised my arm and twirled it in the air, which made it
look like some kind of windmill as it slithered up my arm—you see,
the bracelet was too big and my arm too thin.

Grandmother often observed me moving the things from the past
out of the room and scolded me: "There's nothing you won't play
with, child! You'll never amount to anything."

Though this was what she was saying, still she seemed to gain
some satisfaction from the reminiscences this opportunity to see
these objects from her past in broad daylight afforded her. Consequently, her scolding wasn't particularly harsh at all, and naturally
I paid no heed, but went right on picking up whatever I pleased.

As a result, these things in our house that had not seen the light
of day for the longest time reappeared only because I had brought
them out. Afterwards they either wound up broken or discarded,
until they all finally ceased to exist.

This was how I passed the first winter that I can remember. Although I didn't actually feel lonely, it could never be as much fun as
playing in the rear garden. But then, children forget easily and can
make the best of any situation.

IV

The following summer we planted a lot of leeks in the rear garden
because Grandmother liked to eat dumplings stuffed with leeks. But
by the time the leeks began to appear, Grandmother had become

seriously ill and could not eat them, and since no one else in the family ate leeks, they were left neglected in the garden.

Owing to Grandmother's serious illness the house was all a-bustle; my eldest aunt and my second aunt both came.

Second Aunt came in a carriage owned by her husband's family and pulled by a donkey with a bell around its neck that tinkled loudly as it stood beneath the window.

First out of the carriage was a child who hopped down onto the ground. This child, who was my second aunt's son, was a little taller than I. His nickname was Little Orchid, and Granddad told me to call him Orchid Brother. I don't remember what else happened, and I only recall that before long I was leading him out into the rear garden. I told him that this was a rosebush, this was called a foxtail, and the cherry tree no longer bore any fruit.

I didn't know if he had ever seen me before, but I was sure I had never laid eyes on him. As I was leading him over to look at the plum tree in the southeast corner, he said to me as we approached it: "This tree died the year before last."

He surprised me when he said this. How did he know that this tree had died? I began to experience pangs of jealousy, as I felt that this garden belonged to me and Granddad, and that other people had no right to know anything about it.

"Then you've been to our home before?" I asked him.

He answered that he had.

This made me even angrier; why wasn't I informed that he had been to our home before?

"When were you here?"

He said it had been the year before last, and that he had brought me a little stuffed monkey. "Don't you remember? After you grabbed the stuffed monkey and ran off, you fell down and started to bawl!"

Hard as I tried, I couldn't remember the incident. But at any rate, considering that he had given me a stuffed monkey and was nice to me, I could no longer be angry at him.

From then on we played together every day. He was eight years old—three years my senior—and he told me he was studying in a school. He had even brought a few books along with him, which he took out and showed me in the evenings beneath the light of a kerosene lamp. The words for "people," "scissors," and "house" were printed inside, and since there were illustrations for all of them, I was confident I could read the words the moment I saw them, so I said: "This is read *chien-tao*, for 'scissors,' and this is read *fang-tzu*, for 'house.' "

"No," he corrected me, "this is the single character *chien*, and this is *fang*."

I pulled the book over and looked closely. Sure enough, there was only one character given for each, not two; I had been going by the illustrations, and so I was wrong. I also had a box of flash cards with illustrations on one side and the characters on the other, so I brought them out and showed them to him.

From that time on we played together all day long, every day. I was no longer aware of the state of Grandmother's illness, although I noticed that a few days before she died they put a set of new clothes on her, as though she were going visiting. They said they were afraid that if she died there wouldn't be enough time to dress her in new clothing.

Because of the seriousness of Grandmother's illness there was a great deal of activity at our house, with many relatives coming to call, all of them busily doing one thing or another. Some were noisily tearing out strips and patches of white cloth; off to the side others were sewing these patches together; while still others were filling small jars with rice and sealing the mouths with red cloth. Someone else went out into the rear garden to set up a fire for frying wheat cakes.

"What are those?" I asked.

"These are cakes to ward off dogs."

She told me there are eighteen check stations in the nether world, and when you reach the station of the canines, the dogs there will come up to try and bite you. But if you throw out some of those cakes, the dogs will eat them instead of attacking. It seemed to me that she was just talking to hear herself talk, so I didn't pay any attention to what she was saying.

The more people who came to our house, the lonelier I got. I would walk into a room to ask about this or that, but it was all beyond my comprehension. Even Granddad seemed to have forgotten me. Once, after catching an especially large grasshopper in the rear garden, which I took in to show him, he said without even looking: "That's fine, that's just fine. Now you go out and play in the garden, all right?"

On days when Orchid Brother wasn't with me, I just played in the rear garden all alone.

V

Grandmother was now dead, and everyone else had already been to the services at the Dragon King Temple and returned; as for me, I was still playing in the rear garden.

A light rain started to fall there, so I decided to go inside and get my straw hat. As I walked by the pickling vat (at our house the pickling vat was located in the rear garden), I noticed a couple of drops of water land noisily on the lid, and it occurred to me that since the lid was so large, it would keep the rain off me a lot better than my straw hat. So I flipped it over onto the ground where it rolled around a bit, just as the rain started falling heavily. With a great deal of difficulty I managed to find a way to squeeze myself under the lid, which was really too big for me to handle—it was almost as tall as I was.

I stood up and walked a few steps with it on my head, but I couldn't see a thing; it was so heavy it made walking very difficult. I had no idea where my steps were taking me, and all I noticed was the pitter-patter of rain above my head. Then I looked down at my feet and discovered that I was standing in a patch of foxtails and leeks. When I found a spot thick with leek plants I sat down and was immediately pinned to the ground by the lid, which now must have looked like a little roofed cottage. This was a lot better than standing, because I no longer had to carry the lid on my head—it was now supported by the patch of ground where the leeks were growing. But inside it was so pitch dark I couldn't see a thing.

Meanwhile all the noises I heard seemed to be coming from far away. The big tree was rustling in the wind and rain, but it sounded as though it had been moved over into someone else's compound. The leeks had been planted at the base of the north wall, and I was sitting on the leeks. Since the north wall was a long way from the house, the noises of activity inside the house seemed to be coming to me from a great distance.

I listened very carefully for a while, but, unable to distinguish any of the sounds, I just kept sitting there inside that little cottage of mine. What a great little cottage it was, safe from the wind and the rain. When I stood up I walked off supporting my roof on my head, which made me feel as carefree as can be. Actually, it was quite heavy and made walking very difficult.

I felt my way along, propping up the lid of the vat as I walked over to the back door of the house with the idea of showing Granddad what I was carrying on my head. The threshold of our back door was quite high off the ground, and since the vat lid was so big and heavy, I couldn't step over it. I didn't even have the strength to lift my legs. But with a great deal of effort I was finally able to pull them over with my hands, and I had more or less stepped across. Having entered the house, I still didn't know which way to go to find Granddad, so I shouted at the top of my voice. But before the sound had died out my father gave me a kick that sent me sprawling, almost knocking me into the wood fire burning in the stove. The vat lid had crashed to the ground where it was rolling around.

After being helped to my feet, I looked around: something was very wrong here—everyone was dressed in white clothing. Another look, and I could see that Grandmother was sleeping, but not on her k'ang; she was laid out on top of a long piece of wood.

From that day on Grandmother was dead.

VI

Following Grandmother's death a continuous stream of relatives came to our house. Some of them brought incense and paper money with them, went over and wailed beside the corpse for a moment, then left to return home. Some came with bundles of all sizes and stayed over with us.

While trumpets blared by the main gate, a mourning tent was erected in the courtyard; wailing sounds filled the air throughout the whole noisy affair, which lasted for more days than I could count. Buddhist monks and Taoist priests were brought over, and the commotion of all that eating, drinking, talking, and laughing lasted late into the night.

It was fun for me too, and I was happy then, especially since now I had some little playmates, where before I had had none. Altogether there were four or five of them, some older than I, some younger. We climbed the tree and clambered up onto the walls, and nearly climbed up onto the roof of the house. They took me to catch pigeons on top of the small gate, and moved the ladder over under the house eaves so that we could catch some sparrows. Spacious as my rear garden was, it was no longer big enough to hold me.

I went with them over to the edge of the well and looked down inside. I had never seen just how deep that well was. When I shouted into it, someone down inside answered me; then I threw down a rock, and the noise it made when it hit the bottom came from far away. They also took me over to a grain storeroom and to a grain mill, and on occasion they even took me out onto the street. I had left the confines of my home, and not in the company of anyone in the family. I had never gone so far before.

The fact that there were bigger places than my own rear garden had never occurred to me, and as I stood there at the side of the street I was not so much looking at all the activity or at the people, animals, and carts, but wondering if someday I could travel as far as this all by myself.

One day they took me to the south bank of the river, which wasn't all that far from my house—probably less than a *li*—but since it was the first time I had ever gone there, it seemed to me that it was a long way off, and I worked up a sweat getting there. On our way we passed a loess pit and a military barracks with soldiers standing guard at the entrance. The courtyard in front of the barracks building looked much too large to me, larger than it had any right to be. The courtyard in our house was already big enough, so how could their courtyard be so much bigger? It was so big it had an unappealing look about it, and even after we had passed by I kept turning my head back to look at it.

Then we passed a house on the road where the people had placed some potted plants along the top of the wall. This didn't seem like such a good idea to me, because someone might come along and steal them when no one was looking.

I also saw a small Western-style house that appeared to be ten times better than my own house. If you had asked me what was so good about it, I couldn't have told you, but to my eyes it looked new from top to bottom and not at all worn-down like our house. I had traveled no more than half a *li* or so, but I had already seen an awful lot, which fortified my belief that the south bank of the river must be a long way off.

"Are we there yet?"

"Just about; we're almost there," they answered.

And just as they had promised, as soon as we rounded the corner of the barracks wall the river came into view. This was the first time I had ever seen the river, and I was at a loss to figure out where its waters came from and how many years they had flowed here. It seemed enormous; I scooped up some dirt along the bank and threw it into the river without dirtying the water even a tiny bit. There were a few boats on the river heading in either direction, some of which were being rowed over to the apparently deserted opposite shore, which was lined with willow trees. I looked off even farther, but I didn't know what places I was seeing, since there weren't any people or houses or roads over there, and no sounds to be heard. I wondered whether someday I could go over to that deserted place myself and take a look around.

Beyond the rear garden at my house there was a wide street; beyond the street there was a wide river; beyond the river there was a willow grove; beyond the willow grove there were places even farther away, deserted places where there was nothing to be seen and no sounds to be heard. What else might there be beyond these places? The more I pondered this, the harder it was to come up with an answer.

Without mentioning all the things that I hadn't seen in my life, let's just talk of the courtyard and the potted plants: we had a courtyard and potted plants at my house too, but the barracks courtyard was much bigger than ours, and at our house we put the potted plants in the rear garden, while others put theirs on the tops of walls. It was obvious that there was a lot I didn't know.

And so Grandmother died, while I actually gained in wisdom.

VII

After Grandmother died I began to study poetry with Granddad. Now that Granddad's room was empty, I caused a big scene with my demands to sleep in there with him.

I recited poems in the mornings and in the evenings, and I even recited them when I woke up in the middle of the night. I would recite for a little while until I was drowsy, then go back to sleep. Granddad taught me the verses in the *Thousand Poet Classic*, though we didn't use a book, but relied instead on his memory. He would recite a line and then I would recite it after him.

Granddad would recite:

> I left home young, I return an old man . . .

Then I would recite:

> I left home young, I return an old man . . .

I couldn't have told you just what the words meant, but they sounded good when I said them, so I shouted them out gleefully along with Granddad, though I was always louder than he was.

Whenever I recited poems I could be heard in every room in the house, and since Granddad was afraid I would injure my voice with all that shouting, he often said to me: "You're going to blow the roof right off the house!"

I would smile at this joke of his for a moment, but before long I was shouting again.

In the evening I shouted as always, until Mother scared me by saying if I kept it up she would spank me. Even Granddad said: "No one recites poetry like you do; that isn't 'reciting' poetry, it's just a lot of screaming."

But there was no way I could change my habit of screaming, and if I couldn't shout, what was the use in reciting them anyway? Whenever Granddad started to teach me a new poem, if I didn't like the way it sounded, right away I said: "I'm not going to learn that one."

Then he would choose another one, and if it didn't please me either, I'd say no to it too.

> I slept in spring not conscious of the dawn,
> But heard the gay birds chattering all around.
> I remember, there was a storm at night;
> I know not how many blossoms fell to the ground.

I really liked this poem, and whenever I got to the second line, "But heard the gay birds chattering all around," the words "all around" pleased me no end. I really thought this had a nice ring to it, especially the words "all around."

There was another poem, "Flower Shadows," which I liked even better:

> Layer upon layer they cover the steps;
> The servant, summoned often, still cannot sweep them away.
> Taken from sight with the setting of the sun,
> The moon brings them back at the close of day.

I had no idea what the words, "The servant, summoned often, still cannot sweep them away" meant, and I always said, "Serving some off the sill cannot sweep them away."

The more I recited it the better it sounded to me, and my interest grew with each recitation. Whenever we had company in our home Granddad had me recite my poems, and this is the one I liked doing the most. I don't know if the guests understood what I was saying, but they nodded their heads and complimented me.

VIII

Just memorizing a lot of poems without any understanding of their meaning wasn't the long-range plan, and after I had memorized dozens of them, Granddad explained to me what they meant.

> I left home young, I return an old man;
> The speech is the same, though my hair is thin.

"This is about someone who left home to go out into the world when he was young and returned when he was an old man," Granddad explained. " 'The speech is the same, though my hair is thin' means that the accent of his hometown remains the same even though his beard has all turned white."

"Why did he leave home when he was young?" I asked. "Where was he going?"

"Well, it would be just like your Grandpa here leaving home when he was about your age, then returning as old as he is now. Who would know him after all that time? 'The children see me, not knowing who I am / They smile and ask: "Stranger, where do you come from?" ' You see, he is met by the children, who call out to him: 'Say, where have you come from, white-bearded old man?' "

I didn't like what I was hearing, so I quickly asked Granddad: "Will I be leaving home? Won't even you recognize me when I come home with a long white beard, Grandpa?"

My heart was filled with foreboding, but Granddad laughed and said: "Do you think your Grandpa will still be around when you get old?"

After he said this he could see I was still unhappy, so he quickly added: "You won't be leaving home . . . how could you leave home? Now, hurry up and recite another poem! Let's hear 'I slept in spring not conscious of the dawn'!"

As soon as I began reciting "I slept in spring not conscious of the dawn" out came the shouts again, and my contentment returned. I couldn't have been happier, and everything else was forgotten.

But from then on I made sure that every new poem was explained to me first, and I made sure also that the ones I had already learned were explained. It seemed like my habit of shouting and screaming had changed a little for the better.

> Two yellow orioles sing in the green willows;
> A line of egrets climb into the blue sky.

At first I liked this poem a great deal, because I mistook the word for "orioles" as the word for "pears," and pears were one of my very favorite fruits. But after Granddad explained that this poem was about a couple of birds, I completely lost interest in it.

> This time last year behind this gate
>   her face and the blossoms glowed in the peach trees.
> Now the face is no more; only the blossoms
>   are still smiling in the spring breeze.

I didn't understand this poem either when Granddad recited it for me, but I liked it anyway. That was because peach blossoms were mentioned in it. After all, don't peach blossoms bloom just before the fruit appears? And aren't peaches delicious to eat?

So each time I finished reciting this poem I quickly asked Granddad: "Will there be any flowers on our cherry tree this year?"

Next to reciting poetry, my favorite activity was eating.

I recall that the family who lived to the east of the main gate raised pigs, and there was always a bunch of little pigs following behind their sow. One day one of the little pigs fell down the well, and although someone fished it out with a dirt-carrying basket, it was already dead by the time they got it up. A lot of people had gathered around the sides of the well to see what all the commotion was, and Granddad and I were there to join in the excitement.

As soon as they had gotten the little pig out of the well, Granddad said he wanted it. He carried it home, where he packed it in yellow clay, then stuck it into the stove and cooked it. When it was done he gave it to me to eat. I stood beside the *k'ang* with the whole pig lying there in front of my eyes, then when Granddad split it open, oil oozed out. It was so fragrant—I had never had anything that smelled as good in my whole life, and I had never eaten anything that tasted so delicious.

The next time it was a duck that fell down the well; Granddad also packed it in yellow clay and cooked it for me to eat. I helped him do the cooking—that is, I helped him with the yellow clay, yelling and shouting all the while, just like a cheerleader rooting him on.

The duck tasted even better than the pig because there wasn't much fat on it, and so duck became my favorite food.

Granddad sat beside me watching as I ate, but he wouldn't take any for himself until after I had finished. He said that I had small teeth, which made it harder to bite, so he wanted me to eat the tenderest portions first, then he would eat whatever was left.

Granddad sort of nodded his head with each swallow I took and made lighthearted comments like: "What a greedy little thing you are," or "This little thing sure eats fast."

My hands were dripping with oil, which I rubbed on my lapels as I ate. Granddad said without a trace of anger: "Quickly, add a little salt and some leeks; you shouldn't eat that without anything else, or before you know it you'll have an upset stomach. . . ." So saying, he picked up a pinch of salt and put it on the piece of duck meat I was holding. I opened my mouth and stuffed the whole thing in.

The more Granddad praised my appetite, the more I ate. Starting to worry that I might eat too much, he finally told me to stop, and I put it down. I knew for sure that I couldn't eat another bite, but still I said: "Even a whole duck isn't enough for me!"

From that time on I thought a great deal about eating duck, but the longest time went by without another duck falling into the well. On one occasion I saw a flock of them in the vicinity of the well, so I picked up a stick and tried to drive them into it. But they just scattered and ran round and round the mouth of the well making loud quacking noises, and still none of them fell in. I yelled out to the kids nearby that were watching all the fun: "Give me a hand here!"

While we were shouting and running around, Granddad hurried over and asked:

"What's going on here?"

"I'm driving the ducks over to the well so one of 'em will fall in; then we can fish it out and cook and eat it."

"There's no need to do that; your Grandpa will catch one for you and take it home and cook it."

But instead of listening to him, I kept chasing after the ducks. He stepped in front of me and brought me to a stop, then picked me up in his arms and wiped the sweat off me as he said: "You come home with me now; I'll get a duck and cook it for you."

I thought to myself: Since you can't catch a duck unless it's fallen into the well, does he expect one of them to just walk over and allow itself to be packed in yellow clay and cooked? I struggled to get down out of Granddad's arms as I yelled: "I want one that's fallen down the well! I want one that's fallen down the well!"

Granddad could barely hold me.

4 THE COMPOUND *I*

By the time summer arrived the mugwort had grown as high as an adult's waist and was over my head; if the yellow dog ran in amidst it, you couldn't see a trace of him. The mugwort rustled in the night winds, and since it virtually covered the courtyard, the rustling noise was especially loud as big clumps moved noisily with each gust. When it rained, clouds of mist rose from the tips of the stalks, and even if the rainfall was actually a light one, it seemed to be quite heavy to anyone who was looking at the mugwort. During light drizzles the mugwort took on a hazy, indistinct appearance, as though covered by a layer of fog or an overcast sky. The scene was one of a frosty morning where everything is blurred under a pall of rising vapor.

The courtyard turned dreary with the coming of the winds and rain, and even on a clear day with the sun shining brightly in the sky the courtyard remained dreary-looking. There were no dazzling or eye-catching decorations there, nor a trace of any man-made objects. Everything just followed its own nature: if it wanted to grow this way, it grew this way; if it wanted to grow that way, it grew that way. A natural, primitive scene would have been maintained if only it had been left alone, but something was wrong here. What sort of scenery was this? Off to the east there was a pile of rotten wood, while off to the west the ground was covered with discarded firewood; to the left of the gate a layer of old bricks, to the right a pile of clay drying in the sun.

The clay had been used by the cook when he put up the kitchen stove, and he had just dumped the remainder beside the gate. If someone had asked him whether or not the leftover clay could serve any purpose, I doubt that he could have come up with any, and he had probably just forgotten all about it.

I hadn't the slightest idea what the old bricks were for, as they had been there for a long time, buffeted by the wind, baked by the sun, and drenched by the rain. But since bricks are impervious to water, it really didn't matter that they got rained on. As a result, no one gave them a moment's thought, and just let them get rained on. In fact, there was no reason to bother about them; if it happened that the stove or the opening beneath one of the k'angs was in need of repair, they could still be used for the job. There they were, right in front of you—you merely had to reach out and pick them up, and what could be handier than that? At any rate, the stove seldom needed fixing, and the openings of the k'angs were well put together. I don't know where they found such competent workmen, but the k'ang openings held up for at least a year; if they were repaired in September, by the middle of the following year they were still holding up, and then when September rolled around again a plasterer and a bricklayer were called, who had to use a metal knife to remove and replace the bricks one at a time. And so that pile of bricks by the side of the gate served little purpose the year round. It remained there year after year, though it most likely grew smaller as time went on, with this family taking one to use as a base for a flower pot, and that family taking one for something or other. If the reverse had been true—that the pile had grown bigger as time went on—things would have been in a sad state, for wouldn't they have gradually blocked the entire gate?

But, in fact, the pile did grow smaller. With no interference by man, the natural course of events saw to it that the pile would completely disappear within two or three years. At the time, however, it was still there in front of us, soaking up the sun just like the pile of clay nearby; the two piles kept each other company.

Additionally, there were also the splintered remains of a large vat which had been tossed over by the base of the wall, and an earthen jar with a chipped and broken mouth that rested on the ground alongside it. The jar had been put out there empty, but was now half-filled with rainwater; if you picked it up in your hand by the lip and shook it, you could see a tiny world of living creatures swimming around. Looking a little like fish and a little like insects, they were actually neither, and I could not tell just what they were. Looking at the big vat that was already splintered and standing there very precariously, threatening to topple over, you could see that there was nothing at all inside it. Actually, I shouldn't be saying "inside," since it was split wide open, and there was no longer any "inside" or "outside" to speak of; let's just call it a "vat pedestal." This vat pedestal, on top of which there was nothing, was delightfully smooth and shiny, and it even made a resounding noise when I slapped it with my hand. When I was young I liked to move it from one spot to another, for I was always fascinated by what I found: beneath the vat pedestal were swarms of sowbugs. When I saw them I was startled into running away, but after running off some distance I would stop, turn back and take a long look, watching the sowbugs scurry around for a moment before they crawled back under the vat pedestal.

Then just why wasn't this vat pedestal thrown away? Probably it had been left there for the purpose of raising sowbugs.

Opposite the vat pedestal stood an overturned hog trough. I don't know how many years this hog trough had lain there upside down, but it was already rotting away. The bottom was covered with dark colored mushrooms, small ones that didn't look as though they were edible, and I never could figure out what they were growing there for. A rusty old steel plow was lying in the grass beside the trough.

Strange as it may sound, everything at our house seemed to come in twos; there were only pairs, no single items: The bricks lying in the sun had the clay to keep them company, the broken jar was matched up with the splintered vat, and the hog trough was accompanied by the steel plow. It was as though they were paired or mated to each other. Not only that, each couple brought new life into the world. There were, for example, the fishlike creatures in the jar, the sowbugs beneath the vat, the mushrooms that grew on the hog trough, and so on.

I don't know why, but the steel plow didn't look as though any new life was associated with it; meanwhile, it was falling apart and covered with rust. Nothing was born of it, nothing grew from it—it just lay there turning rusty. If you touched it with your finger, flakes fell to the ground, and although it was made of steel, it had by this time deteriorated so much that it looked as though it were made of clay that was on the verge of crumbling to pieces. When viewed alongside its mate, the wooden trough, there was absolutely no comparison—it was covered with shame. If this plow had been a person it would doubtless have wept and wailed loudly: "I'm made of better stuff than the rest of you, so why has my condition weakened to its present state?"

Not only was it deteriorating and rusting, but when it rained, the rusty pigment that covered it began to run, spreading with the rain water over to its companion, the hog trough, the bottom half of which had already been stained the color of rust. The fingers of murky water spread farther and farther away, staining the ground they touched the color of rusty yellow.

II

My home was a dreary one.

Just inside the front gate, along the eastern wall of the covered gateway, were three dilapidated old rooms, and along the western wall were three more. With the covered gateway in the middle, they gave the appearance of seven rooms standing in a line. From the outside they looked to be very imposing with their tall roofs and sturdy frames of thick, solid wood. The posts were so thick that a child could not wray his arms around one. All the buildings were roofed with tiles, and the ridges were adorned with tile decorations that were a delight to behold when the sun glinted off them. Each end of the house ridge was finished off with a pigeon, which was probably also made of tile. They remained there all year long, never moving. From the outside these buildings didn't look bad.

But to my eyes there was an emptiness about them.

Our family used the three buildings to the west to store grain—

there wasn't all that much grain kept in them, but there were hordes of rats. Holes had been chewed through the granary floors by the rats, whole families of which were eating the grain. And while down below it was being consumed by rats, up above it was being eaten by sparrows. A rank, moldy odor filled the rooms. The broken windows had been boarded up; the dilapidated doors shook on their hinges when they were opened.

The three buildings along the eastern wall beside the covered gateway were rented out to a family of hog farmers. Inside and out, there were nothing but "hogs"—grown hogs and newborn hogs, hog troughs and hogfeed. The only people who came and went there were hog dealers; the buildings, the people, everything was permeated with a horrible stench.

Come to speak of it, that family didn't raise all that many hogs, perhaps eight or ten. Every day at dusk people far and near could hear the sounds of their hogcalls as they banged on the troughs and the tops of the sties. They would shout a few times, then stop; their voices rose and fell, and in the solemn evening air it sounded like they were complaining of the loneliness of their lives.

There were, in addition to these seven rooms standing in a row, six more dilapidated buildings—three run-down huts and three milling sheds.

The three milling sheds were rented out to the family of hog farmers, since they were located right next to the sties.

The three run-down huts, which were in the southwest corner of the compound, had run off by themselves a long way from everything else, and were standing all alone, squalid-looking and leaning to one side or the other.

The roofs of these buildings were covered with lichens, and from a distance appeared as an eye-catching patch of green. When it rained, mushrooms grew on the roofs, which the people climbed up to pick, like they were foraging for mushrooms on a mountain. There was always a bumper crop. Rooftops that produced mushrooms were a rare sight indeed, and of the thirty or so buildings my family owned, none of the others could boast this distinction. So whenever the people who lived there took their baskets up onto the roof to pick mushrooms, everyone in the compound would begin to comment enviously: "Those mushrooms are certainly nice and fresh, so much better than the dried ones we have. If you killed a young chicken and fried it along with them, it would be simply delicious!"

"Fried bean curd and mushrooms—my, wouldn't that be tasty!"

"Even a baby chick isn't as tender as rain-fed mushrooms."

"If you fried chicken with some of those mushrooms, everyone would eat the mushrooms and leave the chicken."

"If you cooked some noodles with those mushrooms, everyone would drink the soup and forget the noodles."

"It would be quite a feat if someone could even remember his name while he was eating those mushrooms."

"If you steamed them and added some sliced ginger, you could eat at least eight bowls of steamed rice along with them."

"It'd be a mistake to treat something like those mushrooms lightly, because they're an unexpected windfall!"

The envious people who shared the compound hated themselves for not having had the good fortune to live in those huts, and if they had known that the crop of mushrooms went with the buildings, they would have insisted they be rented to them. Whoever heard of such luck—renting a house with mushrooms thrown into the bargain! They just stood there sighing and commiserating with one another.

Then, of course, what glory came to the person who was standing on the roof picking mushrooms under the scrutiny of all those eyes! So he picked them very slowly, and a job that should have taken no longer than the time it takes to smoke a pipeful was stretched out to perhaps half the time it takes to eat a meal. Not only that, he purposefully picked several of the larger ones and threw them down, saying as he did so: "Just look at those, will you! Have you ever in your life seen cleaner mushrooms than those? There isn't another rooftop around that has mushrooms like these."

The people down below had no way in the world of knowing just how big the rest of the mushrooms on the roof were, so they had to assume that they were all the size of the ones thrown down, which increased their astonishment no end. They hastily bent over, picked them up, and carried them home; then at dinnertime, when the bean-curd peddler came around, they splurged several coins on a little piece of bean curd and cooked it up with the mushrooms.

But, owing to his feelings of pride, the fellow on top of the house had forgotten that there were several bad spots on the roof, some of which had even sprung holes, and in a careless moment he put his foot completely through the roof. He pulled his foot back up through the hole only to discover that his shoe was missing.

The shoe had fallen from the ceiling straight down into a pot in which water was just then being boiled, and so his shoe was cooked in the pot of boiling water. The people who were sifting bean flour alongside the pot were both intrigued and amused by the sight of a shoe bobbing around in the boiling water; a murky substance oozed from the sole of the shoe, turning all the bean noodles that had already been sifted a yellowish color. But still they didn't fish the shoe out of the pot, their explanation being that the bean noodles were to be sold anyway, and weren't intended for their own consumption.

The roof over this house could produce mushrooms, but it couldn't keep out the rain, and each time it rained, the whole room filled up like a jar of water. Everything in the room was wet to the touch.

Fortunately, the people who lived there were all coarse individuals. There was a child with a crooked nose and staring eyes whose nickname was Iron Child. He held an iron shovel in his hands all day long, which he used to chop things in a long trough. But what exactly was he chopping? When you first entered the place you couldn't see clearly because of the clouds of steam that filled the room and prevented you from discerning what anyone was doing there. Only when you had a chance to look more closely would you see that what he was chopping was potatoes. The trough was filled with potatoes.

This particular hut was rented out as a flour shop where noodles were made out of bean flour. The people there were a coarse lot who could not afford to wear good shoes or socks and owned no decent bedding. There wasn't much difference between them and pigs, so that living in this type of building was very appropriate—if they had lived in a nice home they would probably have turned it into a pigsty in no time. Then, of course, their diet was enhanced by the addition of mushrooms every time it rained.

When the people who lived in this bean-flour mill had mushrooms to eat, they always mixed them with the bean flour they milled: they had fried mushrooms and bean flour, stewed mushrooms and bean flour, and boiled mushrooms and bean flour. When there was no soup they called it "fried," when there was soup they called it "boiled," and when there was slightly less soup they called it "stewed."

Often, after making such a meal, they brought a large bowlful over to give to Granddad. He would wait for the boy with the crooked nose and staring eyes to leave, then say: "We can't eat this; if there were something poisonous in it, we might die of food poisoning."

But no one in the bean-flour mill ever died of food poisoning, and as a matter of fact, they spent the day singing as they sifted the bean flour.

A rack several feet tall had been erected in front of the bean-flour mill, from which shiny lengths of bean noodles hung like cascading waterfalls. All the time the people were hanging out the noodles they were singing to themselves, and after the noodles had dried in the sun, they gathered them in, still singing as they worked. Their songs were not an expression of the joys of their work; rather they were like sounds of someone laughing with tears in his eyes.

Stoically they accepted their hardships: "You say that the life I live is a pitiable one; well, that's all right with me. In your eyes I am in mortal danger, but my life gives me satisfaction. And if I were not satisfied, what then? Isn't life made up more of pain than pleasure anyway?"

The songs that emerged from that bean-flour mill were like a red flower blooming atop a wall—the brighter and lovelier it was, the more desolate the feeling it evoked.

On the fifteenth day of the very first month
Lanterns are hung by one and all;
While others' husbands are reunited at home,
Meng Chiang-nü's spouse labors on the Great Wall.

On clear days, as the bean noodles were being hung out to dry, this song could always be heard. Inasmuch as the hut was located in the southwest corner, the sounds of the singing were more distant than others. Once in a while someone imitating a woman singing "The Daybreak Lament" could be heard.

The hut they lived in was certainly beyond repair. Every time there was a heavy rain a new support had to be placed on the northern side of the building, and eventually there were as many as seven or eight such struts, but still the house leaned farther and farther to the north every day. The lean grew more and more pronounced until it frightened me just to look at it. I could imagine its collapsing to the ground just at the moment I was passing by and pinning me beneath it. No question about it, the hut was in sad shape: the windows, which had originally been square, had become twisted out of shape by the lean of the building. The doorframe was so awry that you couldn't close the door, and the tie beams above the wall seemed on the verge of crashing to the ground; having broken loose they seemed about to leap out of the building. The central beam of the roof ridge moved a little farther north each day, since the tenons had already broken loose from the mortices, and there was nothing left to control it. It was now moving as a free agent. As for the smaller beams that had been nailed to the ridgepole of the building, those that were able to keep up with it just followed along this northward journey as a river follows its course; those that couldn't keep up simply wrested their nails loose and sagged downwards, hanging precariously over the heads of the people inside the bean-flour mill. They didn't come falling down because the other ends were anchored down by the outside eaves, so they just sagged and creaked.

I just had to go inside the mill and see how they sifted the bean flour, but I didn't dare survey the scene around me too closely, for fear that the beams would fall in on top of me.

When winds arose, the entire building creaked and groaned; the beams, the timbers, the doors, the windows—everything strained and moaned.

The rains, too, caused the building to creak, and in the nighttime, even if there was no wind or rain, there were still creaking noises. As night deepened and people noises died out, the creatures of the night began their chorus; how then could this building, whose nature it was to creak, be expected to keep silent?

In fact, its creaking noises could be heard above all else. The other sounds, though audible, were much less discernible, and not very reliable. Perhaps the people's ears were playing tricks on them, and the sounds were not there at all, for these were not the noises that one expected to hear, unlike the sounds of animate creatures like cats, dogs, and insects.

On more than one occasion someone heard a building crying out in the night; he would wonder just whose house it was that could cry out like that, making the plaintive sounds of a living creature, and so very loud. It invariably awakened whoever was sleeping inside. But the person who had been awakened merely turned over and said: "The house is on the move again."

It truly seemed as though he were talking about a living thing, and that the building was betaking itself to a new site. Now, since the building was off to a new location, wouldn't you think that the person sleeping inside would get out of bed? But no, he just rolled over and went back to sleep.

The people who lived in this hut felt no sense of danger regarding the possibility of its collapsing around them; they treated the building with such trust and confidence that one might suppose there was a blood relationship between them. It was as though even if the building did collapse someday, it would not fall on their heads, and even on the chance that it did, their lives would be spared—there was absolutely no danger of losing one's life. I don't know the origin of this extreme self-assurance, but perhaps the people who lived there were made not of flesh and bones, but of iron. Either that or they were like a suicide squad who placed little value on their own lives. Otherwise, how could they be so brave that they scoffed at death?

On second thought, it may be inaccurate to say that they scoffed at death, for on the occasions when the pole from which one of them was taking down strips of bean noodles that were drying in the sun crashed to the ground, that person was frightened speechless.

The noodles had been dashed into small pieces, but he had escaped being hit, and as he scooped up the noodles, he could not take his eyes off the pole; after reflecting for a moment, he commented: "If it hadn't. . . ."

The more he thought, the more bizarre it seemed to him—how could he have missed getting hit, while the noodles were shattered into pieces? He picked up the pole and put it back in place, then stood off a bit and sized it up, experiencing an ever-increasing apprehension. "Aiya! If that had fallen on top of my head . . . !" That truly was too alarming a prospect to imagine, and as he rubbed his head he was aware of just how fortunate he had been. He vowed to be more careful next time.

The truth of the matter is, the pole wasn't as thick as the house's roof beams, but the mere sight of it gave him a scare. From then on, each time he was hanging the bean noodles out to dry he shied away from that pole to the point of refusing to even walk by it, keeping a wary eye on it at all times. He forgot the incident only after the passage of many days.

During thunderstorms the people inside always doused their lights, for according to them, fire is thunder and lightning's mortal enemy, and they were afraid of being struck. Whenever they crossed the river they first threw two copper coins into the water, for legend has it that the river spirit is a rapacious one who often causes people to drown. But if copper coins are thrown in, he is appeased and will spare them.

All of this goes to prove that the people who lived in this creaky hut were just as timorous as anyone else and, like others, spent their days on this earth in mortal fear. That being the case, then why were they unafraid of the prospect of their house's collapsing on top of them?

According to Old Chao, the steamed-bun peddler: "That teetering building just happens to be the very one they want!"

According to the boy with the crooked nose and staring eyes who lived in the mill itself: "This is only a place to live; you don't have to look for perfection as you would in choosing a wife."

According to the two young gentry youths from the Chou family who shared our compound: "You couldn't find a more fitting place for coarse people like that to live in."

And according to Second Uncle Yu: "They're only interested in the cheapest place they can find. Since there are good houses all over the town of Hulan, you wonder why they don't just move, don't you? Well, a good house would cost them money, not like this place of ours. Here they can live for only ten or twenty catties of dry noodles a year, and that's it—why, it's the same as free rent. If your Second Uncle had no family, he would look for a place to live just like that one."

Perhaps there was some truth in what Second Uncle Yu said.

It had long been Granddad's plan to tear that building down, but several times the tenants had come en masse to persuade him not to, and thus it remained standing. As for the questions of whether or not the building would someday collapse, and whether it would bring good fortune or ill to those inside, that was considered by everyone something too far in the future to warrant any thought.

III

The compound in which we lived was a dreary one.

The occupants were some bean-flour sifters who lived on one side and some hog farmers who lived on the other. There was also a miller who lived in one of the side rooms belonging to the hog farmers. This miller would strike his wooden clappers at night, the whole night through. Among the family of hog farmers there were several individuals with time on their hands and little to do, who often got together to sing their Shensi opera to the accompaniment of a two-stringed violin. On clear days the bean-flour sifter in the southwest corner of our compound liked to sing the song "Daybreak Lament."

Now, although they played their two-stringed violins, struck wooden clappers, and sang this song, one must not be misled into believing that these were indications of prosperity or progress; it was certainly not that they could see a bright future ahead of them, nor even that they entertained any hopes for a bright future—it meant none of these things. They could see nothing that could be considered bright, nor could they have recognized it for what it was even if they had. They were like a blind man standing in the sun who, though unable to see the sun, can nonetheless feel the warmth on his head.

These people were like that: they did not know where the brightness was, but they were fully aware of the cold that enveloped their bodies. It was their struggling to break free from this cold that brought them to grief. Ushered into this world by their mothers without any real expectations, they could only hope to eat their fill and dress warmly enough. But they were forever hungry and cold.

Foully the affairs came; fairly they were accepted. Not in the course of their lifetimes did affairs ever come fairly.

The sounds of wooden clappers being struck at night in the mill shed often increased in intensity as the night deepened, and the more vigorously they were struck, the more desolate the sound. That was because they were the lone sounds in the night—there were no others to accompany them.

IV

The compound in which we lived was a dreary one.

A carter and his family lived in one of the siderooms attached to the bean-flour mill. The dance of the sorceress was frequently performed for this family's benefit, so there often arose from that place the sounds of drumbeats and chants. The sound of drums generally lasted late into the night, accompanied by talk of fairies and ghosts, and the ritual of dialogue between the sorceress and her assistant; they were mournful, distant sounds that confused one's sense of time. The old woman of this family was sick the year round, and the dance of the sorceress was performed for her benefit.

This family was more blessed than any other in the compound, with its three generations living together. Their family traditions were the best defined and the neatest: they treated one another with respect, there was mutual understanding and good feelings among the siblings, and a great deal of love between parent and child. There was no one in the family who was an idler or who had time on his hands. No similarity existed between them and the people who lived in the bean-flour mill or the mill shed, who spent so much of their time singing or weeping as the feeling moved them. No, their home was forever quiet and tranquil. Not counting, of course, the dance of the sorceress.

The grandmother in the family—the old woman who was always sick—had two sons, each of whom was a carter. Both of the sons had wives: the elder son's wife was a plump woman in her fifties; the younger son's wife a slim woman in her forties. In addition, the old woman had two grandsons: the elder grandson belonged to the woman's younger son, while the second grandson belonged to her elder son.

As a consequence, there was some small degree of disharmony insofar as relations between the two daughters-in-law were concerned, although it was not all that apparent, and perhaps only the two of them were aware of it. The wife of the elder son felt that the wife of the younger son treated her with less obedience and respect than might be called for, an attitude whose origin she suspected was the fact that her sister-in-law's son was older than her own. The younger daughter-in-law, on the other hand, felt that her sister-in-law was trying to ride herd over her, inasmuch as her son was too young to have a wife. To her, this meant that the elder woman was upset that she herself had no daughter-in-law to control.

With two sons and two grandsons, the old woman was unreservedly pleased with her life. How could the family fail to prosper with such an equitable arrangement for the distribution of family chores?

One need look no further than the operation of the big cart; there was enough combined strength here to handle it completely, and who else could boast of a cart handled by four men of the same family? Everyone—from the one holding the whip to those seated in the rear of the cart—was named Hu, so that no outsider was needed. And whatever the occasional domestic conflict that might arise, they presented themselves to the outside world as a close-knit family. For this reason the old woman had an optimistic view of life though she was constantly ill, and even that could be put out of her mind with the performing of the sorceress' dance. She felt that even if she should die, she would do so with her mind at peace and free of misgivings. But for the moment, there was still life in her body, which meant that she could continue to watch the labors of her sons with her own two eyes.

Her daughters-in-law also treated her quite well, seeing to her every need on a regular basis, and spending whatever was necessary to engage the sorceress to do her dance.

Each time the sorceress danced for her, the old woman reclined on her *k'ang*, her head resting on a pillow; straining into an upright position, she would say to the women and girls who had gathered to watch what was going on: "The arrangements this time were made by my elder daughter-in-law," or "The arrangements this time were made by my younger daughter-in-law." Saying this always gave her feelings of pride and satisfaction, so she said it over and over until she no longer had the strength to sit up. Since she was afflicted with paralysis, she would quickly call for her daughters-in-law to come and help her lie down, an effort that would leave her momentarily gasping for breath.

Among those who had gathered to watch the excitement there

was not a single one who didn't comment on the kindliness of the old woman and the filial behavior of her daughters-in-law. And so people came from far and near each time the sorceress visited her, from the east and west compounds and all the neighboring streets. The one thing they could not do was reserve a place, so the early arrivals sat on benches and on the edge of the *k'ang*, while those who came later had to stand.

At such times the Hu family briefly enjoyed a position of leadership in the community owing to the filial conduct of its members, who served as models for other women. Men, as well as women, made comments: "Providence has smiled on old Hu's family, and one day wealth will come to them as well."

"Of the three factors—weather, land, and morale—morale is the most important. If there is high morale, even if the weather is bad, or if the land is no good, it is still all right."

"You wait and see—today they are a family of carters, but in another five years, if they aren't a second-class family, they'll be at least a third-class one."

Second Uncle Yu's comment was: "You mark my word; before too many years have passed, they will own a stableful of donkeys and horses. Don't be fooled by the fact that they only own a single cart now."

There were no new developments in the disharmonious relationship between the two daughters-in-law, though it never completely worked itself out either.

The wife of the elder grandson, a red-faced young woman, was both capable and obedient. She was neither too fat nor too thin, neither tall nor short, and when she spoke her voice was neither loud nor soft. She was a woman perfectly suited to this family. When the cart returned home she led the horse over to the well to drink, and before the horse and cart left the compound, she fed the animal. To look at her you wouldn't have thought she was made for this type of rough life, but when she worked she seemed no frailer than anyone else, and in this respect suffered little in comparison even with the men.

After she had finished her duties outside the house she began her domestic chores, all of which she handled quite capably. Whether it was needlework, mending, or what have you, she managed everything just as you would expect it to be managed. And though there were no silks or satins in their house to work with, still the coarse materials had to be sewn with fine, even stitches.

Then, as New Year's approached, no matter how busy she might be, she nonetheless found time to make pairs of embroidered shoes for the old grandmother, her mother-in-law, and her aunt. Although she had to do without dainty shoe tops, even if she had only a piece of plain blue cloth to work with, the needlework still had to be delicately done. Since she had no silk thread, she had to use cotton thread instead, but she still managed to make the color combination fresh and crisp. The pair she made for her husband's grandmother were embroidered with large pink lotus petals, those for her aunt were festooned with peonies, and the pair for her mother-in-law were decorated with elegantly simple green-leafed orchids.

Whenever this young woman returned to her mother's home, she was asked how things were at the home of her husband. Her response was that everything was just fine, and that the family was destined someday to make its fortune. She told of her uncle's cautious and attentive nature, and how hard-working and capable of enduring hardship her father-in-law was. "The grandmother," she said, "is a good woman, as is her aunt, and in fact there isn't a person in the family who is anything but good." Everything was just as she would have wished it, and families like that are not easy for a woman to find. Granted that her husband had beaten her, but as she said: "What man does not beat his wife?" And so this did nothing to lessen her complete satisfaction with the way things had turned out.

When the grandmother was presented with the finished embroidered shoes, the fine workmanship caused her to experience a sense of guilt in her treatment of this wife of her grandson. She felt that with her ability to do such fine needlework, it was an insult to have her spend each day slopping the hogs and kicking the dogs. The old grandmother reached out and took the shoes from her, but not knowing what she should say, she held them gently in her hands and nodded her head with a smile on her ashen face.

We have thus seen how good a woman the wife of the elder grandson was. As for the second grandson, even though a wife had already been selected for him, he was still too young for the marriage to take place.

The fact that this girl had not yet been brought into the family was the cause of the ill feelings between the two daughters-in-law. The girl's prospective mother-in-law proposed that she be brought over as a child-bride, while the younger daughter-in-law objected, since the girl was too young to do anything but eat, and what good would that do them? They argued over this matter for some time without ever resolving the issue; it was always: "Wait till the next time we have the sorceress over for the old woman and we'll ask her opinion."

V

My home was a dreary one.

Roosters crowed before the sun was up, and the sound of the wooden clappers from the mill continued even after daybreak. Once the sky turned light, flocks of crows appeared in the sky. I slept beside Granddad, and as soon as he woke up, I asked him to recite some poems; and so he began:

> I slept in spring not conscious of the dawn,
> But heard the gay birds chattering all around.
> I remember, there was a storm at night;
> I know not how many blossoms fell to the ground.

"Someone sleeping on a spring morning slowly awakens to the new day, and the first thing he hears is the sound of birds all around. His thoughts return to the rainstorm of the night before, but he doesn't know how many fallen flowers are on the ground today."

Each reading of a poem was followed by an explanation, for this is what I had demanded.

As Granddad was explaining the poem to me, our family cook had already got up. I could hear him coughing as he carried the water bucket out to the well to fetch some water. Our well was quite far from the rooms where we slept. It was too distant for us to be able to hear the sound of the well rope being pulled up during the day, but in the early morning the sound came through loud and clear.

Even after the old cook had fetched his water, the others in the house were still asleep. Then came the sounds of the old cook scraping the pot. After he had scraped the pot clean he boiled some water for us to wash our faces, and still no one else was out of bed. Granddad and I continued to recite poems until the sun rose in the sky.

"Let's get up." Granddad said to me.

"Just one more poem."

"One more and then we've got to get up."

So we did one more, and when we had finished, I stalled by saying that that one didn't count, and I wanted to do one more.

Every morning we carried on like that. Once the door was opened, out we went into the garden, which by then was already flooded with light. The sun baked down on us as it climbed overhead. Granddad walked over to the chicken coop to let the chickens out, so that's where I went too; Granddad went over to the duck pen to let the ducks out, and I followed right behind him. I tagged along behind him with the big yellow dog following on my heels. I was hopping and jumping; the big yellow dog was wagging his tail.

The dog's head was the size of a small washbasin. He was a large dog, and round, and I was forever trying to ride him as I would a horse, though Granddad wouldn't allow it. Nonetheless, the big yellow dog liked me, and I loved him.

The chickens and the ducks came out of their coops, shook out their feathers, and began to run around the yard, cackling and quacking noisily. Granddad scattered some kernels of bright red sorghum on the ground, and then the golden kernels of some other grains.

Immediately the air was filled with the pecking sounds of chickens as they ate the feed on the ground.

After the chickens had been fed we looked up at the sky to see that the sun had climbed even higher. Granddad and I returned to the house, where we set up a small table; Granddad ate a bowl of rice porridge with sugar sprinkled on top. But I didn't eat. I wanted some baked corn, so he led me back out into the rear garden; then, walking on the dew-covered ground, he went over to the clump of corn stalks and pulled off an ear of corn for me. Our shoes and socks were soaked through by the time he had broken off the ear of corn.

Granddad told the cook to bake the corn for me, but by the time it was ready I had already eaten two bowls or more of sugared rice porridge. I took the corn from him, ate a few kernels, and complained that it wasn't any good—you see, I was by then already full. So what I did was take the corn out into the garden to feed Big Yellow. "Big Yellow" was the dog's name.

From out on the street beyond the wall came the voices of all the different peddlers: There was the bean-curd peddler, the steamed-bun peddler, and vegetable peddlers.

A vegetable peddler was calling out the things he had to sell—eggplants, cucumbers, various legumes, and scallions. After he had passed by with his basket of produce, another followed; but instead of eggplants and cucumbers, this one had celery, leeks, and cabbage to sell.

There was a good deal of noise and commotion out on the street, though our house remained quiet.

The mugwort-covered courtyard was the hiding place of hordes of chirping insects, as well as all sorts of discarded objects.

One would assume that my house was quiet because the day had just begun. But the truth of the matter was that there were a great many buildings, a large compound, and very few people living there. For that matter, even at high noon my house was still placid.

Each autumn, smartweed flowers covered the tops of the mugwort, bringing forth great numbers of dragonflies and butterflies that darted back and forth atop the dreary stretch of mugwort. But instead of bringing a look of luxuriance to the area, as one would expect, their presence increased the sense of gloom and loneliness one felt there.

5   THE CHILD-BRIDE   *I*

Except for the time I spent playing in our rear garden, accompanied by Granddad, I was left to my own devices to find amusement. Sometimes all by myself I pitched a makeshift tent beneath the eaves, then after playing for a while I would fall asleep there.

We had removable windows in our house that, when taken down, would stand up only if they were propped up against a wall, making a nice little lean-to. This I called my "little chamber." I often took naps there in my little chamber.

Our entire compound was covered with mugwort, over which swarms of dragonflies flew, attracted by the fragrance of the red smartweed flowers. I amused myself by catching dragonflies until I grew tired of it, after which I lay down in the mugwort and went to sleep.

Clumps of wild berries grew among the mugwort, looking like mountain grapes, and delicious to eat. I foraged for wild berries to eat among the mugwort, and when I grew weary of that I lay down beside the wild-berry bushes and went to sleep. The dense mugwort served as a kind of mattress for me as I lay atop it, and I also enjoyed the shade the tall grass offered.

One day just before suppertime, as the sun was setting in the west, I lay dreaming on my bed of mugwort. I must not have been sleeping all that soundly, for I seemed to hear a great many people talking somewhere nearby. They were chatting and laughing with real gusto, but I couldn't quite make out just what was happening. I could only sense that they were standing off in the southwest corner, either inside the compound or just beyond it—whether it was inside the compound or not, I simply couldn't tell—and out there somewhere there was quite a bit of excitement. I lay there half awake for a while, and the noise eventually died out; most likely I had fallen asleep again.

After I woke up I went into the house, where I was given the news by our old cook: "The Hu family's child-bride arrived, and you weren't even aware of it; hurry up and eat so you can go have a look at her!"

The old cook was busier than usual that day; he was carrying a platter of sliced cucumbers into Granddad's room with both hands, and his brief but animated conversation with me nearly caused him to drop the plate to the floor. In fact, the cucumber slices did slide off the platter onto the floor.

I walked into Granddad's room, where I found him sitting alone at the supper table with all the dishes laid out before him. There was no one else there to eat with him; Mother and Father hadn't come to supper, nor had Second Uncle Yu. Granddad saw me come in and asked: "How does the child-bride look?"

He apparently thought I had just come from taking a look at her. I told him I didn't know, that I had just come in after eating wild berries amidst the mugwort.

"Your mother and the others have all gone to look at the child-bride over at old Hu's house—you know, the one where the sorceress is always doing her dance." When he finished speaking, Granddad called out to the old cook to hurry up with the plate of cucumbers.

The cucumbers, lying in vinegar sauce and topped by hot-pepper oil, were an eye-catching mixture of greens and reds. I was sure he had had to slice another plateful, since I had seen the original one scattered on the kitchen floor. The moment the cucumber dish arrived, Granddad said: "Hurry up and eat, so we can go have a look at the child-bride."

The old cook stood off to the side, wiping his sweaty face with his apron. Every time he spoke he blinked his eyes and spurted saliva from his mouth.

"There certainly are a lot of people going over to see the child-bride!" he said. "Even the second wife of the grain shop owner took her kids and went over. Little Pockface from the compound behind us is over there too, and several members of old Yang's family from the west compound who climbed over the wall to get there." He said he had seen all this as he was drawing water from the well.

Exhilarated by this news of his, I said: "Grandpa, I'm not hungry; I want to go see the child-bride."

But Granddad was steadfast in wanting me to eat before he would take me over, though I was in such a hurry I didn't eat a very good supper. I had never in my life seen a child-bride, whom I imagined to be beautiful beyond words! The more I dwelled upon it, the more I was convinced that she must indeed be beautiful, and the more excited I grew, the stronger was my conviction that she could not but be a rare beauty. Otherwise, why was everyone so eager to see her? Otherwise, why would even Mother miss her supper?

I grew more and more fidgety, since I was sure that the best part of the show was already over. Now if I left right away, at the very least I would be able to see something worthwhile, but I was afraid I would be too late if I waited much longer. So I pressed Granddad: "Hurry, hurry up and eat, Grandpa, please hurry."

The old cook was still standing off to the side talking a blue streak, while Granddad asked him a question every once in a while. I could see that the cook was interrupting Granddad's meal, but even though I tried to get him to stop talking, he wasn't about to listen to me. He kept on chuckling and laughing, so finally I got down from my chair and literally pushed him from the room.

Granddad still hadn't finished when Third Granny from old Chou's house came over to report that their rooster kept running over to our house, and that she had come to fetch it. But instead of leaving after she had her rooster, she came up to the window and notified Granddad: "The little child-bride has already arrived at old Hu's. Aren't you going over to see her? There are lots of people over there taking a look, and I plan to go over after supper."

Granddad told her that he was going over after supper too, but it seemed to me that he would never finish his meal. First he asked for some more hot-pepper oil, then he wanted some salt. I could see that I wasn't the only one who was growing impatient—the old cook could barely contain himself; his brow was sweating profusely and his eyes were blinking continuously.

The moment Granddad put his rice bowl down, I began dragging him along with me over to the southwest corner of the wall without even letting him light up his pipe. As we hurried along, I experienced feelings of regret every time I saw someone coming back from watching all the fun. Why had I had to wait for Granddad anyway? Couldn't I have run over there by myself a long time ago? The recollection that I had heard some excitement coming from over here while I was lying in the mugwort added to my displeasure. Really, the more I thought about it, the stronger my regrets grew. This affair had already taken up half the afternoon, and I just knew that the good part was over, and that I was too late. Coming now was a waste of time—there was nothing more to be seen. Why hadn't I rushed over to take a look the second I heard all that talking and laughing while I was lying in the grass? My regrets grew so strong that I was getting mad at myself, and just as I had feared, when we drew up next to old Hu's window, there wasn't a sound coming from inside. I was so mad I nearly cried.

When we actually walked in the door, it wasn't at all as I had been led to expect. Mother, Third Granny Chou, and several people I didn't know were all there, and everything was contrary to what I had imagined; there was nothing worth seeing here. Where was the child-bride? I couldn't spot her anywhere until the others pointed and nodded, then I saw her. This was no bride, it was just a young girl! I lost all interest the moment I saw her, and I started pulling Granddad toward the door.

"Let's go home, Grandpa."

The next morning I saw her when she came out to draw some water to wash up. Her long black hair was combed into a thick braid; unlike most young girls, whose braids hung down to about their waists, hers came down almost to her knees. Her complexion was dark and she had a hearty laugh.

After the people in the compound had all taken a look at the child-bride of old Hu's family they agreed that apparently there was nothing wrong with her, except that she seemed a little too proud-spirited and didn't look or act much like a child-bride.

Third Granny Chou said: "She hasn't the least bit of shyness when she's with people."

Old Mrs. Yang from the next compound agreed: "She isn't even a tiny bit shy. Her very first day at her mother-in-law's house she ate three bowls of rice!"

Then Third Granny Chou said: "Gracious! I've never seen the likes of it. Even if she weren't a child-bride, but someone who came to the house already married to the boy, she'd still have to get to know what the people are like her first couple of days in the home. Gracious! She's such a big girl, she must be well into her teens!"

"I hear she's fourteen!"

"How could a fourteen-year-old be that tall? She must be lying about her age!"

"Not necessarily. Some people develop early."

"But how are they going to handle their sleeping arrangements?"

"You've got a good point there, since there are three generations of family and only three small k'angs."

This last response to Third Granny Chou came from old Mrs. Yang, as she leaned over the top of the wall.

As for my family, Mother was also of the opinion that the girl was not at all like a child-bride should be.

Our old cook said: "I've never seen the likes of her, with such a proud bearing and eyes that look right at you."

To which Second Uncle Yu added: "What's this world coming to when a child-bride doesn't look anything like a child-bride ought to?"

Only Granddad had nothing to say on the subject, so I asked him:

"What do you think of that child-bride?"

"She's quite all right," he said.

So I felt she was quite all right too.

Every day she led their horse to the well to drink, and I saw her on many of these occasions. No one properly introduced us, but she smiled when she saw me, and I smiled back and asked her how old she was.

"Twelve," she replied.

I told her she must be wrong: "You're fourteen—everybody says so."

"They think I'm too tall," she said, "and they're afraid people will laugh if they know I'm only twelve, so they told me to say I'm fourteen."

I couldn't figure out how being very tall would cause people to laugh.

"Why don't you come over and play in the grass with me?" I asked her.

"No," she said, "they won't allow it."

II

Before many days had passed, the people in that family began to beat the child-bride. They beat her so severely that her cries could be heard far away, and since none of the other families in the entire compound had any children, cries or shouts were seldom heard there.

As a result, this became *the* topic of conversation throughout the neighborhood. The consensus was that she had deserved a beating right from the start, for whoever heard of a child-bride with no trace of shyness, one who sat up straight as a rod wherever she was, and who walked with a brisk, carefree step!

Her mother-in-law, having led the family horse up to the well to drink one day, said to Third Granny Chou: "We've got to be harsh with her from the outset. You mark my words, I'm going to have to beat her when I go back to the house; this little child-bride of ours is really a handful! I've never seen the likes of her. If I pinch her on the thigh, she turns around and bites me, or else she says she's going home to her mother."

From then on the sounds of crying filled our compound daily; loud, bitter cries accompanied by shouts.

Granddad went over to old Hu's house several times to try to dissuade them from beating her, since she was just a young girl who didn't know much, and if there were problems in her behavior, he recommended trying to educate her. But as time went on the beatings grew even more severe, day and night, and even when I woke up in the middle of the night to recite my poems with Granddad I could hear the sounds of crying and shouting coming from the southwest corner of the compound.

"That's the child-bride crying, isn't it?" I would ask Granddad.

To keep me from being frightened, he would answer: "No, it's someone outside the compound."

"What could they be crying about in the middle of the night?" I would ask him.

"Don't concern yourself about that," he would say, "but just keep reciting your poems."

I got up very early, and just as I was reciting, "I slept in spring, not conscious of the dawn," the crying sounds from the southwest corner started in again. This continued for the longest time, and only when winter arrived did the sounds of her crying finally come to an end.

III

The sounds of weeping had been replaced by those of the sorceress, who came to the southwest corner every night to do her dance. The staccato beats of a drum resounded in the air, as the sorceress first chanted a line, and was then answered by her assistant. Since it was nighttime, the words they sang came through loud and clear, and I soon memorized every line.

There were things like: "Little spirit flower," and "May the Genie let her 'come forth.' " Just about every day the sorceress chanted these kinds of things.

Right after I got up in the mornings I started to minic her chants: "Little spirit flower, may the Genie let her 'come forth. . . .' " Then I went *"bong-bong, bang-bang,"* imitating the sounds of the drumbeat.

"Little spirit flower" meant the young girl; the "Genie" was supposed to be a fox spirit; to "come forth" meant to become a sorceress.

The sorceress performed her dances for nearly the whole winter, until she finally succeeded in causing the child-bride to fall ill. The child-bride soon had an unhealthy look about her, but even though her complexion was no longer as dark as it had been when she first arrived that summer, she retained her hearty laugh.

When Granddad took me over with him to visit her family, the child-bride even came over and filled his pipe for him. When she looked at me she smiled, but on the sly, as though she were afraid her mother-in-law would see her. She didn't speak to me.

She still wore her hair in a thick braid, but her mother-in-law told us she was ill and that the sorceress had been engaged to drive the evil spirits away. As Granddad was leaving their house, the mother-in-law walked out with him, saying in a low voice: "I'm afraid this child-bride isn't going to make it; she's being claimed by a genie who is determined to have her 'come forth.' "

Granddad would have liked to ask them to move, but here in Hu-lan there is a custom that the time for moving in the spring is March and in the autumn, September. Once March or September has passed, it is no longer the time for moving.

Each time we were startled out of our sleep in the middle of the night by the sorceress' dance, Granddad would say: "I'm going to ask them to move next March."

I heard him say this on any number of occasions. Whenever I imitated the shouts and cries of the sorceress and chanted "Little spirit flower," Granddad said the same thing—he'd ask them to move next March.

IV

But during the interim the commotion emanating from the south-west corner of our compound grew in intensity. They invited one sorceress and quite a few assistants, and the beat of drums resounded the day long. It was said that if they allowed the little child-bride to "come forth," her life would be in peril, so they invited many assistants in order to wrest her from the sorceress' clutches.

Whereupon many people volunteered their opinions to the family, for who would not come to the rescue of someone facing death? Every person of conscience and good will extended a helping hand; he would offer a special potion, she would share her magical charms.

Some advocated making a straw figure for the girl, to be burned in the big pit to the south.

Some advocated going to the ornament shop and having them make a paper figure called a "proxy doll," which could then be burned as her substitute.

Some advocated painting a hideous face on the girl, then inviting the sorceress over, with the expectation that when the sorceress saw her she would find her too ugly and reject her as a disciple; that way she would not have to "come forth."

But Third Granny Chou advocated that she be made to eat a whole, unplucked rooster—feathers, feet, and all—on a given star-filled night, then be covered with a quilt. She should be made to sweat it out until cockcrow of the following morning before allowing her to emerge from under the quilt. For after she ate a whole rooster and sweated profusely, a rooster would forever exist in her soul, and spirits, ghosts, genies, and the like would not dare try and possess her body. Legend has it that ghosts are afraid of roosters.

Third Granny Chou told of her own great-grandmother, who had fallen under the power of a genie and was in the throes of this agony for a full three years, on the verge of death. Eventually she was cured by this very method, and was never again ill for the rest of her life. Whenever she was having a bad dream during the night, one which would nearly frighten her to death, the rooster in her soul would come to her rescue by crowing and waking her from her nightmare. She was not ill another day in her life and, strange as it sounds, even her death was extraordinary. She died at the age of eighty-two, and even at that advanced age she was still able to do embroidery work. At the time she was busy embroidering a child's apron for her grandson, and after sitting on a wooden stool and embroidering for a while she felt tired, so she leaned back against the door and dozed off. She died in her sleep.

Someone asked Third Granny Chou: "Were you there to see it?"

"I certainly was," she replied. "Just listen: for three days and nights after she died she could not be laid out, and eventually there was nothing to do but make a special coffin and seat her inside it. Her cheeks were still pink, just as though she were still alive."

"Did you see that too?" someone else asked.

"Gracious! That's a strange question to be asking," she answered. "With all the tales of things that have happened in this world, how many can a person witness in one lifetime? How else can we know about things unless we are told?" She appeared somewhat put out by the question.

And then there was old Mrs. Yang from the west compound, who also had a tonic: She said you needed two ounces of bitters and half a catty of pork, both of which had to be finely chopped and cured over a piece of tile, then pounded into powder and divided into five portions. Each portion was to be wrapped in red paper, then taken individually. This potion's specialty was curing convulsions and a drifting soul.

Her prescription was simple enough, even though the child-bride's illness was neither convulsions nor a drifting soul, and there seemed to be some disparity between the disease and the cure. But then what harm could it do to give it a try—after all, it only called for two ounces of bitters and half a catty of pork. Besides, here in Hulan there was often some cheap pork available. And even though the pork was said to be infected and not entirely dependable, this was, after all, a matter of curing an illness, not eating a meal, so what difference could it make?

"Go ahead and buy half a catty of pork and see how it works on her."

"Anyway, even if it doesn't cure her, it certainly can't do any harm," a bystander said approvingly.

"We've got to try," her mother-in-law said, "because where there's life there's hope!"

And so the child-bride began her cure by eating half a catty of pork and two ounces of bitters.

This prescription was personally prepared for her by her mother-in-law, but the slicing of the pork was the job of the wife of the elder grandson. The pork was all dark and discolored, but there was a portion of bright red meat in the center, which the wife of the elder grandson secretly held back. She figured that it had been four or five months since her husband's grandmother had eaten any meat, so she used this piece of pork she had secretly held back to make a large bowl of meat-and-flour soup for the old woman.

"Where in the world did this meat come from?" the grandmother asked her.

"Why don't you just eat and enjoy it as something your grandson's wife prepared especially for you."

Meanwhile the child-bride's mother-in-law was curing the medicine on a piece of tile over the fire in the stove, saying as she did so: "What I have here is half a catty of pork, not a fraction less."

The pork smelled better each minute as it was being cured, its odor eventually attracting a kitten that came over to snatch a piece. But when the kitten stretched out a paw to take it, the child-bride's mother-in-law reached over and gave it a swat with her hand.

"So you think you can get your paws on this, do you! You greedy little thing, this is someone's medicine—a full half catty of pork—so what makes you think you deserve a bite? If I gave you a piece, there wouldn't be enough medicine to work the cure. Then the responsibility for the girl's death would be yours; don't you know any better! There is exactly half a catty of meat here—no more, no less."

After the prescription was prepared it was pulverized and given to the child-bride together with water. Two portions were to be taken each day. She managed all right on the first day, but on the morning of the second, when the people who had prescribed the remedies came over, there were still three portions lying on the altar where the kitchen god was placed.

Someone present questioned the wisdom of eating bitters, for they were, after all, a cold ingredient, and if someone like her, who experienced night sweats, ate bitters, her vital energy would be driven out; now how could a person get by after her vital energy has been driven out?

"She can't take that!" someone else agreed. "Within two days after she's eaten it she will have passed on to the nether world."

"What'll we do now?" the child-bride's mother-in-law exclaimed.

In an apprehensive voice, the man asked her: "Has she already taken some?"

Just as the mother-in-law of the child-bride opened her mouth to answer, the clever wife of the elder grandson cut her short: "No, she hasn't—not yet," she said.

"Well, since she hasn't taken any yet," the man replied, "then there's nothing to worry about. The Hu family is certainly blessed; your lucky star is watching over you, for just now you came awfully close to throwing away a human life!" Then he offered a potion of his own, which, according to him, was actually not a potion at all, but simply a cure-all that the proprietor of the Li Yung-ch'un Pharmacy on Road Two East often prescribed. The medicine was so effective that a hundred uses resulted in a hundred cures, and it worked for everyone—man, woman, young, and old—every single time. It didn't even matter what the symptoms were—headaches, aching feet, stomachaches, visceral disorders, falls, broken bones, cuts, boils, carbuncles, rashes—whatever the illness, it disappeared with one application of this remedy.

What was this remedy? The more the people heard of the great results it produced, the more eager they were to learn just what it was.

"If an elderly person takes it," he said, "his dimming eyesight will be restored to what it was during his youth.

"If a young man takes it his strength will be great enough to move Mount T'ai.

"If a woman takes it her complexion will be the color of peach blossoms without the aid of rouge or powder.

"If a child takes it, an eight-year-old can draw a bow, a nine-year-old can shoot an arrow, and a twelve-year-old will become a *chuang-yüan*, first on the list at the official examinations."

When he began talking, everyone in old Hu's family was absolutely amazed and awed, but toward the end his discourse somehow lost its effect on them. After all, the men in old Hu's family had always been carters, and there had never been a *chuang-yüan* among them.

The wife of the elder grandson asked the crowd of onlookers to move away a bit, then she walked over to the make-up chest and took out an eyebrow pencil. "Won't you please hurry and write down the ingredients of this prescription for us," she said, "so that we can go to the pharmacy right away and get some of that remedy?"

Now the person who was telling them about this prescription had at one time been the cook at the Li Yung-ch'un Pharmacy, but had not worked there for some three years, ever since the woman with whom he had been having an affair had run out on him, taking with her the little savings he had managed to accumulate over half a lifetime. He had been in such a rage over this that he had developed a touch of insanity. But even though he was slightly mad, he had not completely forgotten the names of the medicines he had committed to memory during his employment at "Li Yung-ch'un." Since he was illiterate he gave a verbal listing of the ingredients:

"Two-tenths of an ounce of plantain, two-tenths of an ounce of honeywort, two-tenths of an ounce of fresh rehmannia, two-tenths of an ounce of Tibetan safflower, two-tenths of an ounce of Szechuan fritillary, two-tenths of an ounce of atractylis, two-tenths of an ounce of Siberian milkwort, two-tenths of an ounce of the euphorbia spurge. . . ."

At this point he seemed unable to recall the remaining ingredients, and nervous beads of perspiration began to dot his forehead. So he blurted out: " . . . and two catties of brown sugar . . .," thereby completing his prescription.

Once finished, he began asking the people around him for some wine: "Do you have any wine here? Give me a couple of bowlfuls."

Everyone in Hulan River knew this slightly mad fellow well; everyone, that is, but the members of old Hu's family. Having moved here from somewhere else, they were taken in by him—hook, line, and sinker. Since they had no wine in the house, they gave him twenty coppers to go out and buy his own. As for the remedy he had prescribed, it was absolutely unreliable, merely a product of his wild imagination.

The child-bride grew more seriously ill with each passing day, and according to her family, she often sat bolt upright as she slept during the night. The sight of another person threw a terrible fright into her, and her eyes were invariably brimming with tears. It seemed inevitable that this child-bride was fated to "come forth," and if she were not allowed to do so, there seemed little hope that she would ever be well again.

Once the news of her plight began spreading throughout the area, all of the people living nearby came forth with their suggestions; how, they said, could we not come to the rescue of someone at death's door? Some believed that she should simply be allowed to "come forth," and let that be the end of it. Others were of the opposite opinion, for if someone of such tender years were to "come forth," what hope was there for her ever living a normal life?

Her mother-in-law adamantly refused to let her "come forth": "Now don't any of you get the wrong idea that I'm opposed to letting her "come forth" only because of the money I spent when I arranged for the engagement. Like the rest of you, I feel that if someone so young were to "come forth," she would never be able to live a normal life."

Everyone promptly agreed that it would be best not to allow her to "come forth," so they turned their collective energies to finding the right prescription or engaging the right sorceress, each extolling the virtues of his own plan.

Finally there came a soothsayer.

This soothsayer told them he had come unhesitatingly from the countryside a great distance away as soon as the news reached him that old Hu's family had recently brought a child-bride into their home, one who had fallen ill shortly after her arrival and remained so even after being seen by many eminent physicians and mystics. He had made the trip into town expressly to have a look for himself, for if he could perform some service that might spare her life, then the trip would have been worth making. Everyone was quite moved by this speech of his. He was invited into the house, where he was asked to sit on the grandmother's *k'ang*, was given tea, and offered a pipeful of tobacco.

The wife of the elder grandson was the first to approach him: "This younger sister of ours is actually only twelve years old, but since she is so tall, she tells everyone she is fourteen. She's a cheerful, sociable girl who up to now was never sick a day in her life. But ever since she came to our house she has grown thinner and paler every day. Recently she lost her appetite for food and drink, and she even sleeps with her eyes open, as she is easily startled. We've given her every imaginable remedy and have burned incense of every kind for her benefit, but nothing has worked. . . ."

Before she had finished, the girl's mother-in-law interrupted her: "I've never abused her all the time she's been in my home. Where else will you find another family that has not abused its child-bride by giving her beatings and tongue-lashings all day long? Now I may have beaten her a little, but just to get her started off on the right foot, and I only did that for a little over a month. Maybe I beat her pretty severely sometimes, but how was I expected to make a well-mannered girl out of her without being severe once in a while? Believe me, I didn't enjoy beating her so hard, what with all her screaming and carrying on. But I was doing it for her own good, because if I didn't beat her hard, she'd never be good for anything.

"There were a few times when I strung her up from the rafters and had her uncle give her a few hard lashes with a leather whip, and since he got a little carried away, she usually passed out. But it only lasted for about the time it takes to smoke a pipeful, and then we always managed to revive her by dousing her face with cold water. We did give her some pretty severe beatings that turned her body all black and blue and occasionally drew some blood, but we always broke open some eggs right away and rubbed the egg whites on the spots. The swellings, which were never too bad, always went down in ten days or a couple of weeks.

"This child is such a stubborn one; the moment I began to beat her she threatened to return to her home. So I asked her: 'Just where do you think your home is? What is this, if not your home?' But she refused to give in. She said she wanted to go to her *own* home. And this made me madder than ever. You know how people are when they get mad—nothing else seems to matter—so I took a red-hot flatiron and branded the soles of her feet. Maybe I beat her soul right out of her body, or maybe I just scared it away—I don't know which—but from then on, whenever she said she wanted to go home, instead of beating her, all I had to do was threaten to chain her up if she even tried, and she would start screaming with fright. When the Great Genie saw this he said she should be allowed to 'come forth.'

"It costs a lot of money to bring a girl into a family as a child-bride. Figure it out for yourself: the engagement was arranged when she was eight years old, at which time we had to hand over eight ounces of silver. After that there was the money we spent for her trousseau, and finally we had all the expenses of bringing her here by train from far-off Liao-yang. Then once she got here, it was a steady series of exorcists, incense, and one potion after another. If she had gotten better as time went on, then everything would have been fine, but nothing seemed to work. Who knows eventually . . . what the outcome will be . . . ?"

The soothsayer, who had come unhesitatingly from so far away, was a most proper and serious man who showed the signs of much travel. He wore a long blue gown under a short lined coat, while on his head he wore a cap with earflaps. He was a man whom others treated with the respect due a master the moment they saw him.

Accordingly, the grandmother said: "Please draw a lot quickly for my second grandson's child-bride and tell us what her fate will be."

The soothsayer could tell at first glance that this family was a sincere and honest one, so he removed his leather cap with the ear-flaps. The moment he took off his cap everyone could see that his hair was combed into a topknot and that he was wearing Taoist headwear. They knew at once that this was no ordinary run-of-the-mill individual. Before anyone could even utter the questions they wanted to ask, he volunteered the information that he was a Taoist priest from such-and-such a mountain, and that he had come down to make a pilgrimage to the sacred Mount T'ai in Shantung. But how could he have foreseen that midway on his journey he would have to cut his trip short for lack of traveling expenses? He had drifted to the Hulan River area where he had been for no less than half a year.

Someone asked him why, if he was a Taoist, he wasn't wearing Taoist garb.

"There's something you people ought to know," he replied. "Each of the 360 trades in this world of ours has its share of miseries. The police around here are really fierce; the minute they see someone dressed as a Taoist, they start in with a detailed interrogation, and since they are disbelievers of the Taoist creed who won't listen to reason, they are all too ready to take one of us into custody."

This man had an alias—the Wayfaring Immortal—and people far and near knew of whom you were speaking when you mentioned his name. Whatever the disease or discomfort, whether the signs were good or evil, life and death was settled for all time with the drawing of one of his lots. He told them that he had learned his divining powers from the head priest of the Taoists himself, Chang T'ien-shih.

He did not have many divining lots—four in all—which he took out of the pocket of his gown one at a time. The first lot he brought forth was wrapped in red paper, as was the second; in fact, all four were wrapped in red paper. He informed everyone that there were no words written on his divining lots, nor were there any images; inside each there was only a packet of medicinal powder—one red, one green, one blue, and one yellow. The yellow one foretold the wealth of gold, the red one foretold ruddy-cheeked old age. Now if the green one were drawn, things could take a turn for the worse, for it represented the devil's fire. The blue one was not very good either, for it meant the cold face of death, and Chang T'ien-shih himself had said that the cold face of death must come to meet Yama, the king of the nether world, whether the person be dead or alive.

Once the soothsayer had finished reciting his chants he called for someone in the afflicted person's family to reach out and draw a lot. The child-bride's mother-in-law figured this to be an easy, uncomplicated task, so she decided to quickly choose one and get some idea of whether it was the girl's fate to live or die. But she had overlooked something, for the moment she reached her hand out, the Wayfaring Immortal said: "Each drawing of a lot will cost you one hundred coppers; if you choose the blue one and are unhappy with it, you can choose another . . . one hundred coppers for each one. . . ."

Suddenly the child-bride's mother-in-law understood everything: this lot-drawing wasn't free after all, and at a hundred coppers apiece, it was no longer a laughing matter. For ten coppers she could buy twenty cakes of bean curd. Now if she bought one cake every three days, then with twenty cakes—since two threes are six—that would be enough bean curd for sixty days. But if one cake were bought only every ten days—that's three cakes a month—then there would be enough bean curd in the house for half a year. Continuing along this line of thought, she wondered who would be so extravagant as to eat a cake of bean curd every three days. According to her, a cake a month was enough for everyone to have a taste every now and then, in which case twenty cakes of bean curd—one each month—would be sufficient for twenty months, or a year and a half plus two months.

Or let's say rather than buying bean curd, she were to buy and raise a plump little pig. If she conscientiously fed it for five or six months until it was nice and fat, just think how much money that could bring in! And if she raised it for a whole year, then we're talking about twenty thousand coppers . . .

Or if she didn't buy a pig, but spent the money instead on chickens, a hundred coppers could buy ten or so chickens. After the first year the chickens would become egg layers, and everyone knows how much an egg is worth! Or if she didn't sell the eggs, but traded one of them for vegetables to feed the entire family—all three generations—for a whole day . . . not to mention the fact that each egg laid meant one more chicken, and by keeping the cycle going they could have an unlimited supply of chickens and an unlimited supply of eggs. Wouldn't they then make their fortune!

But her thoughts weren't really so grandiose; it would be sufficient if everyone had enough to eat and enough clothes to wear. If, by living frugally, she could manage to put a little something aside in her lifetime, that would be enough for her. For even though she had a real love for money, if she had been given the opportunity to actually make a fortune, she definitely would not have had the nerve to do so. The numbers she was contemplating were greater than she could count, more than she could ever remember. With chickens laying eggs and eggs producing more chickens in an unbroken cycle, wouldn't the situation soon have developed where there were as many chickens as there are ants? There would be so many they would cloud her vision, and clouded vision produces headaches.

This mother-in-law of the child-bride had raised chickens in the past; in fact, it was exactly a hundred coppers' worth—no more, no less. To her the ideal number to raise was a hundred coppers' worth. For one hundred coppers she was able to buy twelve little chicks, a number she considered just right. If there were more, she was afraid she might lose some, but if there were fewer, then they wouldn't have been worth a hundred coppers.

When she was buying these newly hatched chicks she picked them up one at a time to take a close look, rejecting one after the other. She rejected all those with black claws, those with spotted wings, and those with marks on the tops of their heads. She said that her mother had become an expert at choosing chickens after raising them for a lifetime. She had raised them year after year, and although she never kept too many, she was never short of household necessities during her lifetime, managing to trade eggs the year round for anything she needed. As a result, she really knew her chickens—which of them would be short-lived and which could be expected to live a long time—spotting the good ones unerringly every time. She could even tell at a glance which of them would lay large eggs and which of them would lay small ones.

As she was buying the chicks she constantly reprimanded herself for not having had the foresight to learn more about chickens from her mother in years past. Ai! Young people somehow never have an eye for the future! She was moved to sighing as she bought the chicks; having picked them out with a great deal of thought, she had done her very best in selecting. The chicken seller had over two hundred chicks for sale, every single one of which she picked over, but whether the ones she finally chose were the best of the lot was something of which she herself was never able to be absolutely sure.

She raised chickens with a great deal of care. She was forever concerned lest they be eaten by cats or bitten by rats, and whenever they dozed during the day she chased the flies away, fearing that the flies might wake them up; she wanted them to get plenty of sleep, for she was concerned that they got too little. If one of them had a mosquito bite on its leg, the moment she discovered it she immediately mixed an ointment of mugwort and water and rubbed it on the bite. According to her, if she didn't rub the ointment on right away, then if the chick later turned out to be a rooster, its growth would be stunted, and if it turned out to be a hen, it would lay small eggs. A small egg could be traded for two cakes of bean curd, while a large one would bring in three. That's what can happen to a hen. As for a rooster, they eventually wind up on the dinner table, and since everyone prefers fat ones, the stunted ones are difficult to sell.

Once her chickens had grown a bit and were ready to leave the house and go out into the courtyard and look for their own food, she put some dye on the top of each of their heads—six red and six green.

In order to determine where she should place the dye she first took a look at her neighbors' chickens to see where they had dyed theirs, after which she was able to make up her mind. Her neighbors had put the dye on the tips of the chickens' wings, so she put hers on the tops of their heads. If her neighbors had dyed the tops of their chickens' heads, she would have dyed the bellies of hers. According to her, people shouldn't dye their chickens in the same place, because then you couldn't tell them apart. Your chickens would run over to my house and mine would run over to your house, and there would be nothing but confusion.

The little dyed chickens were extremely eye-catching with their red or green heads, looking like they were wearing little colored caps. It was as though instead of raising a brood of chicks, she was raising a brood of children.

This mother-in-law of the child-bride had even said during her chicken-raising days: "Raising chickens is a lot more refined than raising children. When someone raises children don't they just leave them to fend for themselves and grow up the best they can? There are always mosquito bites, bedbug bites, and what have you, so that there is hardly a child anywhere who doesn't carry scars on his body. Children who don't have some will be hard ones to raise—they won't live long."

According to her, she didn't raise many children of her own—in fact, only the one son—but even with the small number to care for, she didn't fawn over him. By that time he already had more than twenty such scars on his body.

"If you don't believe me," she would say, "I'll have him take off his clothes and let everyone see for himself . . . he has scars of every size on his body—even one as big as the mouth of a rice bowl. Really, I've never spoiled my child. Not counting the ones from his own falls and spills, some of the scars come from the beatings I gave him with an axe-handle. Raising a child isn't anything like raising chickens or ducks. If you raise a chicken carelessly, then it won't lay any eggs; a large egg is worth three cakes of bean curd, a small one is worth two, and that's nothing to laugh at, is it? It certainly isn't!"

Once her son stepped on a chick and killed it; she beat him for three solid days and nights.

"Why shouldn't I have beaten him? Each chick is worth three cakes of bean curd—chicks come from chicken eggs, you know! In order to get a chicken, you have to have a chicken's egg—half an egg isn't enough, is it? Not only half an egg, but even an egg that's almost whole, but not quite, won't do either. Bad eggs won't do, nor will old eggs. One chicken requires one egg, and if a chicken isn't the same as three cakes of bean curd, what is it? Just think how great a sin it would be to knowingly put three cakes of bean curd on the ground and squash them with your foot! So how could I have not beaten him? The more I thought about it, the angrier I got; every time I thought about it I hit him, day or night, for three whole days. Eventually he fell ill from the beatings and woke up crying in the middle of the night. But I didn't let the matter overly concern me; I just beat on the door frame with the rice ladle to call his spirit back, and he got better on his own."

It had been several years since she had raised chickens, and in the time that had passed since making the engagement arrangements for this child-bride she had spent all the little savings she had managed to put aside. Not only that, she had had to spend money every year for gifts and other expenses, so that things had been tighter than she could have imagined these past few years. So she begrudgingly had to forego raising a few chickens.

Now here was this Wayfaring Immortal sitting across from her asking one hundred coppers for each lot drawn. If he hadn't mentioned money, but had just let her go ahead and draw a lot, then asked for money afterwards, it would have been like she was drawing a lot for nothing. But no, the soothsayer had to mention the hundred coppers *before* he would let her draw a lot. So the child-bride's mother-in-law had a vision of all her money flying off into the distance—a hundred coppers every time she reached out her hand or opened her mouth. If this wasn't throwing money out the window, what was it? Without a sound or a trace it simply disappeared. It wouldn't even be the same as crossing a river and throwing money into the water, for at least when you do that there is the splashing sound and the ripples that spread out. Not a single thing could come from doing it this way—it was the very same thing as losing money when your mind is elsewhere, or meeting up with a robber who takes your money from you.

The child-bride's mother-in-law was nearly moved to tears by the anger welling up in her heart. As these thoughts occupied her, she felt that this was not so much drawing lots as it was paying some kind of tax. Accordingly, she drew back her outstretched hand, quickly ran over to the wash basin, and washed her hands. This was no laughing matter—it was money, a hundred coppers' worth! After washing her hands she went over and knelt before the kitchen god to offer up a prayer, after which she finally drew her lot.

Her first drawing produced the green one, and green wasn't very good—it represented the devil's fire. So she drew again, but this one was even worse—in fact, it was the worst of all; she had drawn the one in which blue medicinal powder was wrapped, the one which meant that the person would have to come face to face with Yama, whether dead or alive.

When the child-bride's mother-in-law saw that both of her choices had been bad ones, by rights she should have burst into tears. But that's not what she did. Ever since the child-bride had fallen seriously ill, the woman had heard every conceivable comment regarding the prospects of living or dying. In addition, they had engaged fox fairies and sorceresses any number of times with all of their chants and witchery, and she had seen a great deal of the affairs of this world in all that time. She seemed to live under the impression that although it is nice to be alive, she wouldn't be particularly grieved to die either, for it seemed to her that the meeting with Yama would not be taking place for the time being.

She then asked the Wayfaring Immortal whether, since both lots she had drawn were bad ones, there was some way to negate their power.

"Bring me a brush and some ink," was his answer.

Since there were no brushes in their home, the wife of the elder grandson ran over to the grain shop next to the main gate of the compound to borrow one.

The proprietress of the grain shop asked her in a heavy Shantung accent: "What's happening over at your place?"

"We're curing our younger sister-in-law's illness," the wife of the elder grandson answered.

"Your younger sister-in-law's illness is a serious one. Has she improved at all lately?"

Now the elder grandson's wife had planned to just get an inkstone and a writing brush and run back home with them, but since the woman had voiced her concern, it would have been impolite to just ignore her, and so she was gone long enough to smoke several pipefuls before heading back home.

By the time she finally came back with the inkstone, the Wayfaring Immortal had already torn some red paper into strips. He took up the writing brush and wrote one large character on each of the four strips of red paper; since the strips were no more than half an inch in width and an inch in length, the large characters looked as though they were about to fly off the edges.

As for the four characters that he wrote, inasmuch as no one in the family knew how to read—even the scrolls hanging on either side of the kitchen god altar had been written by someone at their request—they all seemed to them to be identical, like children of the same mother. For all they knew, they might have been the very same character. The elder grandson's wife looked at them but didn't know what they said, and the grandmother looked at them without recognizing them either. But even though they couldn't read them, they felt certain that they couldn't have bad meanings, for otherwise, how could they be expected to effectively keep someone from having to come face to face with Yama? And so each and every one of them nodded her head approvingly.

The Wayfaring Immortal then ordered them to bring him some paste. Now paste was something they went without the whole year long, as it was so terribly expensive—a single catty of flour cost over a hundred coppers—so when they had to repair shoes they settled for kernels of cooked millet.

The wife of the elder grandson went to the kitchen and scooped a gob of millet off the rice pot. The Wayfaring Immortal spread some of the gooey substance onto the strips of red paper, then lifted the tattered lined jacket off the head of the child-bride and told her to hold out her hands, sticking one of the strips onto each palm. Then he had her remove her stockings, after which he stuck a strip onto the sole of each foot.

When the Wayfaring Immortal noticed the large white scars on the soles of her feet he reckoned they must be from the brandings the mother-in-law had been talking about a short time before. But he feigned ignorance and asked: "What sort of malady did she have here on the soles of her feet?"

The child-bride's mother-in-law quickly reminded him: "Didn't I just say that I had branded her with a flatiron? This girl continually refused to admit the error of her ways. She walked as though she were on the top of the world and soon forgot all the beatings I gave her, so I had to brand her. Fortunately, it wasn't all that serious—after all, young people's skin is so resilient—and after being confined to bed for ten days or a couple of weeks she was just fine."

The Wayfaring Immortal mulled this over for a moment, then decided to throw a scare into the woman by saying that although he had stuck paper strips onto the scarred soles of her feet, he was afraid they might not hold; nothing, he continued, escaped Yama's attention, and these distinctive scars might just stick in his mind, which could make their plans go awry.

When he had spoken his piece, the Walfaring Immortal looked

to see if he had succeeded in frightening them or not; deciding that he had fallen somewhat short, he continued in an even graver tone: "If these scars aren't gotten rid of, Yama will be able to find her within a period of three days, and the moment he finds her he will snatch her away, even though she still be alive. The last lot you drew a while ago was infallible, so these red stickers are absolutely useless."

The Wayfaring Immortal could not have imagined that this chilling prospect would still not have noticeably frightened any of them, from the grandmother down to the grandson's wife, and so he continued by saying: "Not only will Yama snatch the child-bride away, he will likewise come after her mother-in-law in order to seek retribution. For what is branding the soles of someone's feet, if not a form of torture? A woman who tortures her prospective daughter-in-law shall be consigned to a vat of boiling oil, and since the child-bride of the Hu family has been tortured by her prospective mother-in-law. . . ."

His voice grew louder as he went along, until he was on the verge of shouting; it was as though he were a gallant crusader attacking injustice—this demeanor had changed from when he first came. When he reached his point there was not a single member of the Hu family—young or old—who was not gripped by fear. Trembling from head to toe, they felt as though an evil demon of some sort had infiltrated their household. The mother-in-law was more frightened than any of the others; mumbling incoherently about the ghastly prospects that were reaching her ears, she could not imagine that such a thing as torturing one's daughter-in-law was something that ever happened on the face of the earth. She quickly fell to her knees and, with tears streaming down her face, said to the Wayfaring Immortal: "This is all a result of a lifetime of accumulating no virtues, and my sins are being visited upon my children. I implore the Wayfaring Immortal to break this terrible spell in good faith, to use his divine methods to snatch my daughter-in-law from the jaws of death!"

The Wayfaring Immortan changed his tune at once, saying that he had an infallible means of keeping the daughter-in-law from coming face to face with Yama—a guaranteed method. It was extremely simple: the child-bride need only remove her stockings once again; he would then make a mark with his brush over the scars, making them invisible to Yama. So the stockings were removed at once, and he made his mark on the soles of her feet, chanting as he did so. Viewed as an extremely simple act by those who witnessed it, nonetheless, it cost the Wayfaring Immortal such great effort that beads of perspiration dotted his forehead. He performed the act with a deliberate gnashing of teeth, wrinkled brows, and staring eyes as if making these marks had been no easy matter for him; that, in fact, it had been much the same as scaling a mountain of knives. Then, having made his mark, he tallied up his fee: two hundred coppers for the two drawn lots; four strips of red paper stuck onto the palms of his hands and soles of her feet, at fifty coppers apiece—half the normal rate—which amounted to two hundred coppers; and finally the two marks he had made (the usual rate was a hundred coppers per mark, but he had cut his fee in half for them), at fifty apiece, making another hundred coppers. Two hundred plus two hundred, and another hundred, made a total of five hundred coppers.

Accepting his fee of five hundred coppers, the Wayfaring Immortal departed the scene in high spirits.

Just prior to the time the mother-in-law of the cild-bride had drawn the first lot, her heart was gripped by an excruciating pain as she learned that each one would cost her a hundred coppers. Thoughts of how she could have put that money to work raising chickens or raising hogs had crossed her mind. But now that the five hundred coppers had been handed over, she thought no longer about raising chickens or raising hogs. For she figured that when the episode had reached this point she had no choice but to hand it over. The lots had been drawn, the characters written, and it would have been out of the question to withhold payment. What else was one expected to do when affairs had reached this point? Even if it had been a thousand coppers instead of five hundred, what else could she do but hand it over?

And so, with a sense of resignation she handed over the five hundred coppers, which was part of the earnings from the sale of a quarter peck of soybeans that she herself had foraged in the fields in the autumn. She had sold the beans for a total of less than a thousand coppers. Foraging soybeans in the field was no easy task for these people, since after the landlord's harvesting there were precious few beans left on the surface of that vast plot of land. And yet there were hordes of poor people—children, women, old ladies—engaged in the same task, with the result that competition for each bean was fierce. A grand total of a quarter peck of beans had required two or three solid weeks of foraging in the field on her knees, until her back ached and her legs were sore. Ai! Because of those few beans the mother-in-law of the child-bride had had to make a visit to the Li Yung-ch'un Pharmacy to buy two ounces of safflower. This she had been forced to do because the sharp point of a bean plant had pricked her under a fingernail while she was crawling along the ground looking for beans. She hadn't given it any thought at the time, but had merely removed the thorn from her finger and gone on about her business. Since she was there to forage beans, forage is what she would do. But for some unknown reason, after a night's sleep she woke up to find her finger swollen to the size of a small eggplant.

Even this swelling didn't concern her much, since she wasn't royalty and was not used to being pampered. Besides, for those whose lives are at Heaven's mercy, who hasn't occasionally experienced Heaven's wrath? But after being discommoded over this for several days, until she could no longer sleep at night for the searing pain, she finally bought the two ounces of safflower.

Buying this safflower is something she should have done at the very outset. Urged to do so by the grandmother, she chose not to; prompted by the wife of the elder grandson to buy some, still she refused. Her own son, out of sense of filial responsibility, tried to force the issue with his mother, demanding that he be allowed to go and buy some for her. He was rewarded for his troubles by a blow on the head from the bowl of her pipe, which raised a lump the size of an egg.

"You little scamp, are you trying to bring the family to ruin? Your mother isn't even in her grave, and already you're acting like the head of the family! You little devil, now let's see if you've got the nerve to bring up the subject of buying safflower again. We'll see if this big brat of mine has the nerve!" All the while she was cursing she was hitting him with the bowl of her pipe.

But in fact she eventually did buy some, most likely due to the urgency of her neighbors' advice; for if she didn't buy a little safflower, it wouldn't look good at all. Everyone would be gossiping about the wife of the elder son of the Hu family: Any money she accumulated throughout the year would disappear, they would say, as though it had fallen through a crack in the earth the moment it touched her hand; once it had come to her there was no chance it would ever reappear. Now this was not the sort of talk that did a family any good. Besides, after selling the beans she had picked for a price of nearly a thousand coppers, if it was necessary to part with twenty or thirty for a little safflower, then it should be done. All she had to do was grind her teeth once, then go and buy two ounces of safflower and rub it on.

But even though she gave it some serious thought, she still could not make up her mind to go ahead. She put it off for several days, never quite able to bring herself to "grind her teeth."

Ultimately, however, she did buy some. She chose a day when her condition was at its most serious—not only was her finger affected, but the whole hand had begun to swell. A finger that had originally puffed up to the size of a small eggplant was now as big as a small melon, and even the palm of her hand was so huge and puffy it looked like a winnowing basket. For years she had bemoaned the fact that she was too thin, saying that people who were too thin had less than their share of happiness. This was especially true for those with skinny arms and legs, which was an obvious sign of a lack of blessings, and even more so for those with bony hands; looking like a pair of claws, they were a sure indication of ill-fortune.

Now she had a plump hand, but it wasn't a very comfortable way of getting it. Not only that, she had come down with a fever, her eyes and mouth felt dry, and her face was flushed; experiencing hot and cold flashes all over her body, she commented: "Is this hand going to bring me to grief? This hand of mine. . . ."

She said the same thing over and over from the moment she got up in the morning. She could no longer even move this hand, which had grown to the size of a winnowing basket. As though it were the head of a cat or a small child, she put it beside her on the pillow as she lay down.

"I'm afraid this hand of mine is going to bring me to grief!" This she said as her son walked up alongside her; from the tone of her voice he got the impression that this time she was prepared to buy some safflower. So he ran at once to see his grandmother to discuss the purchase of safflower for his mother.

Since their home was arranged with two *k'angs* opposite each other—one facing north and one facing south—even though they carried on the discussion in hushed tones, his mother could hear what they were saying. Yet she pretended that she could not hear, so that no one could later accuse her of having been in on the decision to buy the safflower, or say that the idea had originated with her; it most assuredly wasn't she who had asked them to go and buy safflower!

Grandmother and grandson discussed the matter by the northern *k'ang* for a while, then the grandson said he would ask his mother for some money.

"Go and buy it with my money," his grandmother counseled. "We can talk about paying it back once your mother is well."

She intentionally raised her voice slightly as she said this, evidently wanting to make sure that her elder son's wife had heard her. She had and, for that matter, had heard everything else that was said as well. Yet she lay there without moving, not letting on that she was listening.

After the safflower had been purchased and brought home, the son sat down beside his mother and said: "Ma, rub on some of this safflower tonic."

His mother turned her head on the pillow to face him, looking as though she had been caught completely unawares by the news that some safflower had been bought. "Well!" she exclaimed. "So this little rascal has bought some safflower for me, has he? . . ." But this time she refrained from hitting him with the bowl of her pipe. Instead she calmly put her puffy hand out and let him smear the safflower mixture all over it.

She wondered whether they had bought twenty coppers' worth of safflower, or thirty. If it was twenty, then they had gotten plenty for their money, but if they had paid thirty, then it was a bit too expensive. Now if she had gone to buy it herself, she most certainly wouldn't have bought so much; after all, wasn't it only some safflower! Safflower was merely something red, and who could say whether or not it had any medicinal qualities, or if it was anything more than a little psychological comfort?

These thoughts occupied her for a while, until the coolness of the tonic on her hand, the fragrant aroma of the heated mixture, and the strong medicinal aroma of the safflower combined to make her feel drowsy. She was feeling a good deal more comfortable now, and the moment she closed her eyes she began to dream.

She dreamed that she had bought two cakes of bean curd—big, white ones. Where had she gotten the money to buy it? It had been paid for with money left over after buying the safflower, for in her dream it was she who had bought the safflower, and she had not bought thirty coppers' worth, nor even twenty—she had spent only ten. Figuring it all up in her dreams, not only could she eat two cakes of bean curd that very day, but could eat two more someday when she felt like it! For she had spent only ten of thirty coppers on the safflower.

And yet she had just handed over five hundred coppers to the Wayfaring Immortal. Put in terms of her way of looking at things, just think how much bean curd she could have bought with that much money! But these thoughts did not occur to her now. On the one hand, there was her prospective daughter-in-law, whose illness had involved them all inextricably and had already been a big drain on their finances; on the other hand, there was the Wayfaring Immortal with his savage powers, who had just accused her of torturing the child-bride. Giving him the money and letting him get the hell out of there had been the best way to handle it after all.

Having a sick individual in the house certainly exposes a person to all sorts of unpleasantness. The child-bride's mother-in-law thought about the whole matter, this unexpected calamity which kept growing and growing in her mind. She felt terribly put upon and wronged: wanting to vent her anger, there was no one to rail at; feeling like crying, she found herself unable to; wanting to strike out at someone, there was no one within reach.

Of course there was always the young child-bride, but she could not withstand another beating. Now if she had just then arrived at their house, then of course her mother-in-law could have grabbed hold of her, administered a beating, and let the chips fall where they may. Or if the mother-in-law had broken a rice bowl, she could have taken hold of the young child-bride and given her a beating; if she had lost a needle, again she could have taken hold of the young child-bride and given her a beating; or if she had taken a fall, tearing a hole in the knee of her unlined trousers, once again she could have taken hold of the young child-bride and given her a beating. Whatever the situation, when things were not going well with her, her reaction was to hit someone. Who would that someone be? Who could she get away with hitting? The answer was always the young child-bride.

She couldn't hit anyone whose mother was nearby, and she didn't really have the heart to hit her own son hard. She could hit the cat, but was afraid she might never see it again, or she could hit the dog, but was afraid it might run away from home. If she hit one of the pigs, it might lose a few pounds of weight, and if she hit one of the chickens, it might stop laying eggs. The only one she could hit with impunity was the young child-bride. She wouldn't disappear from sight or run away; she didn't lay eggs; and, unlike a pig, if she lost a few pounds it wouldn't make any difference, since she was never weighed anyway. But as soon as this prospective daughter-in-law of hers started getting beaten, she lost her appetite. Now a lost appetite is nothing to be too concerned about, since she could always drink a little water left over from boiling rice; after all, whatever rice-water was left over was always fed to the pigs.

But these times of personal glory were now all in the past, and it didn't look as though such days of freedom would return for her in the foreseeable future. Not only was beating out of the question now, she couldn't even administer much of a tongue-lashing to her anymore. All of the woman's worries were now subordinated to her fear of the girl's dying. Her heart was constantly in the grip of a dark terror: her prospective daughter-in-law simply mustn't die on her!

As a result, she mustered her self-control to overcome all of her personal difficulties, grinding her teeth with determination, fighting back her tears, and restraining herself from cursing and beating. She would not allow herself to cry, even though she experienced countless sorrows and griefs, often simultaneously. She thought that perhaps the reason she was burdened with the girl in this life was because she herself had done nothing good in a previous one. Otherwise, how could it have reached the point that she wasn't even fated to have a child-bride in her family?

She reflected that she had done nothing evil in her life; with a kindly look on her face and a heart brimming with benevolence, she had always given way before others, allowing herself to get the worst of all matters. Granted that she had not abstained from eating meat and had neglected to chant her sutras, still she had fasted on the first and fifteenth days of each lunar month ever since she was a child. And granted that she had often been remiss in going to the temple to worship and light incense, still she had never once stayed home from the temple festival on the eighteenth day of the fourth lunar month, at which time she lit incense at the Temple of the Immortal Matron and performed her three kowtows at the Temple of the Patriarch. Every year, without fail, she had done what was expected, burning incense and performing her kowtows. Granted, furthermore, that she had not learned to read when she was young and did now know characters, nonetheless she was able to recite the Diamond Sutra and had memorized the prayer to the kitchen god. And granted that she had never performed such charitable acts as mending a road or repairing a bridge, yet she always gave her leftover soup and uneaten rice to beggars who came around over New Year's or other holidays. Finally granted that she had not lived a particularly frugal life, still she had never eaten a single cake of bean curd more than she should have. She could live with herself, for she had a clear conscience. Why then, in Heaven's name, had the seeds of disaster been planted in *her* body, of all people? The more she puzzled over this, the less sense it made.

"Things have turned out this way in my present life because I never performed any good deeds in a former one." When her thoughts reached this juncture, she let them go no further; since matters had already reached this point, what good could come of a lot of hasty thoughts and ideas? So she convinced herself that she must fight back her tears, bite down hard on her teeth, and simply part with that modest sum of money she had so diligently put aside after raising hogs and performing other menial tasks. It was a matter of ten coppers here, ten more there; fifty for this, a hundred more for that.

One neighbor advised the burning of incense and paper money, another prescribed a rare remedy to be taken. She had tried them all: remedies, herbal medicines, sorceresses, exorcists, incense, and divining boards; and although she had spent untold sums of money, nothing seemed to have produced much in the way of results.

The young child-bride talked in her sleep at night and ran a fever during the day. During the night as she slept she talked only of returning to her home. In the eyes of the girl's mother-in-law the words "return home" were the most disquieting of all, for she imagined that the girl might be a reincarnated daughter of hell who was being summoned home by the Queen of Hell herself. And so she sent for a reader of dreams, whose explanation was just as she had feared: "return home" did, in fact, mean going to the nether world.

Thus, whenever the young child-bride dreamed of being beaten by her mother-in-law, or of being bound and strung up from the rafters of the house, or of being branded on the soles of her feet, or even of having her fingertips pricked with a needle, she began to wail and scream, shouting that she wanted to "return home." And the moment her mother-in-law heard her scream that she wanted to return home she reached out and pinched her on the leg. As the days went by, and one pinch followed another, the young child-bride's thighs became a welt of black and blue bruises, making her look like a spotted deer.

Now the woman's intentions were completely honorable: fearing that the girl would really be returning to the nether world, she wanted to quickly rouse her from her sleep. But the young child-bride, heavy with slumber, always imagined that she was actually being beaten by her mother-in-law, and as a result, she would begin to scream more loudly, roll over on the k'ang, and jump to the ground where she thrashed around uncontrollably. At such times her strength was astonishing and her shouts fearfully loud, further strengthening her mother-in-law's conviction that she was seeing ghosts and being visited by devils.

The certainty that this child was possessed by a demon was felt not only by the mother-in-law—the whole family believed it to be true. Hearing what was going on, who could not believe? Shattering the late night calm with her shouts of returning home, she then jumped to the floor upon being awakened, her eyes staring, her mouth agape; wailing and shouting, she was more powerful than an ox, her shouts like those of a pig being slaughtered.

Who could doubt it, especially when the girl's mother-in-law added the information that her eyeballs had turned green, like two little demon fires, and that her screams were more like an animal's roar than the cries of a human being?

And so the talk spread, until there was no one in the neighborhood who doubted. As a result, there were several people of good conscience who felt pity for this young girl who had unquestionably been seized by a demon. Where was there a child who had never had a mother, a person who was not born of flesh and blood? All people cared for their elders and educated their young . . . ; the people's natural compassions were greatly aroused. This family's auntie knew of a rare cure, that family's auntie was privy to a miraculous remedy.

And so it went: sorceresses, exorcists, incense, divining boards; there was a constant clamor at the home of the Hu family. It became the main attraction throughout the area, and anyone who didn't come to watch the dance of the sorceress or the rites of the exorcist was considered ignorant. So many kinds of sorceress' dances were performed for the Hu family that it was a historic time—never had there been such activity. This record-breaking episode had ushered in a new age of sorceress-dancing, and if a person failed to see it for himself, his ears and eyes would henceforth be forever closed.

But these festivities went unrecorded since the town was without a local newspaper. If a person were to suffer paralysis of half his body, or a palsy, or a disease that kept him permanently bedridden, it was considered nothing less than the misfortune of his lifetime, and he was pitied by all. Such a person was feared to be forever cut off from the rest of the world, for he had been unable to personally witness such a momentous occasion.

This place, Hulan River, was much too closed off from the outside world, and there wasn't much culture to speak of. Nonetheless, the local officials and gentry were in the main satisfied, and a Hanlin Scholar of the Ch'ing dynasty had been asked to pen a lyric about the place, which went:

> Natural forests along the Hulan,
> Since antiquity the source of remarkable timber.*

This lyric had been set to a melody imported from the Eastern Sea [Japan] and was sung by all of the elementary school children. Actually there was more to the song than just these two lines, but it was considered quite good enough just to sing the two. By good I

---

*There is a pun here: the word for timber (*ts'ai*) is homophonous with and sometimes used for the word meaning "talent/ability." Here the literal meaning is secondary.

mean that they were sufficient to instill feelings of complacence in anyone who heard them. To illustrate: during the Ch'ing-ming Festival, when trees were planted at the gravesites of ancestors, the children from many of the elementary schools lined up and made a procession through the town, singing this melody as they passed by. When the citizenry along the route heard their singing they felt that Hulan River was a truly magnificent place, and they spoke of it as "this Hulan River of ours." Even the child who collected animal droppings for fertilizer would talk of "this Hulan River of ours" as he walked along with his dung rake. I could never figure out, though, just what Hulan River had ever done for him. Maybe the dung rake he carried was Hulan River's gift to him.

This place, Hulan River, may very well have been blessed with marvelous "timber," but it was still too closed off—it couldn't even support a newspaper. And so the curious tales and strange events that happened here went unrecorded, simply carried away on the wind.

The dance of the sorceress at the home of the Hu family was quite a novel event, as was the bath that the child-bride was given in a large vat in full view of everyone. As the news of these unusual spectacles spread, people came in droves to get an eyeful. As for the paralyzed and the palsied, while no one gave much thought to the tragedy of their physical incapacitation, the fact that they were thus incapable of personally witnessing the public bathing given to the Hu's child-bride was, in their eyes, the calamity of a lifetime.

V

Dawn was ushered in by the beating of drums at the Hu house. All was in readiness: the vat, the boiling water, and the rooster. The rooster had been caught and brought forward, the water heated to a running boil, and the vat placed there ready for use.

People came in an unbroken stream to watch the activities, and Granddad and I came with the others. I went up to the dark-skinned child-bride with the hearty laugh as she lay on the *k'ang* and gave her a marble and a little platter. Commenting that it was a pretty little platter, she held it up in front of her eyes to look more closely at it. Then she said that the marble would be fun to play with as she flipped it with her finger. Seeing that her mother-in-law was not there beside us, she sat up with the idea that she would play with the marble on the *k'ang*. But before she even had a chance to begin, her mother-in-law entered and said: "You sure don't know what's good for you; what are you up to now?" She walked up alongside her and covered her up again with the tattered coat so that no part of her head—not even her face—was sticking out.

I asked Granddad why the woman wouldn't let her play.

"She's sick."

"No, she isn't; she's just fine." Then I climbed up onto the *k'ang* and removed the coat from her head.

The moment her face was visible I could see that her eyes were wide open. She asked whether or not her mother-in-law was gone, and when I answered that she was, she sat up again. But no sooner had she sat up than her mother-in-law reappeared, and once again she covered the girl up, saying: "Don't you even care that people will laugh at you? You're so sick we've had to invite sorceresses and exorcists over; who ever heard of such a thing—sitting up any old time you feel like it!"

After saying this very quietly to the girl, the mother-in-law then turned to the gathered crowd and commented: "She must be prevented from being in a draft, because even a slight one will cause her illness to take a turn for the worse."

As the clamor spawned by all this entertainment grew and grew, the young child-bride said to me: "You wait and see; they're going to give me a bath soon." She said it as though she were talking about someone else.

Before long, just as she had predicted, the bathing began, accompanied by a chorus of screams and shouts. The sorceress started beating her drum and ordered that the girl be stripped naked in full view of the crowd. But she resisted their efforts to take her clothes off, forcing her mother-in-law to wrap her arms tightly around her and ask for several people's assistance to come forward and rip the clothes off her body.

Now although the girl was only twelve years old, she looked more like a girl of fifteen or sixteen, so when her body was exposed, the young girls and married women who were watching all blushed.

The young child-bride was quickly carried over and placed inside the vat, which was brim full of hot water—scalding hot water. Once inside, she began to scream and thrash around as though her very life depended upon it, while several people stood around the vat scooping up the hot water and pouring it over her head. Before long her face had turned beet-red, and she ceased her struggles; standing quietly in the vat, she no longer attempted to jump out, probably sensing that it would be useless to even try. The vat was so large that when she stood up inside only her head cleared the top.

I watched for the longest time, and eventually she stopped moving altogether; she neither cried nor smiled. Her sweat-covered face was flushed—it was the color of a sheet of red paper. I turned and commented to Granddad: "The young child-bride isn't yelling any more." Then I looked back toward the big vat to discover that the young child-bride had vanished. She had collapsed inside the big vat.

At that moment the crowd witnessing the excitement yelled in panic, thinking that the girl had died, and they rushed forward to rescue her, while those of a more compassionate nature began to weep.

A few moments earlier, when the young child-bride was clearly still alive and begging for help, not a single person had gone to rescue her from the hot water. But now that she was oblivious to everything and no longer seeking help, a few people decided to come to her aid. She was dragged out of the big vat and doused with some cold water. A moment before, when she had lost consciousness, the crowd watching all the excitement had been moved to unbelievable compassion. Even the woman who had been shouting, "Use hot water!

Pour hot water over her!'' was pained by the turn of events. How
could she not be pained? Here was a sprightly young child whose
life had suddenly come to an end.

The young child-bride was laid out on the *k'ang,* her whole body
as hot as cinders. A neighbor woman reached out and touched her
body, then another woman did the same. They both exclaimed:
"Gracious, her body's as hot as cinders!"

Someone said that the water had been too hot, while someone
else said that they should not have poured it over her head, and that
anyone would lose consciousness in such scalding water.

While this discussion was going on, the mother-in-law rushed
over and covered the girl with the tattered coat, exclaiming: "Doesn't
this girl have any modesty at all, lying there without a stitch of clothing on!"

Originally, the young child-bride had fought having her clothing
taken off out of a sense of modesty, but she had been stripped on
the orders of her mother-in-law. Now here she was, oblivious to
everything, with no feelings at all, and her mother-in-law was acting in her best interests.

The sorceress beat some tattoos on her drum, as the assistant
spoke several time to her, and the onlookers cast glances among
themselves. None could say how this episode would end, whether
the young child-bride was dead or alive; but whatever the outcome,
they knew they had not wasted their time in coming. They had seen
some eye-opening incidents, and they were a little wiser in the ways
of the world—that alone made it all worthwhile.

As some of the onlookers were beginning to feel weary, they
asked others whether or not the final act of these rites had drawn to
a close, adding that they were ready to go home and go to bed. Seeing that the situation would turn sour if the crowd broke up, the
sorceress gathered her energies to make sure she kept her audi-
ence. She beat a violent tattoo on her drum and sprayed several
mouthfuls of wine into the child-bride's face. Then she extracted a
silver needle from her waistband, with which she pricked the girl's
fingertip. Before long the young child-bride came to.

The sorceress then informed the people that three baths were required—there were still two to go. This comment injected new life into the crowd: the weary were given a second wind, renewed vigor came to those wanting to go home to bed. No fewer than thirty people were gathered there to watch the excitement; a new sparkle in their eyes, they were a hundred times more spirited than before. Let's see what happens! If she lost consciousness after one bathing, what will happen when she takes a second? The possible results of yet a third bath were completely beyond their imagination. As a result, great mysteries crowded the minds of the onlookers.

As anticipated, the moment the young child-bride was carried out to the large vat and dumped into the scalding water, her eerie screams began anew. All the time she was shouting she was holding on to the rim of the vat, trying desperately to pull herself out. Meanwhile, as some people continued to douse her with water, others pushed her head down, keeping her under control until once again she passed out and collapsed in the vat.

As she was fished out this time, she was spurting water from her mouth. Just as before, among the onlookers there was no one of conscience who was not moved to sympathize with the plight of this young girl. Women from neighboring families came forward to do whatever they could to aid her. They crowded around to see whether or not she was still alive. If there was still a spark of life, then they need not worry about rescuing her. But if she was breathing her last, then they must hurriedly douse her with cool water. If there was still life in her, she would come around of her own, but if her life was ebbing away, then they would have to do something quickly in order to bring her to. If they didn't they would surely lose her.

VI

The young child-bride was bathed three times that evening in scalding water, and each time she passed out. The commotion lasted until very late at night, when finally the crowd dispersed and the sorceress returned home to go to bed. The onlookers, too, returned to their homes to retire.

On this winter night the moon and stars filled the sky, ice and snow covered the ground. Snow swirled and gathered at the base of the wall, winds beat against the window sills. Chickens were asleep in their roosts, dogs slumbered in their dens, and pigs holed up in their pens. All of Hulan River was asleep.

There were only the distant sounds of a barking dog, perhaps in White Flag Village, or possibly a wild dog in the willow grove on the southern bank of the Hulan River. Whatever the case, the sound was coming from a great distance away and belonged to those affairs that occurred outside the town of Hulan River. The whole town of Hulan River was fast asleep.

There was no longer any hint of the dancing and drum-beating of the sorceress from the previous evening, and it was as though the shouts and cries of the young child-bride had never happened, for not a single trace of all of this remained. Every household was pitch dark, its occupants all sound asleep. The child-bride's mother-in-law snored as she slept.

Since the third watch had already been struck, the fourth watch was nearly upon them.

VII

The young child-bride slept as though in a trance the whole day following, as well as the day after and the day after that. Her eyes were neither completely open nor completely closed; a small slit remained, through which the whites of her eyes were visible.

When members of her family saw how she lay there, they all said that she had undergone a great struggle, but that her true soul still had a grip on her body; if that was the case, then she would recover. This was the opinion not just of her family, but of the neighbors as well. As a result, not only did they feel no anxiety over her condition—neither eating nor drinking, and always in a sort of half-consciousness—but on the contrary, they felt it was something over which they should rejoice. She lay in a stupor for four or five days, which were four or five happy days for her family; when she had lain there for six or seven days, they were six or seven happy days for her family. During this period not a single potion was used, and not a single type of herbal medication was put to the test.

But after six or seven days had passed she remained in a coma, neither eating nor drinking, and giving no indication at all that she was on the road to recovery. The sorceress was called back, but this time she said nothing about effecting a cure; she said it had now reached the point where there was no alternative but for the girl to "come forth," to become a sorceress herself.

The family then decided to apply the true methods of exorcism, so they went to the ornaments shop; there they had a paper image of her made, which they dressed in cotton clothing made especially for it (the cotton clothes were to make the image even more lifelike). Cosmetics were applied to the face and a colorful hankie attached to its hand; the result was a delight to behold—dressed completely in colorful clothes, it looked just like a maiden of seventeen or eighteen years. The image was carried by people down to the big pit on the south bank of the river where it was burned.

This procedure is called burning a "proxy doll," and according to legend, when this "proxy doll" is burned, it takes the place of someone's real body, sparing that person's life.

On the day the "proxy doll" was burned, the child-bride's mother-in-law showed proof of her devotion by engaging a few musicians, who filed in behind the people hired to carry the image; the procession made its way to the big southern pit to the accompaniment of the musicians' tooting and clanging. It would have been accurate to call the procession a boisterous affair, with the trumpets blaring the same tune over and over again. But it would have been no less accurate to call it a mournful affair, for with the paper figure going in front and three or four musicians bringing up the rear, it looked like something between a funeral procession and a temple excursion.

There weren't many people who came out onto the street to watch all the commotion, since the weather was so cold. A few folks did stick out their heads or venture out to take a look, but when they saw there wasn't much worth seeing they closed up their gates and went back inside. Therefore the paper figure was burned in the big pit in a mournful ceremony with little fanfare.

The child-bride's mother-in-law experienced pangs of regret as she burned the figure, for had she known beforehand that there weren't going to be many people looking on, she could have dispensed with dressing the figure in real clothing. She felt like going down into the pit to retrieve the clothing, but it was already too late, so she just stood there watching it burn. She had spent a total of more than a thousand coppers for that set of clothes, and as she watched it burn, it was as though she were watching more than a thousand coppers go up in smoke. There was both regret and anger in her heart. She had by then completely forgotten that this was a "proxy doll" for her prospective daughter-in-law. Her original plan had been to intone a prayerful chant during the ceremony, but it slipped her mind completely until she was on her way back home, at which time it occurred to her that she had probably burned the "proxy doll" for nothing. Whether or not it would prove effective was now anybody's guess!

VIII

Later we heard that the child-bride's braid had fallen off one night as she slept. It had simply fallen off beside her pillow, and no one was quite sure how that could have happened.

The mother-in-law was firmly convinced that the child-bride was some kind of demon, and the detached braid was kept around and shown to everyone who dropped by. It was obvious to anyone who saw it that it had been snipped off with scissors, but the mother-in-law insisted that such was not the case. She stuck to her story that it had simply fallen off by itself one night while the girl slept.

Eventually, as this curious news made the rounds throughout the neighborhood and outlying areas, not only were the members of her family unwilling to have a demon among them, even others in the same compound felt that it was a terrible situation. At night, while closing their doors and windows, the people commented: "The Hu family's child-bride is a demon for sure!"

The cook at our house was a real gossip, who was forever telling Granddad one thing or another about the Hu family's child-bride. Now there was something new to report: the girl's braid had fallen off.

"No it didn't," I retorted. "Someone cut it off with a pair of scissors."

But as far as the old cook was concerned, I was too young, and to ridicule me, he stopped me by putting his finger over my mouth and saying: "What do you know? That young child-bride is a demon!"

"No she isn't. I asked her in secret how her hair had fallen off, and she had a grin on her face when she said she didn't know!"

"A nice child like that," Granddad interjected, "and they're going to kill her."

A few days later the old cook reported: "The Hu family is going to arrange a divorce; they're going to divorce away that little demon."

Granddad didn't hold the people in the Hu family in very high esteem. "Come March I'm going to have them move," he said. "First they nearly kill someone else's child, then they just abandon her."

IX

Before March rolled around, however, that dark-complexioned young child-bride with the hearty laugh died. Early one morning the elder son of the Hu family—the carter with the sickly face and big eyes—came to our house. When he saw Granddad he brought his hands together in front of his chest and bowed deeply.

Granddad asked him what had happened.

"We would like you to donate a small plot of ground to bury our young child-bride."

"When did she die?" Granddad asked.

"I was out with my cart and didn't get home till daybreak," he replied. "They say she died during the night."

Granddad agreed to his request, telling him to bury her on a piece of ground on the outskirts of town. He summoned Second Uncle Yu and told him to accompany them to the place. Just as Second Uncle Yu was about to leave, he was joined by the old cook. I said I wanted to go along too and watch them, but Granddad absolutely would not allow it: "You and I will stay home and trap some sparrows for us to eat. . . ."

And so I didn't go along, though I couldn't take my mind off the whole affair. I waited and waited for Second Uncle Yu and the old cook to return so that I could hear how things had gone, but they didn't come right back. It was after one o'clock when they finally returned, having first stopped over somewhere to have some wine and some lunch. They returned with the old cook in the lead, followed by Second Uncle Yu, the two of them looking like a couple of fat ducks; moving hardly at all, they walked slowly and with great complacence.

The old cook, who was in front, was red-eyed and his lips were glistening with oil. Second Uncle Yu, who was behind him, was flushed from his ears all the way down to the thick tendon below his neck. When they entered Granddad's room, one of them said: "The wine and food weren't half bad. . . ."

". . . The egg soup was boiling hot," the other commented.

Not a word about the burying of the young child-bride. It was as though the two of them had returned from a New Year's celebration, feeling nothing but satisfaction and happiness. I asked Second Uncle Yu how the young child-bride had died and what had happened at the burial.

"What's the idea of asking me that? The death of a human being isn't as noteworthy as that of a chicken . . . just stick your legs out straight and that's the end of that. . . ."

"Second Uncle Yu, when are you going to die?"

"Your Second Uncle isn't going to die . . . now you take a rich man who lives in comfort all his life; the longer he hopes to live, the younger he is when he dies. Not even burning incense in the temple or going into the mountains to worship the Buddha will change the outcome. But then take someone like me who's been poor all my life; I get stronger with each passing year. I'm just like a rock that never dies! Like the old saying goes: 'The rich get but three measures of life; the poor hang on forever.' Second Uncle Yu is one of those poor ones, and King Yama won't even stoop to look at the likes of me."

That evening the Hu family invited the two of them, Second Uncle Yu and the old cook, over again to drink some more wine. This was their way of paying them back for all their help.

X

Not long after the Hu family's child-bride died, the wife of the elder grandson ran away with another man.

Later on the grandmother passed away.

As for the wives of the two sons of the family, one of them lost the sight of one eye because of the affair with the child-bride; she had cried every day over the fact that all of the family's wealth—more than fifty thousand coppers—had been squandered on behalf of the child-bride.

The other wife had suffered untold shame over the fact that her son's wife had run away with someone, and she spent every waking minute of each day sitting beside the stove smoking a pipe, never combing her hair or washing her face. If someone walked by when her spirits were high, she would ask them: "Is everyone in your family well?" But when her spirits were low she would spit in the person's face.

She had become half mad.

From then on few people ever thought about the Hu family.

XI

Behind our house there was a Dragon King Temple, to the east of which there was a big bridge we called Great Eastern Bridge. The ghosts of wronged people congregated below this bridge, and during inclement weather people crossing over it could hear the weeping sounds of those ghosts.

People were saying that the ghost of the child-bride had also come to this spot below Great Eastern Bridge. They said that she had been transformed into a big white rabbit who came to that place under the bridge once every few days to weep.

Someone might ask her why she was weeping.

She would say she wanted to go home.

If the person responded by saying, "I'll take you home tomorrow. . . ." then the white rabbit would wipe her eyes with her big floppy ears and disappear. But if no one paid any attention to her, she would continue to weep until the crowing of chickens ushered in the new day.

Epilogue

The little town of Hulan River, in earlier days it was where my Granddad lived, and now it is where he is buried. When I was born Granddad was already in his sixties, and by the time I was four or five he was nearly seventy. As I approached the age of twenty Granddad was almost eighty; soon after he reached the age of eighty Granddad was dead.

The former masters of that rear garden are now gone. The old master is dead; the younger one has fled.

The butterflies, grasshoppers, and dragonflies that were in the garden may still return year after year; or perhaps the place is now deserted.

Cucumbers and pumpkins may still be planted there every year; or perhaps there are no more at all.

Do drops of morning dew still gather on the flower-vase stands? Does the noonday sun still send its rays down on the large sunflowers? Do the red clouds at sunset still form into the shape of a horse, only to shift a moment later into the shape of a dog?

These are things that I cannot know.

I heard that Second Uncle Yu died.

If the old cook is still alive, he will be getting on in years.

I don't know what has become of any of our neighbors.

As for the man who worked the mill, I haven't the slightest idea how things have gone with him.

The tales I have written here are not beautiful ones, but since my childhood memories are filled with them, I cannot forget them—they remain with me—and so I have recorded them here.

December 20, 1940
Hong Kong

APPENDIX I

Preface to *The Field of Life and Death*[1]
Lu Hsün

I recall it was four years ago in February that my family and I were trapped in the line of fire at Shanghai's Chapei district, and there I witnessed the extinction of the Chinese population as they fled or died. Later, with the assistance of a few friends, we gained entrance into the peaceful British Concession. Although refugees filled the streets, the residents there were living in peace and comfort. We were no more than four or five *li*, I suppose, from Chapei, and yet it was such a different world. How then could our thoughts have been on Harbin?

When this manuscript reached my desk, it was already the spring of this year. I had long since returned to Chapei, which was once again bustling with people. But in the manuscript, I was seeing a Harbin of five years ago, or even earlier. This is, of course, nothing more than a brief sketch whose narration of events and scenic descriptions are superior to its characterizations. And yet the tenacity of survival and the resistance to death forcefully permeate the pages. Keen observations and an extraordinary writing style add considerably to the book's vividness and beauty. Its spirit is robust. Even those who have an abhorrence of literature or those of a practical bent cannot help but be moved by this work.

Having heard that the Literature Society was willing to publish this work, I submitted the manuscript to the Publications Censorship Committee of the Central Propaganda Department. It was held up there for half a year; ultimately, approval was denied. Very often people become wiser only after an event, and on reflection, the outcome was never in doubt. The themes of tenacity of survival and resistance to death are, I'm afraid, contrary to the doctrine of "political tutelage."[2] In May of this year this haughty committee was suddenly and completely dissolved as a result of an article entitled "Short Talks on Emperors." This, then, is an application of the great object lesson of "using oneself as a model."

The offer of the Slave Society to use its meager, hard-earned funds to publish this book came half a year after our superiors had "used themselves as a model." I was asked to write a short preface. However, during these past few days, rumors have been circulating, and the bustling crowds of residents of Chapei are once again scurrying around like rats. Constant streams of cars bearing luggage and pedestrians pass through the streets, while on both sides foreigners, both yellow and white, watch the antics of our *civilized* nation with amusement. Newspapers from publishing companies located in the safe zones call these fleeing people "commoners" and "fools." For my part, I consider them wise. At least they have learned, through past experience, not to trust the pompous, official-sounding pronouncements. They still remember.

It is now the night of November 14, 1935, and I have just finished rereading *The Field of Life and Death*. All around me there is a deathlike stillness. Gone are the sounds of neighbors talking, which I've grown so used to hearing, and gone are the cries of the street vendors selling food. Now and then I hear the faint sound of dogs barking in the distance. I can imagine that a similar condition does not exist in the British and French Concessions, nor, for that matter, in Harbin. The residents in those places and I harbor different feelings and live in different worlds. But at this moment my heart feels like the stagnant water at the bottom of an abandoned well, devoid of ripples. In such a mood I have mechanically penned these few words. This then is the heart of a slave—and yet, if these words can stir the hearts of the readers, assuredly we are not yet slaves.

But, rather than listen to these jeremiads uttered in comfort, you will do better to turn quickly to *The Field of Life and Death* which follows. It will infuse in you the strength to persevere and to resist.

Notes

1. Lu Hsün's preface appeared in the 1935 Slave Series edition of *The Field of Life and Death*, but has been excised from the Hong Kong photo-offset reprinting. It is included in a 1958 Hong Kong version.

2. One of the three phases of the "National Reconstruction Process"—the political tutelage phase of provisional government—put into effect by the Kuomintang in June 1931.

APPENDIX II

Epilogue to *The Field of Life and Death*[1]
Hu Feng

I have read articles referring to Sholokhov's *Virgin Soil Upturned* and to his description of the peasants' fondness for their cows and horses, and of their reluctance to part with the animals that were being sent to the collective farms. That, the articles declared, is a portrait of the very souls of certain peasants in a transition period. Although the author of *The Field of Life and Death* has not read *Virgin Soil Upturned*, yet her rendering of the peasants' affection for their livestock (goats, horses, and cows) is so realistic and sincere that nowhere else in our corpus of peasant literature can we come across such moving poetry.

Needless to say, there is no comparison between the lives of the peasants here and those of the peasants in the Paradise-like Soviet Union. Existing like ants, there was neither logic to their reproduction nor order to their dying. Fertilizing the soil with their blood, sweat, and lives, they brought forth food and raised livestock. They squirmed, diligently and painfully, beneath the might of two tyrants—nature and man.

But this kind of chaotic existence could not continue for long. The "Black Tongue" swept in and cars and airplanes proclaiming the "Kingly Order" whizzed by. The Japanese flag had replaced the Chinese flag, and the four sizable provinces of Manchuria were lost without a struggle. Why did the Japanese rob us of our land? How could the rulers of China let them get away with the robbery? The pillagers wanted to reduce the soil-enriching peasants to more servile and direct slaves, while the pillaged wanted to demonstrate their docility and vie for the stature of slaves.

And yet the pillaged people were "untameable." Even though they had been branded as "nationless slaves," their blood completely drained by the mouthful, raped and murdered, they resisted. Aside from that, they could go into the city or could enter a convent, but none could escape this world where men prey on each other.

In hard times obstinate old Mother Wang characteristically stood up. So did the penitent and conscientious Chao San; and even the cautious Two-and-a-Half *Li*, who, for all the world, could not see beyond his goat, finally stood up. When the widows responded: "Yes, even if we are cut into a million pieces"; when old Chao San wept and cried out: "Wait until I'm buried . . . then plant the Chinese flag over my grave, for I am a Chinese! . . . I want a Chinese flag. I don't want to be a nationless slave. Alive I am Chinese, and when I'm dead I'll be a Chinese ghost . . . not a nation . . . nationless slave"; and when everyone knelt before the muzzle to take his oath, saying: "If I am not sincere, may Heaven slay me; may this gun end my life. The bullet has eyes, is all-knowing and sacred," these antlike, ignorant men and women, sad but resolute, stood on the front line of the sacred war of nationalism. Once they were like ants, living in order to die. Now they were titans, dying in order to live.

This is merely an account of an isolated village in the vicinity of Harbin in its first stage of awakening. However, in it dwells the real and suffering Chinese peasantry. In it we see a spontaneous surge of truth. The village "represents a part and also the whole of China, the present and the future, the way of life and the way to death."[2]

What I found exciting about the book is that it not only records the joys and tribulations of these ignorant men and women, it also depicts the blood-spattered earth beneath the blue sky. Moreover, this book, which illuminates the ironclad will to fight, came from the pen of a young woman. In it we can discern subtle, feminine sensibilities as well as a vigorous, manly mentality. The former pervades the entire work; of the latter I shall cite a couple of examples:

> The mountain snow blown by the wind seemed to want to bury this little house near the hill. The trees howled; the wind and snow swooped down on the little house. A wind-swept tree on the hillside toppled over. *The winter moon, fearful of being shattered by all that pandemonium, retreated to the edge of the sky.* At that moment, from next door came a pitiful plea. (p. 68)

and, as I have already mentioned, after the women had echoed their oath: "Yes, even if we are cut into a million pieces," this is what follows:

> The shrill, piercing voices stabbed painfully like an awl at the heart of everyone present. *For a brief moment, intense sorrow swept through the crowd of bowed heads. The blue sky seemed about to fall.* (p. 118)

Old Chao San spoke tearfully of dying and placing the Chinese flag before his grave. Then comes the following account:

> The concentrated, nondiffusible grief caused even the trees to bow down. Standing before the red candles, *Chao San knocked hard on the table twice. In unison, the crowd directed their supplications and tears toward the blue sky.* The whole crowd fell to weeping and wailing. (pp. 118–119)

Like a steel spear being brandished in the air, swishing and shimmering, her style of writing is, I must say, a rarity.

And yet, I am not saying that the author is without her faults or weaknesses. First, there isn't sufficient organizing of the materials; the entire work comes across as a series of random sketches, without leaving an impression that a central theme is being developed, and thereby preventing the reader from experiencing the tension that he should feel. Second, a great lack of imaginative work in bringing unity to the characters depicted is evident. Looking at them individually, her characters give the appearance of life, but their personalities lack definition, and they tend not to be like other people, thus they fail to come alive truly to the reader. Third, the syntax of her sentences is rather too unusual, partly because of her desire to introduce a fresh new frame of mind, and partly because of the dialect in which she writes, but mostly because of a lack of experience and skill in rhetoric.

I believe that were it not for these few weak points, this epic poem, though not noted for fine details, would elicit a closer identification and a more intense response from the readers.

But then, these are only the unreasonable demands of a meddler like me, intended as food for thought for the author and her readers. At present we should be satisfied with the author's efforts, for it is through *Village in August* and the present work that we can actually visualize a persecuted people of a pillaged land, and can finally embrace them closely.

November 22, 1935, 2:00 A.M.

Notes

1. Hu Feng's epilogue to *The Field of Life and Death*, dated November 22, 1935, a few weeks before the novel was published in the series he and Lu Hsün created, appears in both the 1935 Shanghai and the Hong Kong photo-offset editions, but not in the 1958 Hong Kong version.

2. From Lu Hsün's preface to *Village in August*, which was written by Hsiao Hung's common-law husband, Hsiao Chün, and published in the same series in August 1935.

APPENDIX III

Preface to *Tales of Hulan River*[1]
Mao Tun

I

This April, rather sick at heart, I paid my third visit to Hong Kong. When I made up my mind in Chungking to take this round-about route back to Shanghai, I did so with mixed feelings and a sinking heart, afraid to travel by the way I myself had chosen, afraid Hong Kong would revive old memories which I wished to forget, yet was eager to recapitulate one last time before they were forgotten.

I stayed first in Canton for one busy, hectic month, so busy I hardly had time to dwell on the past, though I never relinquished hope of reliving it once before forgetting it. I planned to go to Prince Road in Kowloon to see the house where I lived during my first stay in Hong Kong, to see Butterfly Valley where my daughter liked to take her girl friends to play, and to find the American comics my son collected so carefully in those days. I would have a look too at the house on Kennedy Road where I lived during my second stay in Hong Kong, and the Dancing Academy on Tennessee Road where we took refuge after fighting broke out in Hong Kong on December 8. Most of all I was eager to visit Hsiao Hung's grave by Repulse Bay.

I kept these fond hopes secret, though they gave me no peace whenever I was free; but I never summoned up the courage to realize them, and throughout my stay in Hong Kong went neither to Kowloon nor to Repulse Bay. As if against my own will, I kept away or found some pretext or other to postpone the visit, not that I had declared my intention to anyone or was being urged to go.

In the last twenty years and more I have had my full share of the joys and sorrows of life. If there is anything which, while not exactly enraging me or making me despair, nevertheless weighs so heavily on my heart that I long to forget it yet cannot easily do so, it is an early death, a lonely death. Somehow a death in battle distresses us less than that of one who has given up childhood's pleasures to search for truth and studied hard to be of use to her country and people, only to die when her student days are over, like a bullet never fired from a gun—this transcends the bounds of simple grief and pity.[2] An untimely death had dealt me a cruel blow, one I longed to forget yet could not easily banish from my mind. So it was futile, during that third visit to Hong Kong, to think of going back to Butterfly Valley. That was not the only place hallowed by memory, and even had I gone I doubt if I could have buried my sorrow there.

Those whose high hopes of life are repeatedly dashed must feel lonely. Even more lonely was she who had confidence in her ability and an ambitious plan of work, yet was so depressed by the cruelty of life that she became unhappy and frustrated. When on top of her spiritual loneliness she suddenly discovered that her days were numbered and there was no remedy for anything, her lonely anguish must have passed all telling. Her lonely death, too, weighed heavily on my heart; I longed to forget it yet could not easily do so. That is why I meant to go to Repulse Bay but against my will put off going time and again.

II

Hsiao Hung's grave lies alone by Repulse Bay in Hong Kong.

During the bathing season each year the place is gay with crowds of pleasure-seekers, but Hsiao Hung lies lonely there.

In December 1940, a year or so before she died and while her health was still fairly good, Hsiao Hung finished her last book, *Tales of Hulan River*.[3] But even then she was lonely.

Moreover, *Tales of Hulan River* shows us what a lonely childhood she had. Read the brief epilogue to the book and you sense Hsiao Hung's loneliness as she recalled her lonely childhood days.

In April, the year after she finished this work, Hsiao Hung was urged by Agnes Smedley to go to Singapore. (Agnes spent nearly a month in Hong Kong on her way back to the States. When Hsiao Hung asked about the situation in the Pacific, she said the Japanese were bound to attack Hong Kong and the South Seas, and Hong Kong could not hold out for more than a month, but Singapore was virtually impregnable, and even if it fell there would be more ways of escape there.) Hsiao Hung tried to persuade my wife and me to go too. But I did not want to leave Hong Kong, and had work to keep me there. Imagining Hsiao Hung was afraid of being caught in Hong Kong when it fell (if war actually broke out there), I did my best to reassure her. Little did I know that her eagerness to leave arose from her sense of loneliness in Hong Kong, and that she hoped by leaving Hong Kong to escape from that fearful loneliness. This was just after the Southern Anhwei Incident,[4] when many writers and artists from the interior had gone to Hong Kong, so that there was more cultural activity there than ever before. Such being the case, it was hard to understand Hsiao Hung's sense of isolation. By the time I knew and understood it, she had been buried for nearly a year by Repulse Bay.

In the end, instead of going to Singapore, Hsiao Hung fell ill and entered St. Mary's Hospital. In hospital, naturally, she was even more lonely; but her will to live was strong, and hoping to recover she put up with the loneliness of hospital life. Her case was a complicated one, and the attitude of the doctors was outrageous: when finally they diagnosed tuberculosis, they told her they had no drugs to cure her. Still, Hsiao Hung was convinced she would recover. Even after fighting broke out in Hong Kong and the shelling seemed just as likely to carry her off as illness, she dreaded the first possibility more; although the greatest threat to her remained her sense of loneliness.

She did not recover from the final operation. Hong Kong had already fallen by then, and most of her friends were away when she breathed her last, so that she departed this life in loneliness.

Tales of Hulan River shows us the loneliness of Hsiao Hung's childhood.

Life was dull for the precocious little girl. Year after year they planted cucumbers and pumpkins; year after year her playground was the backyard where on fine days there were butterflies, grasshoppers and dragonflies, or the dark, dusty back room piled high with junk. Her only companion was her kindly old grandfather, still a child at heart. In bed in the morning she recited the Tang poems the old man taught her. In the daytime she pestered him to tell the stories she knew only too well, or watched the neighbors, so set in their ways it seemed nothing could change in their lives in a thousand years. If a ripple sometimes disturbed this stagnant pool, it was only when the child-bride in the Hu family fell ill, they summoned a soothsayer, and she finally died; or when Harelip Feng suddenly acquired a wife and baby, when later on his wife suddenly died, leaving him with a second child, a new-born baby.[5]

Life in the little town of Hulan River was equally dead and dull.

Life followed a strict pattern the whole year round: dances to exorcise spirits, *yangko* songs, a lantern festival, operas performed in the open, the big fair at the Immortal Matron's Temple on the eighteenth of the fourth month . . . and the other big, boisterous festivals every year. Yet these festivals were as dull and dead as their ordinary life.

Not that life in the little town lacked sound and color.

From every street, lane and thatched hut, from behind every wicker fence, rose the sound of nagging and quarreling, weeping and laughter, even delirious raving. In every season of the year, the big boisterous festivals which followed each other in due order stood out against the gray background of everyday life like splashes of red and green, bright primitive colors.

Of course, most of them were kindly folk on the banks of the Hulan.

Their thoughts and lives were governed by traditions handed down for thousands of years. They might seem apathetic at times, but in fact they were highly sensitive and particular: they could spend three days and three nights debating and fighting about some trifling matter. They might seem stupid and barbarous, but they did not want to harm others or themselves. They just "did what had to be done" according to their lights.

Of course, we sympathize with the sad fate of the child-bride in old Hu's family. We pity her and hate the unfair way she was treated. Yet our hatred is not directed against her mother-in-law because we pity Mrs. Hu, too, regarding her as another victim of the age-old traditions. Her "stand," which calls more for pity than for hatred, is shown in the way she gladly spends five hundred coppers to hire a soothsayer to cure the child-bride. She made no bones about her attitude, saying:

> "I've never abused her all the time she's been in my home. Where else will you find another family that has not abused its child-bride by giving her beatings and tongue-lashings all day long? Now I may have beaten her a little, but just to get her started off on the right foot, and I only did that for a little over a month. Maybe I beat her pretty severely sometimes, but how was I expected to make a well-mannered girl out of her without being severe once in a while? Believe me, I didn't enjoy beating her so hard, what with all her screaming and carrying on, but I was doing it for her own good, because if I didn't beat her hard, she'd never be good for anything."

Why did Mrs. Hu believe so firmly that she must teach the child-bride a good lesson? What displeased her about the girl? The day that the child came to her house, the neighbors' comments were:

"She hasn't the least bit of shyness when she's with people."

"She isn't even a tiny bit shy. Her very first day at her mother-in-law's house she ate three bowls of rice!"

"She's big for fourteen!" (That was unseemly too.) Because she did not measure up to the neighbors' idea of what a child-bride should be, Mrs. Hu had to teach her a lesson; and because the spirited girl would not knuckle under but screamed and shouted and wanted to go home, she had to be beaten hard for a month or more.

The neighbors naturally had no feud with the girl but felt this was for her own good, to make her behave like a normal child-bride. So when as a result of this "discipline" she fell ill, Mrs. Hu gladly went to the expense of hiring a soothsayer and trying other means to cure her, while the neighbors eagerly rallied round with advice.

And the result? The result was that a "dark-skinned, laughing" child of twelve, who passed for fourteen and was taller and stronger than most girls of fourteen, was hounded out of this life to her "final home."

The little town of Hulan River was full of sound and color of every kind, yet it was dead and dull.

Life in the little town was lonely.

Hsiao Hung passed her childhood in these lonely surroundings. It goes without saying that they left an indelible mark on her mind.

The child-bride, who all unconsciously defied the age-old traditions, died; and Hsiao Hung, who consciously defied these traditions, recollected the lonely little town with a smile but with tears in her eyes. Her heart remained lonely even in the great age of a mighty struggle.

IV

Some readers may not regard *Tales of Hulan River* as a novel. They may argue: No single thread runs through the whole book, the stories and characters in it are disconnected fragments, the work is not an integrated whole.

Others may look upon *Tales of Hulan River* as an autobiography of an unorthodox sort.

To my mind, the fact that it is not an orthodox autobiography is all to the good and gives it an added interest.

And we may counter: The main point is not that this work is not a novel in the strict sense, but that it has other qualities more "attractive" than those to be found in the average novel. It is a narrative poem, a colorful genre painting, a haunting song.

Satire is here, and humor. At the start you read with a sense of relaxation; then little by little your heart grows heavier. Still there is beauty, slightly morbid perhaps but bound to fascinate you.

You may complain that the work contains not a single positive character. Nothing but poor creatures, full of self-pity, yet choosing to be slaves to tradition. And the author's attitude toward them is perplexing. Flaying them ruthlessly, she nevertheless sympathizes with them. She shows us the stupidity, obstinacy and sometimes the cruelty of these slaves to tradition, yet presents them as by nature good, not given to cheating, hypocrisy, or living in idle comfort, but very easily satisfied. This is true of Second Uncle, the old cook, the whole of old Hu's family, and the men who make bean noodles. Like the lowest forms of plant life, they can live with a minimum of water, soil and sunlight—even with no sunlight at all. Harelip Feng of the mill has the most vitality of them all, so much so that we cannot but admire his spirit. And yet we find nothing outstanding about his character, apart from the tenacity of his will to live, and that is a primitive tenacity.

If we search for a weakness in the author's outlook, we shall probably find it not in the absence of positive characters but in the impression their nightmare existence makes on readers. If not for their own stupidity and conservatism, and the trouble they bring on themselves, their life has its pleasanter side. We are shown no trace of feudal oppression and exploitation, no trace of the savage invasion of Japanese imperialism. But these must surely have weighed more heavily on the people by the Hulan than their own stupidity and conservatism.

V

When Hsiao Hung wrote this book, she was lonely.

She was virtually "hibernating" in Hong Kong. It is hard to understand how a woman with her high ideals, who had struggled against reaction, could "hibernate" in such stirring times as the years just before and after 1940. A friend of hers, trying to explain her frustration and apathy, ascribed them to a series of emotional shocks which confined this poet richer in feeling than intellect within the small circle of her private life. (Although she condemned this circle, some inertia kept her from breaking boldly with it.) She was cut off completely from the tremendous life and death struggle being waged outside. As a result, although her high principles made her frown on the activities of the intellectuals of her class and regard them as futile talk, she would not plunge into the laboring masses of workers and peasants or change her life radically. Inevitably, then, she was frustrated and lonely. This has cast a shadow over *Tales of Hulan River*, evident not only in the mood of the whole work but in its ideological content as well. This is to be regretted, just as we deeply regret Hsiao Hung's untimely death.

Notes

1. This translation appeared in the magazine *Chinese Literature*, No. 2 (1963), 25–32. The present translator has made some corrections and revisions. The original, dated August 1946, appeared only in the 1947 Shanghai edition of the novel.

2. This passage refers to the writer's daughter.

3. *Ma Po-lo* (Part II) was completed in 1941.

4. A Communist-Nationalist confrontation in January 1941.

5. A translation of "Harelip Feng" by Gladys Yang appeared in *Chinese Literature*, No. 2 (1963), pp. 3–24.

A SELECTED BIBLIOGRAPHY
OF WORKS BY HSIAO HUNG[1]

The Field of Life and Death (Sheng-szu ch'ang), 1935 (novel)
Market Street (Shang-shih chieh), 1936 (reminiscences)
The Bridge (Ch'iao), 1936 (stories and essays)
On the Oxcart (Niu-ch'e shang), 1937 (stories)
A Remembrance of Lu Hsün hsien-sheng (Hui-yi Lu Hsün hsien-sheng), 1940 (biographical sketch)
Prose Writings of Hsiao Hung (Hsiao Hung san-wen), 1940 (essays)
A Cry in the Wilderness (K'uang-yeh ti hu-han), 1940 (stories)
Ma Po-lo, 1940 (novel)
Ma Po-lo (Pt. II), 1941 (novel)[2]
Tales of Hulan River (Hu-lan-ho chuan), 1942 (novel)[3]
Selected Works of Hsiao Hung (Hsiao Hung hsüan-chi), 1958 (novels and stories)[3]
Spring in a Small Town (Hsiao-ch'eng san-yüeh), 1961 (stories)[3]

PUBLISHED ENGLISH TRANSLATIONS
(in CHRONOLOGICAL ORDER)

"Hands" (Richard L. Jen). *T'ien Hsia Monthly*, No. 4, 1937, pp. 498–514.
"A Night in a Stable" (Chia Wu and Nym Wales). *Asia Magazine*, September, 1941, pp. 487–489.
"Hands" (Gladys Yang). *Chinese Literature*, No. 8, 1959, pp. 36–52.
"Spring in a Small Town" (Sidney Shapiro). *Chinese Literature*, No. 8, 1961, pp. 59–82.
"Harelip Feng" (Gladys Yang). *Chinese Literature*, No. 2, 1963, pp. 3–24.[4]
"On the Oxcart" (Howard Goldblatt). *ASPAC Quarterly*, Spring, 1976, pp. 56–64.

---

1. For a more complete list see Howard Goldblatt, *Hsiao Hung* (Boston, 1976), pp. 153–155.
2. Published in magazine serialization only.
3. Published posthumously.
4. Chapter Seven of *Tales of Hulan River*.